NORTHBROOK PUBLIC LIBRARY
1201 CEDAR LANE
NORTHBROOK, IL 60062

OCT 1 3 2009

Northbrook Public Library

3 1123 00901 8071

Programming
A Beginner's Guide

Richard Mansfield

D1412450

New York Chicago San Francisco
Lisbon London Madrid Mexico City
Milan New Delhi San Juan
Seoul Singapore Sydney Toronto

The McGraw·Hill Companies

Library of Congress Cataloging-in-Publication Data

Mansfield, Richard, 1945-
Programming : a beginner's guide / Richard Mansfield.
        p.   cm.
    ISBN 978-0-07-162472-5 (alk. paper)
    1. Computer programming.   I. Title.
  QA76.6.M3575   2009
  005.1—dc22   2009022768

McGraw-Hill books are available at special quantity discounts to use as premiums and sales promotions, or for use in corporate training programs. To contact a representative please e-mail us at bulksales@mcgraw-hill.com.

Programming: A Beginner's Guide

Copyright © 2009 by The McGraw-Hill Companies. All rights reserved. Printed in the United States of America. Except as permitted under the Copyright Act of 1976, no part of this publication may be reproduced or distributed in any form or by any means, or stored in a database or retrieval system, without the prior written permission of publisher, with the exception that the program listings may be entered, stored, and executed in a computer system, but they may not be reproduced for publication.

All trademarks or copyrights mentioned herein are the possession of their respective owners and McGraw-Hill makes no claim of ownership by the mention of products that contain these marks.

1234567890 FGR FGR 019

ISBN   978-0-07-162472-5
MHID   0-07-162472-4

Sponsoring Editor   Roger Stewart
Editorial Supervisor   Janet Walden
Project Manager   Smita Rajan, International Typesetting and Composition
Acquisitions Coordinator   Joya Anthony
Technical Editors   Todd Meister and John Paul Mueller
Copy Editor   Lisa Theobald
Proofreader   Susie Elkind
Indexer   Karin Arrigoni
Production Supervisor   Jean Bodeaux
Composition   International Typesetting and Composition
Illustration   International Typesetting and Composition
Art Director, Cover   Jeff Weeks
Cover Designer   Jeff Weeks

Information has been obtained by McGraw-Hill from sources believed to be reliable. However, because of the possibility of human or mechanical error by our sources, McGraw-Hill, or others, McGraw-Hill does not guarantee the accuracy, adequacy, or completeness of any information and is not responsible for any errors or omissions or the results obtained from the use of such information.

This book is dedicated to my friends David and Cliff, for their many kindnesses.

About the Author

Richard Mansfield has written hundreds of magazine articles and two columns. He began writing books full time in 1991. This his 41st book. Overall, his books have sold more than 500,000 copies worldwide and have been translated into 12 languages. His recent titles include *How to Do Everything with Second Life* (McGraw-Hill), *CSS Web Design For Dummies* (Wiley), *Office 2003 Application Development All-in-One Desk Reference For Dummies* (Wiley), *The Visual Basic .NET Power Toolkit* (Sybex, with Evangelos Petroutsos), and *The Savvy Guide to Digital Music* (SAMS).

About the Technical Editors

Todd Meister has been developing using Microsoft technologies for more than ten years. He has been a technical editor on more than 50 titles ranging from SQL Server to the .NET Framework. In addition to technical editing titles he is an Assistant Director for Computing Services at Ball State University in Muncie, Indiana. He lives in central Indiana with his wife, Kimberly, and their four remarkable children.

John Paul Mueller has technically edited 63 books, written 82 books of his own, and written more than 300 articles for various publishers. He has more than 34 years of programming experience. When John isn't working at his computer, he enjoys making soap and working with wood, among other things.

Contents at a Glance

Contents

Acknowledgments

I want to thank editorial director Roger Stewart for his thoughtful guidance during the entire process of creating this book. Roger understands authors and knows how to get the best out of them.

I was also lucky to have five editors work with me on this book. Roger helped shape the book in a variety of ways and always kept the big picture in mind.

Janet Walden made a number of improvements to the book, and was both judicious and gracious in her suggestions and modifications to the text.

A close technical edit by Todd Meister contributed to the book's accuracy. Todd was indefatigable: He verified each code listing, even the short snippets of code. And he offered a variety of interesting suggestions about both themes and content.

My sometime co-author on other books, John Mueller, provided a valuable edit of this book. He also helped me ensure that the book's audience—beginners—were well-served by improving the book's clarity and technical accuracy.

Special thanks go to project manager Smita Rajan who was highly effective in all her jobs: shepherding, diplomacy, scheduling, and offering intelligent suggestions about style and many other issues as the book moved through the production stages. Her acumen and her grace were much appreciated.

Copy editor Lisa Theobald proved thoroughgoing and systematic. She paid particular attention to the passive voice, split infinitives, and ending sentences with a preposition. Overall, her efforts were as exhaustive as they were painstaking.

Production supervisor Jean Bodeaux offered good suggestions about improving elements of the book, and also provided valuable technical assistance.

Joya Anthony diligently coordinated the editorial submission processes. And she gave me some helpful guidance in other areas as well.

To these, and all the other good people at McGraw-Hill who contributed to the book, my thanks for the time and care they took to ensure quality at each station along the way from initiation to publication.

Finally, I want to give special thanks to my agent, Matt Wagner of Waterside Productions, who has been offering me good advice for many years.

Introduction

The great secret about programming is that it is often easy and fun. Like sports, collecting, or cooking, programming can be a wonderful pastime.

True, *anything* you are forced to do in life can become frustrating or boring. But lots of amateurs and many professionals truly enjoy creating new programs. You might, too.

This book is for the curious. If you have wondered about programming and want to give it a try, I believe you will find this book an enjoyable introduction. If you end up writing programs as a hobby, you will have endless hours of pleasure. As a bonus, you will get to customize and improve your programs until they work exactly how you want them to work.

Amateur programming is alive and well, so if you choose to work solo you can even make a good living by writing and selling your programs as shareware (see Chapter 13).

If you decide to study programming formally, or to continue on and make a career in computers, you are unlikely to have problems finding work. The demand for computer professionals remains strong. This book will not only help you prepare for that career, but will also help you understand exactly what is involved in the profession of programming, both the pros and cons.

Three Common Misconceptions About Programming

Most people who have never written a computer program have several misconceptions.

Myth #1: Programming Involves Math and Science   First, programming is not related to math. I quit studying math in the ninth grade and have been professionally programming and writing books about programming for 30 years. True, "computer science" is often part of the math department in academia, but nobody can explain why. Well, yes I can: At my local university, urban planning is part of the geography department. There is our answer.

In any case, studies have shown that the best, most talented natural programmers are English and music majors. Programming, after all, is an act of *communication*, albeit with a machine. So if your strengths tend more to the liberal arts than the sciences, do not make the mistake of thinking you will struggle to write programs. You might actually be quicker, and more capable, than your more scientifically talented friends. You might, however, struggle to get a degree in computer "science" because, among many other hurdles, you'll likely be expected to master subjects such as Calculus.

Of course, some kinds of programming do involve complex math (such as sophisticated data analysis, NASA rocketry, and games). But my point is that programming is not *intrinsically* a mathematical activity. Most programming does not require advanced math any more than most driving requires a pilot's license.

Myth #2: Make a Mistake and You Can Physically Harm the Computer   Another myth: Do not worry that you might somehow hurt or break the computer physically by making errors in your programming. This cannot happen any more than you can hurt a piece of paper by misspelling a word. Similarly, a computer cannot make you feel inadequate or stupid. Only you can do that.

Myth #3: Programming Is Difficult   This is the biggest myth of all. It is a major misconception that programming is hard. People who do not program sometimes call people who do *computer geniuses.* Believe me, this is a total misunderstanding and I know plenty of programmers. They are intelligent, but only a fraction of them are brilliant. Brilliance is just not necessary.

In fact, programming can be surprisingly easy when you use a programming language like BASIC, as you will discover in this book. BASIC is designed to be, among other things, a learning language. Therefore, many of its commands are ordinary English words.

You already know English, so you already know what BASIC means by words such as *Time, Stop, Day, Next, Return, End, Date, Empty, While, Hour, True,* and *False.*

But do not assume that BASIC is somehow lightweight: It can produce exactly the same programs created in any other language. In fact, as you will see in the final chapter, BASIC programs can be automatically translated into the more complicated (though no more powerful) language called C#. By *automatically*, I mean you can just paste your BASIC programming into a web site and click a button to generate C#. By *complicated*, I mean C# uses fewer recognizable words, inverts syntax, abbreviates, and relies more on symbolic punctuation. Chapter 13 compares BASIC and C# in detail.

Of course, some programs *are* difficult to write, no matter what language you use, just as some books are hard to read. But you can choose to work with easy programs or find easy ways to accomplish difficult tasks. And you have already chosen a book that is easy to read—clarity has been a major goal while I was writing this book. But if you do run into a problem, just e-mail me.

Write Me If You Have a Question

I am happy to assist readers, so if you have any kind of difficulty while using this book, write me at

earth@triad.rr.com

I will try to get back to you the same day. And remember, the only foolish question is one that is unasked. We have all been beginners at some point, so do go ahead and send an e-mail. If you are totally embarrassed, sign your e-mail *Shirley* and I will think you are Shirley instead of your real self.

Tech Tip

Why would anyone use C# if it is harder to use and does not provide anything that you can't already get in Visual Basic? The short answer is that currently professional programming almost always requires a knowledge of C# or similar languages. (Chapter 13 explores this topic in detail.) And, to be fair, C# does include at least one feature not available in VB. It is a highly specialized technique: the use of *unsafe pointers*. This practice is way beyond beginners and indeed is rarely employed by advanced programmers. But it does offer you

(continued)

an edge in certain kinds of esoteric application development. Using unsafe pointers is a unique kind of programming, and you are unlikely ever to need to make use of it. If you're interested in this topic, read more about unsafe pointers at these sites:

- www.c-sharpcorner.com/UploadFile/gregory_popek/ WritingUnsafeCode11102005040251AM/WritingUnsafeCode.aspx
- www.codeproject.com/KB/cs/csunsafeintro01.aspx

Throughout this book, you will find occasional Tech Tips. Think of these as footnotes—not essential information, but worth reading if the topic interests you.

Getting Started

In Chapter 1, you will discover exactly what programming is (and is not), and then in Chapter 2, you will install the Visual Basic 2008 Express language (VB for short) that we will use throughout this book. It is free, efficient, understandable, and very powerful.

In Chapter 2, you will also write your first program. Like the other programs in this book, the Timer program in Chapter 2 is actually *useful*. It is not just a theoretical exercise, as is the case in so many programming books. You will probably find yourself using and customizing this handy utility in the future.

Later in the book—while exploring all the elements of programming such as loops and branches—you will write a couple of larger programs. First, you will build a Quiz program that can be used to help with homework, prepare for a civil service exam, or practice for any other kind of test.

You will finish the book by writing a Diary program where you can type in your secret thoughts, store your passwords, and otherwise conceal private information. You will protect the diary in two different ways: by creating a password entry system and by encrypting the entire contents of the diary.

And you will also see how to make your programs look professional, complete with their own standard Windows-style setup system. Astound your friends and family by giving them copies of these programs for their own use. They will think you are a computer genius. (The truth about how fun and easy all this is will be our little secret.)

OK, now it is time to get started. For many of you, programming will become a lifelong fascination. It has been for me.

Downloading the Code for This Book

To avoid having to type in the code, you can copy and paste it from this book's web site. Here's how:

1. Go to www.mhprofessional.com/computingdownload.

2. The Free Downloads: Samples and Code page appears.

3. Under the Free Downloads heading, scroll down the list, or use the links on the letter ranges, to find Programming: A Beginner's Guide.

4. Click the link to begin the file download process, choosing either to open or save the .zip file that contains all this book's code.

Part I

Introduction to Programming

Chapter 1

Introduction to Programming

Key Skills & Concepts

- The elements of programming
- Programming is easier than most people think
- No math needed
- Data + processing = ingredients + recipe
- Moving step-by-step

Once you understand the main concepts presented in this book, you'll find that programming is usually surprisingly easy. Of course, if you use a complicated programming language, such as C, you'll have difficulties. Even many experienced programmers struggle with C (and similar languages such as Java or C++).

But in this book we'll use BASIC, a language originally developed to teach people how to write programs. Over the years, BASIC has become just as powerful as the alternative languages, while retaining the English-like qualities that make it so understandable, easy to use, and efficient.

True, computer programs that control a moon rocket are not simple, but that's only because tasks such as calculating rocket trajectories are inherently hard to do—not because programming itself is hard. So unless you work for a place like NASA, much of the programming you'll write for your own use will be simple and understandable.

The first concept you should understand about communicating with computers (*programming*) is that computers, in some ways, resemble an *autistic savant—savant* because you can write a few words of programming and the computer will instantly tell you how many days fall between any two dates. But if you put a single comma in the wrong place in your instructions, the computer won't understand at all what you want it to do. So the first thing to remember is that computers are extremely literal. Your instructions to the computer—your programming—must be precise.

Fortunately, many kinds of programming errors (*bugs*) are obvious to BASIC, and it will display a message telling you where it found the error. Or it will show you where the problem is in your *source code* (the lines of programming you write) with a blue, sawtooth underline, as shown in Figure 1-1.

Think of it this way: You can write a program to help your son or daughter do geography homework, for example, because you have a fair understanding of how to quiz a child.

```
Label1.Text = Label1.Tex & "  CORRECT!"
```
'Tex' is not a member of 'System.Windows.Forms.Label'.

Figure 1-1   Visual Basic can show you where many kinds of errors are located and suggest how to fix them.

Later in this book, you'll actually write a flexible program that can be used to quiz a student on any topic. You might also find this program useful if, for example, you need to pass a test to get into the postal service, or you want to help a friend who is trying to get a driver's license.

Why Does Programming Have a Bad Reputation?

Writing our quiz program will be straightforward and undemanding. It's not rocket science. Why, then, do most nonprogrammers think that programming is so hard to do? Why the popular belief that communicating with computers is only possible for "computer geniuses"?

Let's bust a few myths. The main reason that programming is believed to be difficult is that professional or academic programmers have no incentive to tell you otherwise. Like most of us, they like to be thought of as specially talented. There's also job security to consider.

Programming Isn't About Math

Another misunderstanding results because schools usually put programming in the math department and require that students jump over all kinds of hurdles (unrelated to their eventual success as a programmer) before they can be certified as "official" programming professionals.

For example, a student in computer science might be required to takes courses in probability theory, advanced math, physics, engineering, graphics, or other topics not directly related to most actual programming. To be "certified" with a diploma, you sometimes have to demonstrate persistence in the face of irrelevance.

I was an English major and at various times had to take classes in topics such as French, geology (for the "science requirement"), and so on. To be honest, I now enjoy knowing French and understanding the geology I see in road cutaways. But don't think that the fog of peripheral academic requirements—particularly math requirements—surrounding computer science programs has any more relevance to real-world programming than geology does to Shakespeare.

As for mathematics, programming *can* be used to mathematical ends (rocket trajectories), but many programs have nothing at all to do with math.

Programming is multipurpose, and most amateur programmers want the computer to do simple jobs around the house, like quizzing junior on his upcoming history test (see Chapter 6) or providing a diary that nobody can read without knowing the secret password (see Chapter 9). As you will see in this book, these kinds of jobs, like the great majority of programs, have very little to do with math.

Computers are general-purpose machines, like cars. Just as a car can be driven to many destinations, so, too, can a computer do all kinds of jobs for you.

Some Programming Languages Are Complex

Why did I choose BASIC (Beginner's All-purpose Symbolic Instruction Code) as the language to use in this book? The people who created BASIC had several goals in mind. One of their original goals was to keep the word order, terminology, and other features of their new computer language as close as possible to English. Because you already know English, learning BASIC goes much faster than learning most other programming languages.

For example, to end execution of a BASIC program, you use the command End. To print or display something, you use the command Print.

To print the numbers between 1 and 20, the BASIC programming code is easy to understand (the Debug command here is used while testing, or *debugging*, a program):

```
For number = 1 To 20
  Debug.Print number
Next number
```

What could be more sensible or understandable than everyday words used in everyday sentences? For comparison, here's the same task written in C programming code:

```
for (number=1; number<=20; number++)
{   printf(" %d\n", number); }
```

For several decades, BASIC was the most popular programming language of all. It remains the easiest to use and teach, as these examples illustrate. What's more, BASIC has evolved to equal the other programming languages in power and capability.

What Is a Program?

Computers use two primary types of information: data and programming. *Data* is raw information like today's date, your dog's name, or the current gasoline tax. *Programming* is a series of instructions describing how to manipulate data, how to *process* it. That's why computers are sometimes called *data processors*.

This distinction between data and program is quite similar to the two main elements in an ordinary recipe. A typical recipe—such as the following one for tasty spaghetti sauce—is divided into two major sections that correspond to data and processing.

The list of ingredients is equivalent to the *data*. It's the raw materials you'll be working with. And the step-by-step directions *tell you what to do with the data*—how to process that data into a result. In this case, the result is a simple, yet elegant, pasta dish:

```
6 cups plain Hunts tomato sauce
3 tablespoons sugar              } Data
3 tablespoons butter
```

```
1. Simmer the sauce, sugar, and butter about 10 minutes.
2. Cook 1 lb. spaghetti.                                    } Program
3. Mix sauce into spaghetti.
```

Another way to view this distinction is that data is made up mostly of nouns (*sauce*, *sugar*, and so on) along with adjectives that modify the nouns (*plain*, *Hunts*, *6*). Data rarely contains verbs. But a program always contains verbs, actions that are taken to modify the data, such as *simmer*, *cook*, and *mix*.

Figure 1-2 shows an actual program. It calculates sales tax. At the top is a list of data (Dim declarations as they're called) followed by the processing (a statement that multiplies the cost of the TV by the sales tax).

This program defines two items of data and then processes them (multiplies them, in this case). When this program runs, or *executes*, the result of the data processing is displayed to the user. The user can see that the sales tax on a $1400 TV is $98. (Don't worry about those Dim commands—this method of entering data is very simple, and you'll soon understand it well.)

```
Dim SalesTax = 0.07
Dim SamsungCost = 1400

MsgBox(SalesTax * SamsungCost)
```

WindowsApplication1

98

OK

Figure 1-2 The top two lines of this program contain the data, and the third line does the processing.

Moving Step-by-Step

Notice that the instructions in the recipe are a numbered series of steps. This tells you the order in which to carry out the various tasks that the program requires. Obviously, some kind of order is necessary because later steps depend on earlier steps. You can't carry out step 3 until you've completed steps 1 and 2.

Likewise, when you write a program, you write a list of steps to be taken by the computer to achieve your goal. This list of steps is often called the *source code*, and it is made up of a series of *instructions* (also called statements).

In the early days, the steps in a computer program—the list of instructions—were actually numbered in the source code, like this:

```
1 Dim SalesTax = 0.07
2 Dim SamsungCost = 1400
3 MsgBox(SalesTax * SamsungCost)
```

Although you can optionally use line numbers if you want, to indicate the steps in your programs, most people don't do that anymore. Instead, the computer can tell the order of the instructions merely by the order in which you type in your lines of source code. And you can read your programs the same way you read ordinary sentences in a book—no numbering needed.

TIP

Sometimes you don't even have to write an entire program yourself because so much source code has already been written by others. For example, as you'll see in Chapter 12 there are thousands of programming examples that you can copy and paste into your own programs. Using other people's tested source code can make it easier to learn to program, and it can also speed up the writing of programs. Why reinvent the wheel if somebody has already written a piece of source code that does a job you want to do? True, you usually have to modify imported code to make it work in your program, but that can sometimes be easier than starting from scratch. Very few programmers can remember all the precise ways that commands must be written, so example code is often a valuable shortcut.

Chapter 2

Writing Your First Program

Key Skills & Concepts

- Installing Visual Basic Express

- Installing the MSDN library

- Creating your first computer program

- Understanding and entering code

- Expanding a program

Most of us learn best by plunging right into a real-world example, so in this chapter you'll write a small, but useful, program. You'll also see how to use Microsoft Visual Basic's full-featured Code Editor. Visual Basic's Code Editor is to programming what Microsoft Word is to writing—an extremely powerful, fully customizable, and well-tested application.

Just as most of us don't use more than a couple dozen or so of Word's features when writing, you'll probably employ only a small group of the Code Editor's features when programming. But it's nice to know that all those other tools are available if you ever need them.

NOTE

The Visual Basic 2008 Express Edition that we use in this book is composed of three primary elements: the Visual Basic language itself, the Microsoft Programming Editor (something like a word processor), and a vast help system called the MSDN Library. They work seamlessly together, offering a beginner everything needed to learn to write programs. Indeed, they offer everything needed for nearly any programmer—including professionals.

Now let's begin our programming career by installing what I consider the finest programming system available today. And it's free. All you have to do is register it and you can use it all you want.

Installing Visual Basic Express

Follow these steps to install VB Express:

1. Go to www.microsoft.com/express/vb/.

2. Locate the Visual Basic 2008 Express Edition box, as shown in Figure 2-1, and click the Download link.

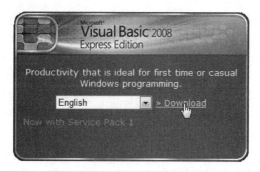

Figure 2-1   Click this Download link to begin the installation of VB Express.

3. A download dialog box opens. Choose the Run option to install VB Express.

4. Follow the setup instructions (clicking the Next button in the Setup dialog when asked to).

5. You may be asked for permission to install Silverlight and SQL Server. Grant permission by leaving the check boxes checked and click Next.

6. Permit the program to install in the default folder Microsoft Visual Studio 9.0. Click the Install button.

The setup process will take a while because, among other things, 154MB worth of files have to be downloaded to your hard drive. If you have a broadband connection to the Internet, however, the download itself should be over in a couple of minutes. After the files are downloaded, it may take 30 or more minutes before the actual installation is completed, depending on the speed of your computer.
And don't be worried about all the mysterious files that are being installed. Remember that in this book (and for most of your typical programming tasks), you'll only need to deal with a couple dozen features on the surface of Visual Basic. You won't need to worry about mechanical work down below in the engine room or about many of the hundreds of specialized tools that VB and its editor make available.

7. After installation is complete, choose Restart Now to finalize the installation process. Again, this will take quite a long time. It may seem that nothing is happening for 10 minutes, so be patient.

8. When the process completes, you'll see a dialog box announcing "Setup complete." You're also asked to register, which is a good idea. There's a 30-day time limit on nonregistered VB Express. You don't want your copy of VB turning into a zombie just as you're getting to the really good stuff in a later chapter.

When you first run VB Express, complete the registration process. Find the registration link on the first page displayed (it's called the *Start Page*). During registration, you're asked if you're willing to allow Microsoft to send statistics about your use of VB Express. This is up to you, but it helps Microsoft better understand how the product is used by real people in real-world programming situations. This seems a small favor to grant in return for getting a free programming language and editor. (However, if you listen to streaming radio a lot or don't have a high-speed Internet connection, this feature can become annoying.)

For now, click Exit to close the dialog box and proceed to the next step, installing the MSDN library.

Installing the MSDN Library

You'll also want to install the Express Edition of the MSDN Library—a vast help system that includes code examples, white papers, and tutorials. The Microsoft Developer Network has been around for many years, and it's a gold mine of usable programming snippets, illustrations of various programming concepts, explanations of the VB language's built-in commands, and other helpful information.

TIP

The term *code* is used by programmers to describe the programming they type into a programming editor. Programming code is also known as *source code*.

Follow these steps to install the MSDN Library:

1. Go to www.microsoft.com/express/download.

2. Locate the MSDN Express Library graphic, as shown in Figure 2-2, and click the Download link.

3. A download dialog box opens. Choose the Run option. This time you're downloading 360MB of data!

Figure 2-2 Click this Download link to install the MSDN Library.

4. Continue to follow the Setup Wizard's instructions, clicking the Next button in the Setup dialog when asked to.

Once the MSDN Library is installed, you can press F1 in the VB editor, click the Contents tab at the lower-left corner of the Help window, and access a huge amount of information for VB Express programmers, as shown in Figure 2-3.

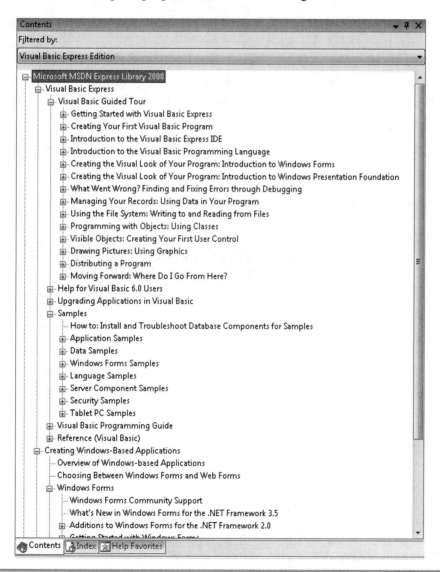

Figure 2-3   MSDN puts a huge library of sample code, tutorials, reference books, and other data at your fingertips.

Writing Your First Program

Now we'll build a handy little program that illustrates several important points about programming and shows you the simplest way to use the editor. Start VB Express and you'll be greeted with a screen that looks something like Figure 2-4.

To start creating a new program, follow these steps:

1. Choose File | New Project, or click the New Project icon on the far left of the default (Standard) toolbar, as shown in Figure 2-5.
A New Project dialog box opens where you'll see a list of different types of VB projects. In this book, we'll focus on writing ordinary Windows applications rather than the more specialized kinds of programs such as class libraries or Internet programs.

2. Double-click the Windows Forms Application icon shown in Figure 2-6.

You now see a blank form in the upper left-hand corner, as shown in Figure 2-7.

Figure 2-4 VB is fired up and ready to respond to your commands.

Figure 2-5   Click this button to start a new project.

While you're designing your application in the programming Editor, you work with *forms*. But when the user runs your application, the forms are displayed as traditional windows. I'll get to forms and windows shortly. For now, let's keep things as simple as possible.

And don't worry about understanding the commands you'll use in this program, the many features of the editor, or other aspects of writing a VB program. I'll cover these

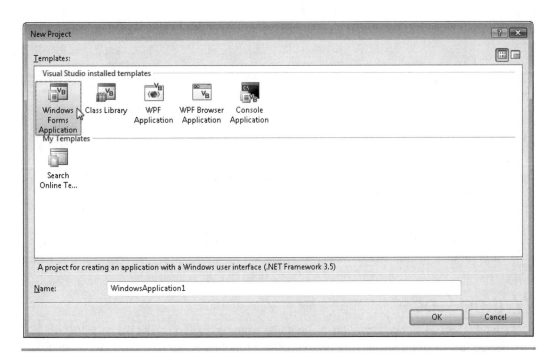

Figure 2-6   Choose the ordinary Windows program option.

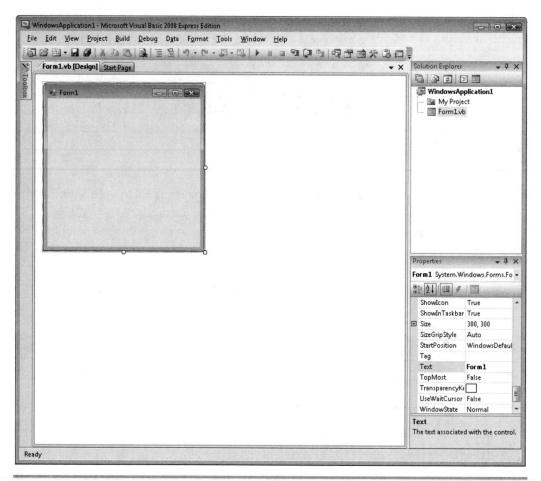

Figure 2-7 You see this blank form whenever you start programming a new Windows application in VB.

topics throughout the book. For now, you're just getting your feet wet and writing your first program.

Writing Code

Behind a form is a code area—the place in the editor where you write the code (instructions) that makes up your program. To get to the Code Editor, just double-click anywhere in the form (see Figure 2-7). You'll see the editor transform itself into a code window, as shown in Figure 2-8.

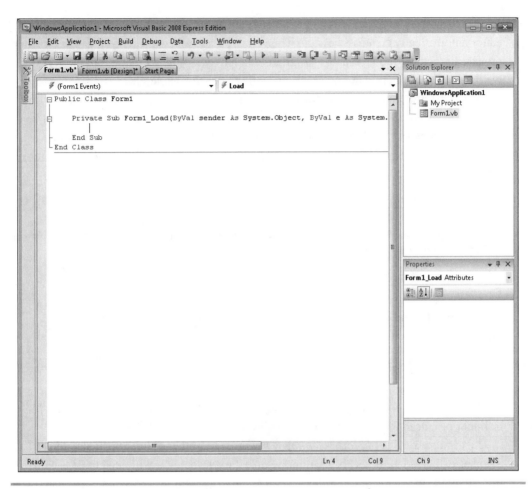

Figure 2-8   Here's where you write your programming commands.

Figure 2-8 shows the *code view*, also called the *code window* or the *code editor*. Figure 2-7 shows the *design view*, also called the *design window* or the *design editor*. You type programming code in code view; you design the user interface (that is, adding buttons, text boxes, and other user interface components to a form) in design view.

Let's get a few concepts nailed down at this point. Look at the tabs at the top of the code window: Form1.vb, Form1.vb [Design], and Start Page. Click the Start Page tab. You're taken back to the original page you first saw when you started VB running, as shown in Figure 2-4. Now click the Form1.vb [Design] tab. You see the form design view window. Finally, click the Form1.vb tab, and you return to the code window.

These tabs are an easy way to switch between the various windows in the editor. The editor automatically creates a new tab whenever you add a new form or other item to your project. Larger and more complex programs can have multiple windows, but in this book we'll create only single-window programs until we reach Chapter 9.

Your first program is a single-form application. Consequently, there will only be one design and one code window, both automatically named *Form1* by the editor. (You'll be surprised at how many effective programs display only a single window to the user.)

Now you should be back looking at the code window (if not, click the *Form1.vb* tab). Let's examine the code that VB has automatically written for you:

```
Public Class Form1

    Private Sub Form1_Load(ByVal sender As System.Object, ByVal e As
System.EventArgs) Handles MyBase.Load

    End Sub
End Class
```

Fortunately, you can ignore almost all of this for most programs you write. The important parts are these:

```
    Sub Form1_Load
    End Sub
```

The rest of the code that VB includes is both distracting and functionally useless for beginner or indeed for programmers at any level.

Just ignore *system objects, eventargs, mybase,* and other elements displayed automatically by VB. It will be extremely rare, if ever, that you will need to deal with these features in your programming. I've been programming for 25 years, and I can recall only once that I had to use the *eventargs* feature. Focus your attention on `Sub Form1_Load` and `End Sub`.

OOP Is Not for Beginners

You may have noticed in the code window that VB automatically adds the lines `Public Class Form1` and `End Class` when a new form is created. Ignore these lines of code as well. Classes (*object-oriented programming*, or *OOP*) can be useful, particularly in advanced professional programming when you're working with other programmers as a team. And some people like to employ OOP when writing their own personal programs, too.

However, OOP is definitely not for beginners, and it's overkill when you're writing simple, relatively straightforward programs. (We won't write OOP code in this book's programs.)

One Editor Line = One Programming Statement

Notice the length of that `Private Sub` line. When printed in this book, the line wraps around and actually becomes two lines in the text, like this:

```
    Private Sub Form1_Load(ByVal sender As System.Object, ByVal e As
System.EventArgs) Handles MyBase.Load
```

However, you must always ensure that long lines like this remain on a *single line in the code window* when you paste or type them. Don't press ENTER to make this (or other long lines) spread over two lines in the editor. VB interprets each line as a single, logical programming statement.

If you break a long line into two, VB will think you're trying to write *two* statements. That's not what you intended. They'll be incomplete statements and VB won't be able to understand what you're trying to do.

Let's see what happens if you *do* break a statement in two. Here's the line we're talking about, now broken because the ENTER key was pressed to snap it in half:

```
Private Sub Form1_Load(ByVal sender As System.Object,
ByVal e As System.EventArgs) Handles MyBase.Load
```

When the line is broken like this, the editor will display a sawtooth error indicator (see Figure 2-9). And the editor will not be able to execute this code.

Notice in Figure 2-9 that the editor underlined the comma and the `ByVal` command with a sawtooth. This clearly shows you where the problem is: the line is broken here. And when you hover your mouse pointer over the sawtooth, the problem is described as a "Syntax error." We'll explore error messages in detail in Chapter 11.

Press F5. This executes the program currently in the editor. Now take a look at Figure 2-10. When you press F5, the editor displays a message saying that it can't "build" this program; asks if you want to run a previous, good version; and opens a window showing a list of errors at the bottom. The error list shows you a description of the error and tells you at which line and column the error is located.

```
    Private Sub Form1_Load(ByVal sender As System.Object,
    ByVal e As System.EventArgs) Handles MyBase.Load
    Syntax error.
```

Figure 2-9   The editor can't understand these two lines of code, because really they are only one line, snapped in half.

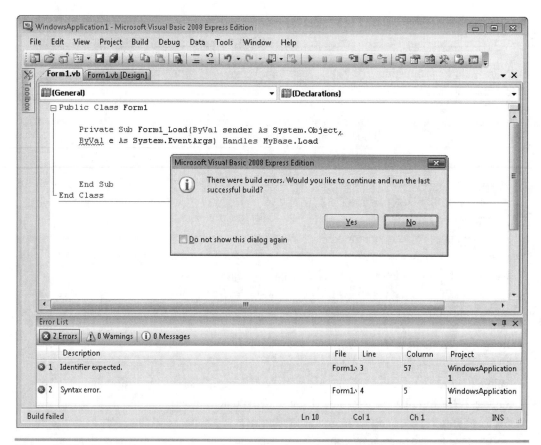

Figure 2-10 Try to run a program with a broken line of code and the editor refuses to execute the program.

You can find plenty of books on OOP if you're interested in it, but while you're learning the elements of programming, I strongly advise you to avoid it. If you decide to go into professional programming, most companies will require you to know OOP. But for now, let's not muddy the waters. VB always adds these lines involving class, and you should always leave them in your code—but just ignore them. I cover OOP briefly in Chapter 13.

Understanding the Word Sub

So, what do the *significant* parts of the code mean, the parts you should not ignore? What, in other words, is a Sub? It's essentially a container. Most programs have multiple subs (also called *events*, *event handlers, subroutines,* or *subprocedures*). Subs are used to subdivide a program into specific tasks. Subs are roughly similar to paragraphs in a letter.

If you create a really simple program that only prints something, you could write all the code in a single sub. But if the program both prints *and* saves the text to a file on your hard drive, you would probably use three subs: one to print, one to save the text, and one to fetch the text back from the file.

It's really up to you, but dividing your program into small, self-contained tasks is very helpful. It makes the program easier to write and easier to fix if a bug (a problem) crops up. It also makes the program easier to read, just as paragraphs make ordinary text easier to read.

Typically, every VB program includes a Form_Load sub that is automatically added by the editor when you start a new program.

For this first program, we'll put all our code in the Form_Load sub. Form_Load is a special sub because the code inside it is executed when the form loads (but before it's displayed as a window to the user). In other words, the Form_Load sub gets executed first when the program is started by the user. Because we're writing such a simple program in this chapter, we'll use only this single sub.

Entering the Code

Now type in the program as shown in the following paragraph. Remember that VB has already entered some of the housekeeping code (most of which you just ignore, as I said earlier). All you need to type is shown here in boldface.

The code window should look like this after you finish typing your part of the code into the editor:

```
Option Strict Off
Option Explicit Off

Public Class Form1
    Private Sub Form1_Load(ByVal sender As System.Object, ByVal e As
System.EventArgs) Handles MyBase.Load
```

```
answer = InputBox("Please type in the delay in minutes...")

MsgBox(answer)

End

        End Sub
End Class
```

TIP

To avoid having to type in the code, you can copy and paste it from www.mhprofessional.com/computingdownload. See "Downloading the Code for This Book" in the Introduction for specific instructions.

Turn off Two Options

Make sure that you add those two lines of code at the very top of the code window that turn off the `Strict` and `Explicit` options. Life is easier for beginners when at least the `Strict` option is turned off. I'll explain these options in Chapter 5.

Note that as you type in your code, you'll see several small "helper windows" opening, as shown in Figure 2-11. Ignore these "IntelliSense" features for now. I'll cover them in the next chapter.

Now press F5. There you go! Your program executes, just as if the user were running it normally by launching it from the Start menu or Windows Explorer. An input box is first displayed to get information from the user, as you can see in Figure 2-12.

After the user clicks OK to close the input box, a message box appears and shows the user what was typed, as shown in Figure 2-13.

TIP

If the Editor freezes up and won't respond normally for some reason after you press F5, just choose Debug | Stop Debugging in the Editor's menus, and things will return to normal. In fact, any time the editor is executing a program, you'll see a blue Stop Debugging button on a toolbar in the editor.

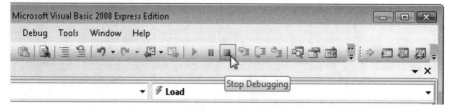

Click the Stop Debugging button shown in the illustration to halt execution (the button will then turn gray). This button is a handy indicator that tells you whether your program is currently executing in the editor. If the button is blue, a program is running (F5 was pressed). If gray, no program is running, and you're free to type in new code or edit existing code.

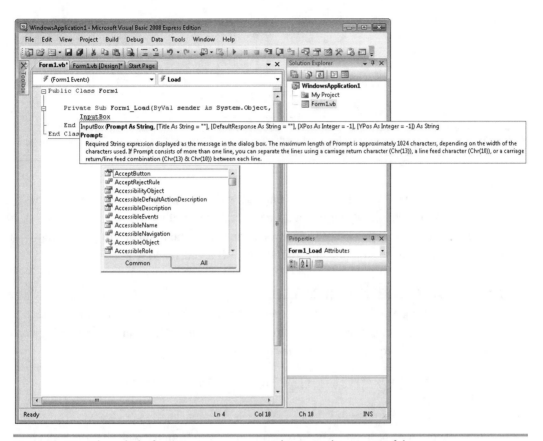

Figure 2-11   These help features in pop-out windows can be very useful.

Figure 2-12   This program displays this small dialog box, asking the user to type in a number.

Figure 2-13 The program remembers what the user typed into the input box and displays it.

This program isn't useful, but you *did* at least write and test an actual program. Now let's conclude this chapter by writing a little utility that *is* useful.

We'll create a timer that you can use when you need to be reminded of something—perhaps that it's time to stop playing around with VB and drive to work.

Expanding the Program

First, delete the code you wrote in the preceding example, but be sure not to delete the two Option lines or the Sub and End Sub statements. Just delete this programming you wrote *within* the sub container. Leave the container:

```
answer = InputBox("Please type in the delay in minutes...")
MsgBox(answer)
End
```

To write our next program, type in (or copy and paste from the web site) the code shown here in boldface:

```
Option Strict Off
Option Explicit Off

Public Class Form1

    Private Sub Form1_Load(ByVal sender As System.Object, ByVal e As
System.EventArgs) Handles MyBase.Load

        EndTime = InputBox("Please type in the delay in minutes...")

        EndTime = EndTime + Minute(Now)

        Do While CurrentTime < EndTime

            CurrentTime = Minute(Now)

        Loop
```

```
MsgBox("Time's Up!")

End

    End Sub
End Class
```

This is a complete Timer program. Press F5, and when asked by the input box, enter **2**. Click the OK button to close the input box. Now, nothing will happen until 2 minutes pass, and then the message "Time's Up!" appears. Just like a kitchen timer.

You may notice a sawtooth line underneath the CurrentTime variable. Just ignore this. (We're ignoring a lot of things, but so what. They're extraneous, insignificant, and distracting.) VB isn't pointing out an error here; it's just offering a little warning that you need not worry about.

Down inside the computer, all kinds of things happen when you write BASIC commands such as InputBox and then press F5 to execute them. Think of it as similar to the famous BBC series *Upstairs Downstairs:* You're upstairs and you write a few instructions telling the maid to bring breakfast to your room. You don't have to bother spelling out all the tasks that must be performed down in the kitchen to make breakfast happen. You just give a command and the details are handled for you by the staff downstairs. Similarly, when you write a line of BASIC code, you're writing commands that BASIC will carry out for you when the program executes.

With the InputBox command, for example, you don't have to tell VB how to display a little dialog box, what color to make it, what typeface to use, or many other details. BASIC handles all these tasks for you.

Recall that each separate line of code in your program is roughly equivalent to an ordinary sentence in a human language, but instead of calling it a sentence, VB refers to each line as a *statement*. Each statement is made up of one or more commands, just as each English sentence is made up of one or more words.

Some lines of code contain only a single word, such as Loop and End in our Timer program. But even a brief line is a statement, a complete idea that VB can understand and carry out for you.

Other lines require a little more information to completely specify what you want to happen. Take the line MsgBox ("Time's Up") for example. You could try to type in the word MsgBox alone, but without some text to display to the user, what's the point? A message box should display a message, and the VB editor knows this. If you just type MsgBox with no parentheses containing any text, VB displays an error message complaining that you didn't include a *prompt* (text message) to be displayed in the message box (see Figure 2-14).

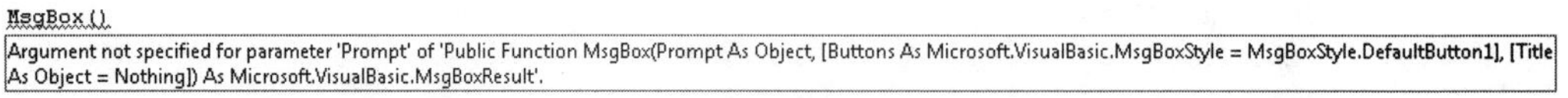

MsgBox ()

Argument not specified for parameter 'Prompt' of 'Public Function MsgBox(Prompt As Object, [Buttons As Microsoft.VisualBasic.MsgBoxStyle = MsgBoxStyle.DefaultButton1], [Title As Object = Nothing]) As Microsoft.VisualBasic.MsgBoxResult'.

Figure 2-14 The editor is complaining that you didn't include a prompt (text message) for this message box.

So, unlike the End command (which shuts down your program without any additional info needed), the MsgBox command always requires that you include the message you want displayed. Makes sense. And notice that in these situations VB always helps you when you forget to add a piece of needed data or forget to type in a complete statement.

But that's enough explanation for now. I'll revisit this Timer program in the next two chapters, explain in detail how each command works, and make some improvements to the timer application. Some of you might have noticed that our Timer program is a little *too* simple. Like most programs you (or I) create, the first time we write it, it contains a bug or two. And this Timer program is no exception. We'll fix the Timer program's bug in Chapter 4.

Chapter 3

Exploring the Editor

Key Skills & Concepts

● Understanding the editor's role

● Using parameter info and auto list members

● Examining the Timer program, step-by-step

● Debugging the Timer program

Computer programming editors work pretty much like word processors—you type or paste lines of code into the editor, and it helps you organize, test, and revise your program.

The Visual Basic Express Editor that you're using is one of the best, most popular, and most useful of all programming editors. The Express Editor is in many ways identical to Microsoft's powerhouse Visual Studio Integrated Development Environment (IDE) used by the majority of professional programmers. So what you learn while using the VB editor will be valuable to you no matter how far you pursue programming in the future, either as an amateur or as a professional.

In this chapter, you'll learn the fundamentals of the VB editor and also explore in detail the Timer program you created in Chapter 2.

IntelliSense: Help with Grammar and Syntax

You doubtless noticed little windows popping up in the editor as you typed in the Timer program in Chapter 2. They can be turned off if you want. (The editor is marvelously customizable; I'll show you how to turn off these windows later in this chapter.) These little windows probably do provide a bit *too* much information for beginners. But many people find these context-sensitive help windows quite useful. They assist you by displaying the purpose, syntax, punctuation, and optional variations of any command.

Collectively, these context-sensitive help windows are referred to as *IntelliSense*. The IntelliSense windows appear and disappear as you write a line of code. IntelliSense can even help you learn to program. Here's how you can use IntelliSense windows to learn Visual Basic more quickly:

1. Start VB.

2. Press CTRL-N to begin a new VB program. (Choose Discard if a dialog box asks what to do with an existing program in the editor.) The New Project dialog box opens.

3. Click the OK button to select the default Windows-style program and close the dialog box.

4. You'll see a blank window (or *form*, as VB calls it) displayed in the upper left of the design window under the Form1 and Start Page tabs. You'll design a form in Chapter 4, but for now, just double-click anywhere inside Form1 to open the code window.

5. You see the default `Private Sub Form1_Load` procedure, with the blinking cursor placed between the `Sub` and `End Sub`—just the place for you to add some code that will execute when this program first runs. (Remember that in a single-form program, that form's `Load` event executes its code first thing when the user runs the program. Even before any window or other item is displayed to the user.)

Using Auto List Members

One of the IntelliSense help features is called *auto list members*. This feature involves a pair of boxes. First, there is a list box that shows you all possible commands that begin with the letter or letters you have typed. Second is a box with a yellow background providing the command's syntax and a description of its purpose. Now start to type in the `MsgBox` command, but just type the letter **M**, as shown in Figure 3-1.

Click the All tab at the bottom of this list so you can see all the available commands, not just the most common ones.

Because you typed *M*, VB thinks you might be typing the `Mid` command, so it shows you a description of how that command can be used (to replace some of the text in a string). However, you want to use the `MsgBox` command, so type **Ms**.

You now see the correct command, `MsgBox`. If you press the ENTER key now, the command is added to the code for you. But don't do that yet. Just type **Ms**, and then click `MsgBox` in the list to open a yellow box which shows you both the *syntax* (the elements of the command and their correct order) and a *description* of what the `MsgBox` command does.

Examining the Syntax

Here's the full syntax for the `MsgBox` command that's displayed by the auto list members feature:

```
Public Function MsgBox(Prompt As Object, [Buttons As Microsoft
.VisualBasic.MsgBoxStyle = MsgBoxStyle.OKOnly], [Title As Object
= Nothing]) As Microsoft.VisualBasic.MsgBoxResult
```

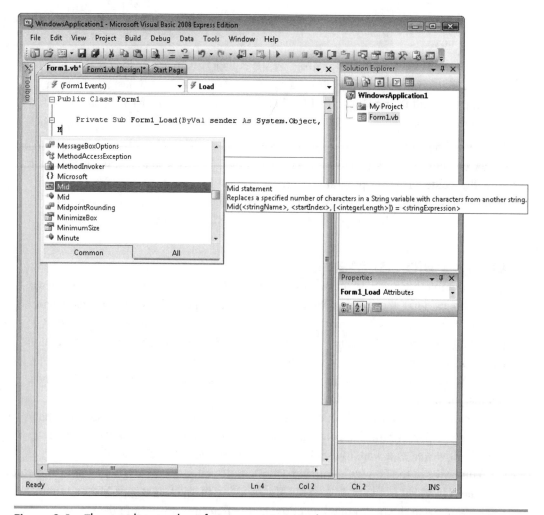

Figure 3-1 The auto list members feature anticipates what command you're typing and describes both its purpose and its syntax.

Fortunately, you can ignore most of what's displayed in most commands' syntax. For the message box, here's the important part (shown in boldface in the preceding full syntax code):

```
MsgBox(Prompt)
```

Pay no attention to the rest of the syntax for now. Commands always include `Public Function`, and there's lots of other redundancy here as well, such as `Microsoft .VisualBasic`.

Also note that whenever you see something inside brackets [ ] in a syntax statement, it's optional. It's up to you to decide whether you want to employ optional elements.

The MsgBox command, like many other commands, is followed by parentheses. This is where you can modify the command with what are called *parameters* (or *arguments*). As you can see in the syntax, the MsgBox command has three parameters: Prompt, Buttons, and Title. However, only the Prompt command is required; the other two parameters are optional because they are enclosed in brackets.

The Prompt parameter is the actual message—the text that you display to the user in the message box. An empty message box would make no more sense than a blank wedding invitation.

Optional parameters sometimes have a default: the default for the message box's buttons parameter is an OK button. So unless you type in an alternative, your message box will by default display that single OK button.

The Title parameter can display text in the message box's title bar (but the default is listed as Nothing; the project's title is displayed). Notice that the syntax does provide you with an idea of the defaults for optional parameters, stating that the MsgBoxStyle is OKOnly and the Title defaults to Nothing. If you wanted to display a title in your message box, you would first list the message, then two commas, and then the title, like this:

```
MsgBox("This is my prompt", , "This is the title")
```

Why the two commas? Parameters are always separated by commas. That's how VB knows when one parameter ends and the next begins. In a *parameter list* like this, you must use commas, even if you're not changing one of the optional parameters. The order of the parameters is important.

In the MsgBox parameter list, the first item is the message, then the button style, and then the title. So here, even though we are not specifying a button style, we must insert a comma for it all the same. You'll get used to parameter lists—they're easy to work with after a while.

Examining the Description

The yellow box in the auto list members feature also includes this description of what the MsgBox command does: *Displays a message in a dialog box, waits for the user to click a button, and then returns an integer indicating which button the user clicked.* (An integer is just an ordinary number with no fraction, such as 2 or 6.)

Because we're only displaying the default OK button, we don't need to know which button was clicked—so we'll just ignore the "returned integer." You *can* make a message box more complicated by displaying additional buttons (such as OK and Cancel, or Yes and No) if you want. In that case, the user can communicate with your program by choosing which button to click. Then, based on the button clicked, the program can take some action. But most of the time you'll use the `InputBox` command if you need to get information back from the user. A message box is primarily used to just show messages.

Getting Comprehensive Help

For really extensive help, including code examples, click the command in your code that you need help with (clicking puts the blinking insertion cursor on that command). Then press F1. Try it now: Type the full command name, **MsgBox**, in the code window. Click `MsgBox` and then press F1. You'll see the VB Help system open a new window with quite a bit of information about this command, including helpful information about how to use the parameters (see Figure 3-2).

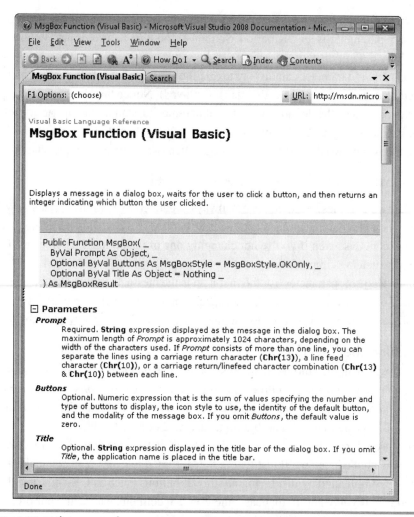

Figure 3-2 VB's Help system shows you everything you wanted to know about the `MsgBox` command.

NOTE

If you don't see the information in Figure 3-2, use the VB editor's menus to add this feature. Choose Tools | Options, and then open the Help options under the Environment category in the left pane of the Options dialog box. Then in the right pane, under *Show Help Using,* choose *External Help Viewer.*

Now scroll down a bit in the right pane to see all the different kinds of button styles you can use, as shown in Figure 3-3.

Scroll farther and you'll see a list of the various return values (shown in Figure 3-4). These values tell your program which button the user clicks to close the program. You can use either the numeric value, such as 2, or the spelled out word, Cancel (called a *constant*).

Notice that in Figure 3-4 that I've now closed the index pane on the left (visible in Figure 3-3). To close the pane, you click the close box (the X) at the top-right corner of the pane. We're not searching right now or using the index list, so closing that pane makes the main help pane on the right easier to read. You can always restore the index pane by clicking the Index option on the Help toolbar, as shown in Figure 3-5.

Finally, at the bottom of the Help page for the MsgBox command is a code example written in VB that shows you one way to employ this command in your own program (see Figure 3-6). You can even copy and paste this code into the code editor, and then modify it to suit your program's needs.

The example code shown in Figure 3-6 really puts the MsgBox command through its paces. It's a rather advanced example. For one thing, it uses the Or command to combine several style parameters:

```
MsgBoxStyle.DefaultButton2 Or MsgBoxStyle.Critical Or MsgBoxStyle.YesNo
```

It also demonstrates how to use the information about which button the user clicks to take action in your program using an *If...Then* structure. We'll explore these topics in future chapters. For now, just notice that the Help system provides quite a bit of valuable information, not least of which is this code sample and the accompanying text description telling you what's going on in the example.

The moral of this story is this: Press F1 when you get perplexed. (And remember that everyone does it, though some pretend they don't.)

Another often useful approach when you're struggling to figure out a programming problem is to Google it. Just type **"Visual Basic" MsgBox** into the Google search box, for example, and you'll see a list of many examples, discussions, tutorials, and answered questions. Several excellent web sites are devoted to Visual Basic, and they're easy to find via a Google search. Chapter 12 explores in-depth the various ways to get help while programming VB.

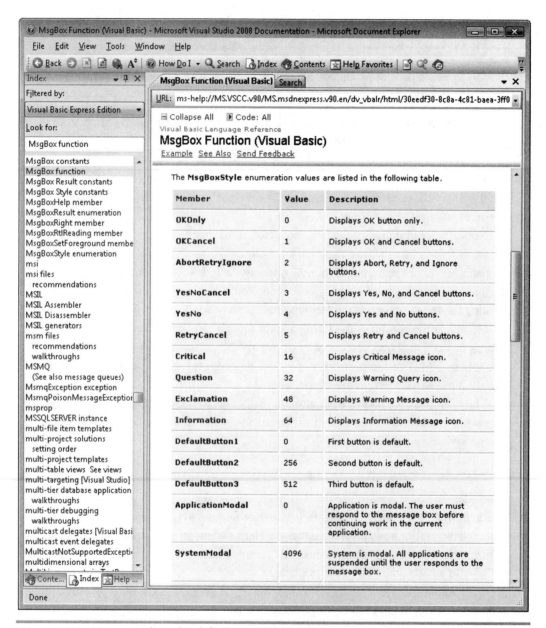

Figure 3-3 You can replace the default `MsgBoxStyle.OKOnly` with a `YesNoCancel` style or any of these listed alternatives.

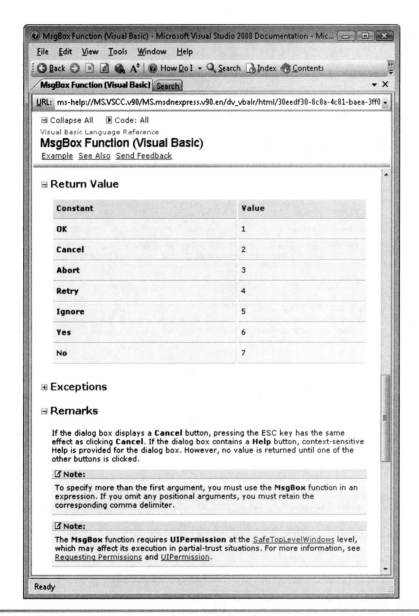

Figure 3-4 Help also displays the set of return values for a `MsgBox`.

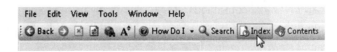

Figure 3-5 Click this button to reopen the Index pane in Help.

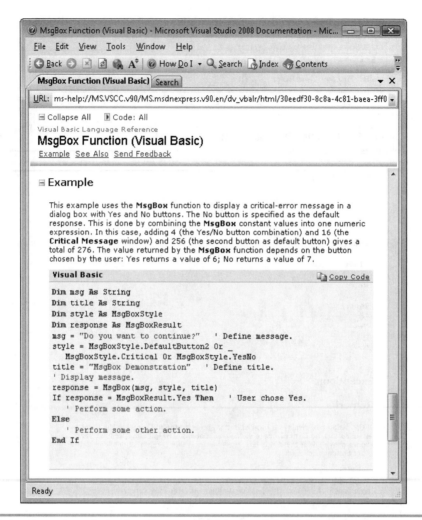

Figure 3-6 Example code is often the most useful part of the Help system.

Using Parameter Information

The second major IntelliSense help feature is called *parameter information*. This feature is displayed once you have finished typing a command and are now typing inside the parentheses that follow most commands. Recall that items inside parentheses after a command are called the command's *parameters*. Everything inside the parentheses is called the command's *parameter list*.

So, to open the IntelliSense parameter information for the `MsgBox` command, you'd type this:

`MsgBox(`

Once you've typed the left parenthesis, the parameter information window opens, as shown in Figure 3-7.

For the first parameter of a `MsgBox` command, the `Prompt` parameter, you're told that it's the "String (text) expression displayed as the message in the dialog box." That pretty much sums it up. I couldn't have put it better myself. But additional helpful information is also displayed: how long the text (string) can be and how to display a multi-line message.

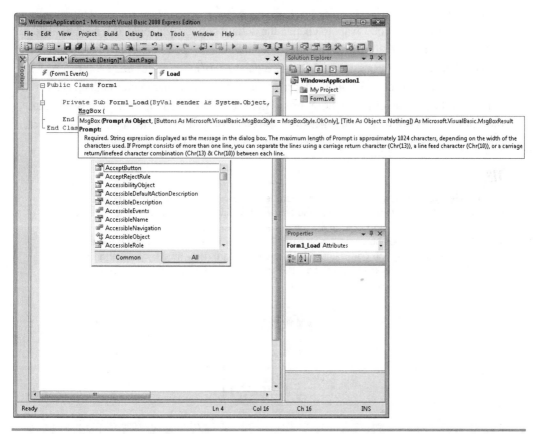

Figure 3-7 This help feature shows you how to use a command's parameters.

```
MsgBox("Well, hello there!",,"Welcome
```
```
MsgBox (Prompt As Object, [Buttons As Microsoft.VisualBasic.MsgBoxStyle = MsgBoxStyle.OkOnly], [Title As Object = Nothing]) As Microsoft.VisualBasic.MsgBoxResult
Title:
    Optional. String expression displayed in the title bar of the dialog box. If you omit Title, the application name is placed in the title bar.
```

Figure 3-8   Because the `Title` parameter appears in boldface in the parameter information box, you can see that you're now working on the `Title` parameter in your code.

Parameter information tells you all about each parameter as you type it in. Remember that parameters are separated in the parameter list by commas, so each time you enter a comma, parameter information changes to describe the next parameter. The parameter currently being entered by you in your code (and thus currently described in the yellow parameter information box) is shown in boldface in the syntax statement.

Figure 3-8 illustrates a couple of points about parameters. First, I want to display the title *Welcome* on this message box. (The title appears at the top of the box in the title bar, as shown in Figure 3-9.)

In this example, I don't want to change the default button style, but I still need to include that comma where the `ButtonStyle` parameter would be specified. That's why you see two commas between the `Prompt` and the `Title` parameters in my code: `hello there!",,`

Also notice in Figure 3-8 that a description of the `Title` parameter is displayed at the bottom of the parameter information box. This is a helpful info, because it tells you that this parameter is optional, that it's a string (text) displayed in the title bar, and that if you don't specify it in your code, the name of your program will be displayed instead.

TIP

If you prefer, you can turn off the auto list members or parameter information features. Choose Tools | Options, and then click the Show All Settings check box in the lower-left corner of the Options dialog box. In the left pane, click Text Editor | Basic | General. Then deselect their check boxes in the Statement Completion section. But even if these features are turned off, you can still turn them on temporarily any time by choosing Edit | IntelliSense or by using keyboard shortcuts. Pressing CTRL-J displays auto list members and CTRL-SHIFT-I shows parameter information.

Figure 3-9   The `Title` parameter (*Welcome* in this example) is displayed in the title bar of the message box.

Understanding the Timer Program

Now let's take a stroll down through the Timer program you created in Chapter 2. We'll look at the program line-by-line, explaining how each line does its job and why that line is important to the overall success of the program.

Press CTRL-N to start a brand-new program in the VB editor. (If a dialog box appears asking you what you want to do with the existing code, click the Discard button.)

In the New Project dialog box, click OK to accept the Windows-style default program type.

Double-click anywhere on the form to open the code window. Then copy and paste the Timer program found at the end of Chapter 2.

TIP

All this book's code can be found at the McGraw-Hill web site at www.mhprofessional .com/computingdownload. See the section titled "Downloading the Code for This Book" in the Introduction for specific instructions.

Now the code is in the editor, ready for you to explore. Recall that you'll see a sawtooth error indicator under the word `CurrentTime`. Ignore that. It's called a "null reference," but it's unimportant to us. It won't cause us any problems. It's only a *suggestion* from the editor, not an error message. (It's like when your mother told you to wear a hat in case it rains.)

But if you see any *other* sawtooth error messages in this code after you paste it, you've pasted the code in wrong. Compare what you see in the editor with the complete code listing at the end of Chapter 2, in the section titled "Expanding the Program." Fix the code in the editor so it looks *exactly* like the code listing in Chapter 2.

Recall that a program is a list of tasks—normally one task is described per line. And when the program runs, those tasks are carried out in order (with a few exceptions such as a *loop,* which we'll look at in a minute). And I don't expect you to totally understand looping fully in this chapter, so don't be concerned for now. By the end of Chapter 7, you'll fully grasp the concept of loops.

Actually, now that I think about it, it's unlikely that you'll completely understand most of the details we're going to explore at this point, but follow along anyway. All you need to do in this chapter is come away with a general sense of how VB executes a program: starting at the first line, and then moving down performing the task specified in each line, in turn.

An InputBox Gets the User's Answer to a Question

To figure out when the user wants our Timer program to *go off* (in other words, how long the timer should run), we need to ask the user to enter how many minutes to delay. An easy way to get info from a user is to display an *input box*. The user can enter 12 or 2 or 88—or whatever number of minutes they want to set the timer delay.

The `InputBox` line of code looks like this:

```
EndTime = InputBox("Please type in the delay in minutes...")
```

When this line executes, a dialog box is displayed to the user with some text (the prompt in quotes) telling the user to type in the delay.

Notice the equal sign. This means: *After this line finishes executing, the number typed in by the user will be stored in the variable named* `EndTime`. In other words: `EndTime` will equal that number: `EndTime =`. Then, later in our code, we can use the word `EndTime` to represent the user's requested delay.

You'll often see a variable followed by an equal sign: This process is sometimes called *assigning* a value to a variable. A *variable* is just a container that holds information that might change while a program runs. (Chapter 5 is all about how to use variables.) A variable can hold a number, a piece of text (called a *string*), or other information such as the time. This program has two variables. Both hold information about time—the current time (when you start the timer) and also the delay, the duration the user specifies in the input box for the timer's countdown.

Each variable can hold only a single item of information. You can't, for example, put both the number 31 and the number 4112 in the same variable. You would need to use two variables—one to hold each item of information.

You, the programmer, create variables. Usually with the `Dim` command. And you can name variables pretty much anything you wish (except for names VB itself already uses for commands, such as `End` or `MsgBox`). People usually choose variable names that are descriptive of whatever data the variable will hold. We named this program's variables `CurrentTime` and `EndTime`.

Manipulating a Variable

When the `InputBox` command executes, VB displays the that dialog box and automatically pauses the program until the user responds to the `InputBox`. VB just waits around until the user presses ENTER or clicks the OK or Cancel button to close the dialog box. Then the input box disappears and VB resumes execution by moving down to the next line of code, which is

```
EndTime = EndTime + Minute(Now)
```

This interesting line takes the number of minutes entered by the user (which is held in the variable EndTime, remember) and adds (+) these minutes to the current minute according to the computer's clock.

In other words, if the current time is 1:15 and the user enters 10, the variable EndTime will contain the sum of the minutes 15 + 10, which is 25 minutes. That's when the timer will "go off," having finished its delay. In this case, the timer would go off at 1:25.

Again, notice the equal sign. That means the result of whatever is to the *right* of the equal sign—EndTime + Minute(Now)—will be *assigned* (stored in) to the variable EndTime.

Basic has many time- and date-related commands, but the Minute command used with the Now command gives the exact current minute.

Testing While Programming

Let's try an experiment now to ensure that this program is doing what we want it to do. I've been programming in Basic for more than 25 years, and I wasn't absolutely certain that the code Minute(Now) would give me the current minute.

Almost no programmers can simply write perfect, working code right off the bat. Most programmers test their code as they go along to be sure they're remembering how to accomplish the various tasks that their program must carry out. Always remember that computer languages are extremely literal; they don't *infer* or *guess* your intent. You must get the commands, the word order (syntax), the spelling, and punctuation *exactly* right.

It's common to test parts of a program while you're writing them. To test this line of code, I inserted a *temporary* message box to display to me the value in the variable EndTime. This message box isn't for the user—it's for me. I'll remove it after I use it for this test.

I used the following line of code (in boldface) to test my assumption that the Minute(Now) commands would give me the current minute:

```
EndTime = InputBox("Please type in the delay in minutes...")

EndTime = EndTime + Minute(Now)

MsgBox(EndTime)
```

Try this yourself. Type in the line **MsgBox(EndTime)** where shown in the code. Press F5 to run this program. Enter **3** when asked to type in the delay. Then see what the message box displays as the end time. Look at your watch or clock. The EndTime value should be the current minute, plus 3 minutes. So if it's 11:12 on your watch, the message box should display *15*.

At this point, the program is actually *running* in the editor (you pressed F5). You won't see anything happening when you close the message box because the timer is counting down. But you want to go back to writing code, because the test is over.

However, the editor is going to remain unresponsive until you stop the executing program. When you press F5 in the editor to execute the code, you enter *debugging mode*. You need to get back to *editing mode* (also called *design mode*).

Recall from Chapter 2 that you stop execution and leave debugging mode by clicking the blue Stop Debugging button in a toolbar, shown next.

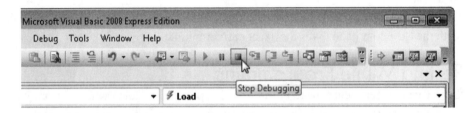

Click that blue button now. The program stops and any little debugging panes displayed on the bottom of the editor (Immediate Window, Error List, whatever) are closed. You're now back in edit mode, ready to continue writing your program.

Delete the line `MsgBox(EndTime)`, because you don't need it any more. The test was successful. Inserting a temporary message box like this to see what's in a variable is a common way to quickly test a program.

The Program Repeats Within a Loop

OK. What happens after our Timer program learns what the end time is? The program goes to the next line of code, where it enters a *loop*. The program will spend most of its time repeating the following three lines of code, called a loop:

```
Do While CurrentTime < EndTime
    CurrentTime = Minute(Now)
Loop
```

Loops are at the heart of many programs. They loop (continue to repeat something) until a particular condition is satisfied. In this case, the condition being tested is whether or not the end time has been reached.

This line of code `Do While CurrentTime < EndTime` means "continue to repeat this loop as long as the current time is less than the end time."

What happens here is that execution of the program is trapped within these three lines—between the `Do` and the `Loop`.

These lines are executed over and over as long as the value in the variable `CurrentTime` remains less than (the < symbol represents the concept of "less than") the value in the variable `EndTime`.

For example, let's assume that the current time is 1:12 and the `EndTime` variable holds 15 (meaning that the user specified a delay of 3 minutes). This loop will continuously repeat for 3 minutes. Each time through the loop, the variable `CurrentTime` is assigned whatever minute the computer's clock provides: 12, 13, 14, and so on. The loop continues.

The Loop Stops Looping

As soon as the minute reaches 15 (1:15), the loop condition is *satisfied*. The value in `CurrentTime` is no longer less than the value in `EndTime`. Instead, they are now equal.

So at this point, the loop structure is exited. The program stops looping and resumes its line-by-line execution. The program now moves down to the line of code immediately below the `Loop` command. And that line of code is

```
MsgBox("Time's Up!")
```

At this point, a dialog box is displayed, telling the user that the timer has finished its countdown. Time's up. And the program ends because we typed in the command `End` on the following line. That command always shuts down a program.

Debugging

Removing *bugs* (errors) from programs is an ongoing process—and in longer, complicated applications (programs), it is *never* really finished. That's because the bigger the program, the more unexpected interactions, unintended side-effects, can occur.

It's like throwing a party. If you invite only two friends who get along well, things should go predictably smoothly. But the more people you add, the greater the possibility that a hissy fit or fight will break out between some of them. Or somebody will fall into the punch bowl, or some other tedious behavior will occur—like slapping or shoving. To put this phenomenon in programming terminology: the more variables, the more possible unexpected interactions.

Nobody's Perfect

Recall that earlier in this chapter we temporarily inserted a MsgBox to test the Timer program to see if the variable `EndTime` really contained the minute that we wanted the delay to end. I wasn't sure.

Some programmers, teachers, and people who write books about programming don't admit that they stumble through the process of creating a program. That it's a trial-and-error process, like sculpting or raising kids. They pretend that they type a program in correctly the first time, out of their brilliance, the way Mozart wrote symphonies.

The truth is, you'll be guessing when you write many lines of code. You'll assume that a command behaves a certain way, trusting your memory or the Help system. You try it out in your program. Sometimes the line works as you hoped, and sometimes not. More often not, especially while you're learning.

If not, you fiddle around until you figure out how to use the command correctly, or else you find out that an entirely different command or technique is needed.

Maybe a few virtuoso programmers *don't* grope around as they write code. They just sit there and type in a perfect list of statements that work exactly as they expect. But most of us pretty much continually guess which code will work, and we just try it and see.

So don't assume that your fumbling attempts to get code right is somehow your fault. You'll *always* fumble. We all do (well, nearly all of us). As time goes on, you'll fumble somewhat less, but not that much less. Coding is sometimes called *hacking* because, like a sculptor, you chop away at the project until it gradually starts to take shape. You have a goal in mind, but exactly which hacks with the hammer and chisel will bring out the statue hiding inside the block of marble can't really be known in advance—by most of us.

My Personal Confessions

Fortunately, the VB editor contains an excellent suite of debugging tools that we'll explore in Chapter 11. For now, let me describe to you what happened when I tried to fix a problem with our Timer program. And there *is* a serious bug in this program.

While I was writing Chapter 2, I realized that the code had a flaw that needed correcting. It's this: picture a clock. As soon as the minute hand goes past 12, the minute changes from 60 back to 0. What happens if the user enters an end time that goes past the hour? For example, what if it's currently 1:50 and the user enters *20* as the delay?

The way our program works, *50* (the current minute) is added to *20*, giving us an end time of *70*! No clock has 70 minutes on it.

If this happens, our loop will never stop repeating itself. It keeps going until the current time is less than the end time. But with an end time of 70, *the current minute will never reach 70.* The loop cannot stop. Minutes only go up to 60. Thus, the current time will always be less than an end time of 70. That's a well-known type of bug: a loop that can never exit is called an *endless* or *infinite loop.*

Two confessions: I didn't realize this would be a problem when I first wrote the program. And second, I didn't immediately know how to fix it. How would I rewrite the code to avoid this problem?

I spent about 20 minutes with a pad and pencil trying to figure out the relationship between `EndTime`, `StartTime`, and the current time (`Minute(Now)`). Maybe you can see an answer to this problem right away. I didn't. I often don't, and most of you, dear readers, won't either.

So once again you see how programming is. For most of us, it's a process of approximation: We try different approaches until, eventually, the correct approach is discovered.

I probably *could* cobble together a few lines of code that would handle this problem, and then fix the program to make it work right. (For example, the `Now.AddMinutes` command would probably provide a solution.)

But I know a better way. Give up! Rather than spending more time fiddling around trying to fix this flawed version of our Timer program, I'll just toss it out completely. I'll try an entirely new approach to writing a Timer program in Chapter 4. That approach will not only work, but it will also be better in several ways than the one we currently have. Among other things, it will have a better user interface because we'll design a form (a window the user will interact with) rather than just using an input box.

Tech Tip

We've barked up the wrong tree with our Timer program. Not only does it have a serious bug in it (it can't deal with a timer delay that goes past the hour), but it also employs bad programming practice. I'm using a loop to time something, and that's just not the best way to pause a program.

Using a loop as a timer hogs the computer. Our current version of the Timer program has the computer looping as fast as it can until the requested delay is over. When this book's tech editor ran the Timer program on his computer, the program went through the loop about 54 million times in 1 minute and raised the central processing unit (CPU) utilization to more than 50 percent during that time. Although the computer won't get tired, or start smoldering, you *are* hogging its CPU—its brain. For one thing, other programs running at the same time will be forced to compete with this lame version of the timer, this time hog.

So we really have several reasons to abandon our original, sketchy approach and start a new timer program all over from scratch in Chapter 4. Some of you may wonder why I didn't just present the correct, polished version of the Timer program right off the bat. Why all this stumbling around? The reason is that I want you to understand that the process of writing a computer program is simply not straightforward, except for those few Mozarts among us.

This *approximation*, this *hacking* and fumbling, is not just the way you, a beginner, will write programs. In fact, it's the way everyone below the genius level writes programs. (And I have my suspicions about some of these geniuses, too.)

To Review

Here are some concepts to remember:

- Pressing F5 runs your program within the VB editor, just as if a user had double-clicked it in Windows Explorer (except the editor remains open). You can test a program while you're writing it by pressing F5 at any time. When you're done testing, click the blue Stop Debugging button.

- Programs carry out your instructions (commands) line-by-line down through the code, with a few exceptions such as a loop, which circles round and round until the loop's exit condition is met.

- Commands are often followed by parameters (in parentheses). Parameters modify how the command works. For example, the statement `MsgBox ("Time's Up!")` begins with the `MsgBox` command, and that command is modified by the `Prompt` parameter you specify in parentheses.

- Writing a program is a trial-and-error process for almost all programmers. You write some code, test it, and if it doesn't produce expected results (and it often doesn't), you rewrite it until you get it to work. Or you throw it out and try a whole new approach, starting over from scratch. Some programmers like to test every few lines of code; some test only when they're unsure about something; others wait until they've finished with the first draft of the program. It's a matter of taste: how often you test, and when, is your choice.

Chapter 4

Creating a User Interface

Key Skills & Concepts

- Using the code and design windows

- Building a form: our Timer program gets dressed up

- Employing the toolbox

- Understanding controls and properties

- Programming events

Now you're going to have some real fun. Designing the surface of a VB application—the windows the user sees and interacts with—is usually both easy and entertaining.

In the previous chapters, you built a Timer program from the *bottom up*: You wrote the code and then added an input box and message box to communicate with the user. You used the editor's code window exclusively in those chapters.

Now we'll switch to the design window and sketch in our program's visual components before writing any code. In this chapter, we won't work from the bottom up. We'll take a different, but popular approach. We'll create the surface, the user interface, first. And then we'll write code "underneath" that interface to make the interface do its job.

It's rather like sketching in a new, sleek car design, and then worrying later about how to make the sun roof move or the door locks work.

Top-down Designing

Working from the surface down is called *top-down* design. And as you might expect, in this chapter you're going to create a more visual version of the Timer program. Let's get started. Follow these steps to start your new program:

1. Start VB.

2. Press CTRL-N to open the New Project window. (Click the Discard button if you're asked what to do with an existing project.)

3. Click the OK button to accept the default Windows Forms Application style for your new project.

You now see an empty form, ready for you to add visual components to it, such as buttons and labels.

Whenever you start a new project, the editor opens the design window by default rather than the code window. This is because most people create programs these days from the top down. They start by designing the form, and then switch later to the code window to type in the code.

This approach makes sense, because when you know what visual components the user will interact with, you have a pretty good general idea about what code you need to make those components do their jobs.

You could design a Timer program in many ways, but we'll keep it simple by adding only three components (usually called *controls*). We'll use a *button* control that the user clicks to start the timer, a NumericUpDown control to allow the user to specify the number of minute's delay for the timer, and a special control called a *Timer* that will keep time for us.

To create the user interface, follow these steps:

1. Click the toolbox tab on the left side of the editor. If it's not visible, choose View | Toolbox. The toolbox is a collection of controls you can drag and drop onto your form, as you can see in Figure 4-1.

2. Drag the Button control from the toolbox and drop it in the lower-right corner of the form, as you can see in Figure 4-2. When you drop the button, the toolbox gracefully withdraws so you can see your form. If you want to move the button, just drag it around on the form. For finer positioning, move the button by holding down the arrow keys on your keyboard.

3. Take another look at Figure 4-2. Notice that the button is surrounded by small "drag handles." You can pull any of these little squares to resize the control. These handles also show you which control (or the form) has the *focus* (is currently *selected*).

4. By default, on the right side of the editor are two *panes* (small windows). They can be repositioned or hidden. The top one, the Solution Explorer, lists all the forms in the current project. Since this is a simple application, we're going to use only one form, so there's no real value in displaying the Explorer while we're working on this program. Click the close box in the upper-right corner of the Solution Explorer pane to close it.

   At this point, the Properties window automatically expands vertically to take up the space previously used by the Solution Explorer. (If some other pane shows up, click its x to close it as well. We're interested in the Properties window only.)

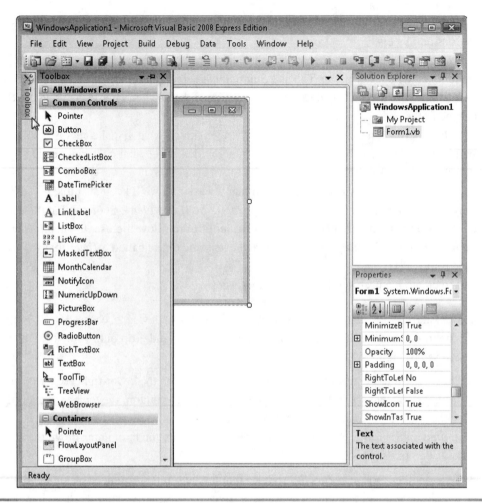

Figure 4-1 You can drag any control from the toolbox onto your form.

5. The Properties window is extremely useful while you're designing a form and working with controls. It's where you can modify the qualities of a control—change its text (caption), its color, its font, and so on. We're not going to enlarge our form, so we've got some room in the editor to widen the Properties window. Drag the left side of the Properties window to make its contents more easily readable, as shown in Figure 4-3.

6. As you can see in Figure 4-3, by default the button is automatically given the name *Button1* (and its text caption also defaults to *Button1*). Each time you add a control to a form, that control is given a default name by VB. For example, when we add a

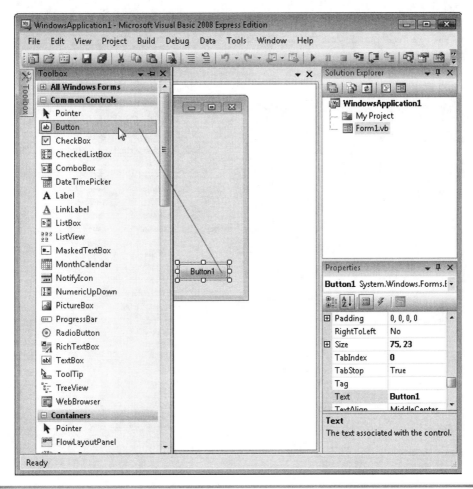

Figure 4-2 Drag-and-drop a Button control onto your form.

NumericUpDown control in a few minutes, it will be automatically named *NumericUpDown1*. If you add a second button to this form, it will be given the default name *Button2*.

7. We want the button's text (caption) to say *Start*, so the user knows to click it to start the timer. If the button isn't currently selected (doesn't have the small boxes around it indicating it has the focus), click the button to give it the focus. This ensures that the Properties window is displaying the button's properties.

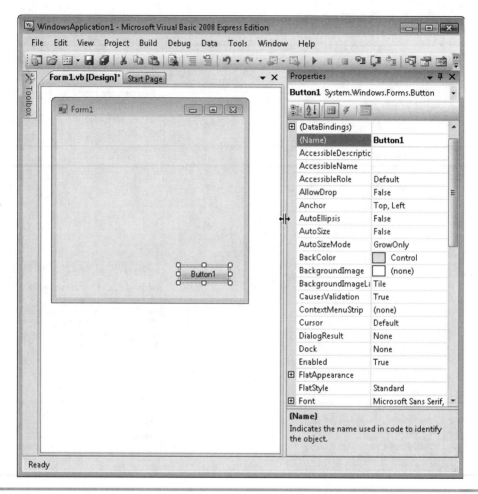

Figure 4-3 Drag the left side of the Properties window to widen it and expose more of its contents.

8. Scroll the Properties window until you see the Text property. Click the Text property. A down arrow appears. Click that down arrow, and a small text box opens. Recall that VB has provided a default caption, *Button1*, just as it provided that same default Name property. But we don't want users to be confused by seeing a button displaying meaningless (to them) *Button1* text. Delete the default text *Button1* and replace it by typing **Start**, as you can see in Figure 4-4.

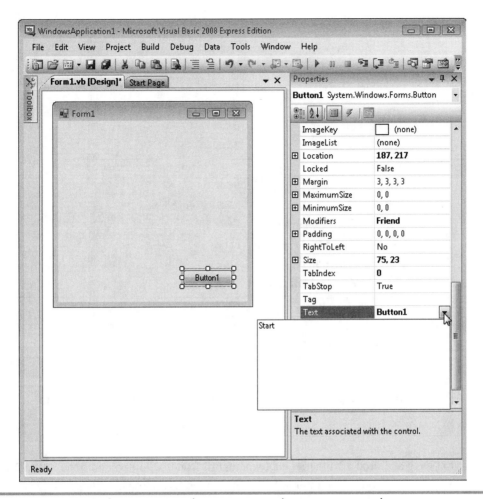

Figure 4-4   You can change a control's properties in the Properties window.

9. Press ENTER to commit this revised caption. Notice that the caption has also now changed on the button itself displayed in the form.

TIP

You need not actually open the text box shown in Figure 4-4. Most controls permit you to just click the right side of the property entry, and just edit the property right there (see Figure 4-5).

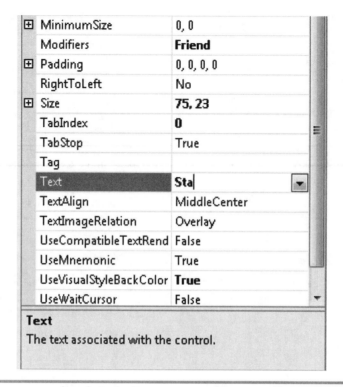

⊞ MinimumSize	0, 0	
Modifiers	**Friend**	
⊞ Padding	0, 0, 0, 0	
RightToLeft	No	
⊞ Size	**75, 23**	
TabIndex	**0**	
TabStop	True	
Tag		
Text	**Sta**	▼
TextAlign	MiddleCenter	
TextImageRelation	Overlay	
UseCompatibleTextRend	False	
UseMnemonic	True	
UseVisualStyleBackColor	**True**	
UseWaitCursor	False	▼

Text
The text associated with the control.

Figure 4-5 You can type directly in the Properties window to modify most properties.

10. Next Drag and drop a NumericUpDown control from the toolbox onto the form. Drag it to position it where you think it looks best on the form. You can always move it or resize it later if you want to.

11. Finally, open the toolbox one more time and scroll down until you see the Components section. At the very bottom of this section, you'll see the Timer control. Drag and drop a Timer onto the form.

Notice that after you drop the Timer control, it is displayed below the form (at the bottom of the design window), not on the form (see Figure 4-6). This is because a Timer control is never visible to the user. Instead, it works behind the scenes, assisting our program with timing issues, but it is visible only to us programmers while we're designing in the editor.

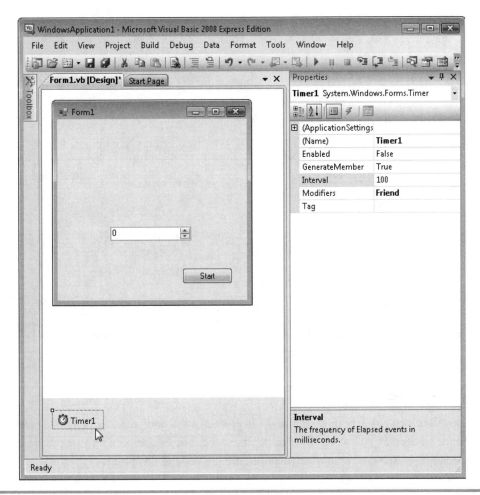

Figure 4-6   A Timer control works behind the scenes, invisible to the user—so it's placed off the form.

TIP

As an alternative in step 8, type **&Start** (rather than Start). Then the user can press ALT-S (a speed key) rather than clicking the button with the mouse. Using speed keys not only makes your program easier to use for typists (they don't have to take their hands off the keyboard and reach for the mouse), but it also addresses accessibility needs for readers who have mobility or sight issues. Speed keys are underlined in a control's caption (text property), so they cue the user that this control can be accessed with an ALT- key combination. See Figure 4-7.

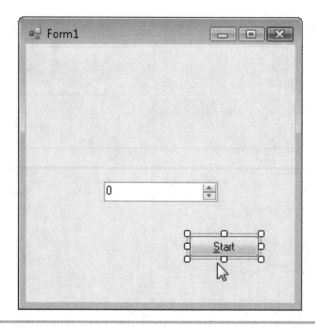

Figure 4-7 When a letter is underlined in a control's Text property, this means it can be triggered by an ALT-key combination (in addition to a mouse click).

Writing the Code

I know that you're being thrown into the deep end of the pool here, and no doubt you'll flounder a little as you work through this next section. Just remember that you're not expected to understand how to write programming code at this point.

When you've completed this book, you'll have a much better idea about what various controls and code statements do, and how to use them in your own programming. For now, just relax and follow along.

We've now finished adding all the controls necessary to design our form. So it's time to switch from design view to code view, where we'll write a few lines of programming to make this Timer program do its job.

Switching to Code View

The easiest way to switch to code view in the editor is to double-click a control. Go ahead and double-click the Start button control on the form to open the code window displaying the `Sub` (event) that is most often used with the button control.

It's no surprise that for a button, its `Click` event is the most popular. (*Events* get *triggered* while a program runs. A button's `Click` event, for example, is triggered—executes its code—when the user clicks that button.)

Now we've switched to the code window. While working on the programming code, you don't need the Properties window open, so if you want you can click the x (close box) in the upper-right of the Properties window to close it. You can always reopen it later by choosing it from the View menu or by pressing F4.

Programming the Button

We want to start our timer when the user clicks the Start button. So type the following code into Button1's `Click` event:

```
    Private Sub Button1_Click(ByVal sender As System.Object, ByVal e
As System.EventArgs) Handles Button1.Click

        Timer1.Interval = NumericUpDown1.Value * 60000

        Timer1.Start()

    End Sub
```

When the program runs, the user types into the NumericUpDown control whatever delay they want to set (or alternatively, they can click that control's small up-and-down arrows to specify the delay).

When the user clicks the Start button, our program finds out how many minutes the user has specified for the delay. This number is in the NumericUpDown control's `Value` property. Whatever number is displayed on the NumericUpDown control is its `Value`. If the user changes that number in the control, the `Value` property automatically and immediately changes too.

A Timer control has an `Interval` property. A timer counts down from its interval to zero, just like a kitchen timer does after you set it to specify how long the timer should count down before the bell goes off.

But why do you have to multiply the `NumericUpDown` value by 60000?

```
Timer1.Interval = NumericUpDown1.Value * 60000
```

A Timer control is very precise—it counts in *milliseconds*—one thousandth of a second. So each second is 1000 milliseconds, and there are 60 seconds in a minute. Thus, 60×1000 means there are 60,000 milliseconds in each minute.

This isn't some weird thing you have to figure out each time you use a Timer control in one of your programs. Just remember that to measure time in minutes, multiply by 60000. And if you forget, press F1 to read the help information about the Timer control, which will remind you about this 60000.

VB's creators could have made the Timer work in seconds or minutes, but that would be crude. Instead, because it uses milliseconds, you can write programs that measure time very precisely.

We are telling VB to multiply the user's entry in the NumericUpDown control by 60000, and then store (assign) the result into the Timer's `Interval` property when it executes this line in our code:

```
Timer1.Interval = NumericUpDown1.Value * 60000
```

As you saw when we modified the Button's Text property from *Button1* to *Start*, properties can be changed in the Properties window. But many properties can also be changed while a program is running, by the programmer writing the necessary code, or directly by the user.

In this program, the NumericUpDown control's `Value` property is changed by the user. And then you, the programmer, change the Timer's `Interval` property by commands you write in your code (`Timer1.Interval =`).

To specify a control's property in your programming code, use the control's name, a period, then the property name, like so:

```
Timer1.Interval or NumericUpDown1.Value
```

Finally, the last statement (line of code) in this event just turns on the timer using its `Start` command: `Timer1.Start`. Technically, `Start` is not a *property* of the Timer control. `Start` is a *method* of the Timer.

Properties are generally qualities, such as color, text, or intervals. Methods are generally capabilities, tasks that an object can carry out, such as starting, stopping, moving, and so on. It's not a perfect analogy because there are some exceptions, but you can think of properties as adjectives and methods as verbs.

Programming the Timer Control

Now we'll finish our programming by entering some simple code into the Timer control's `Tick` event.

Opening the Timer's Tick Event

You can get to the Timer's events by using a pair of drop-down lists that are displayed at the top of the code window. Follow these steps:

1. Click the down arrow to display the contents of the list on the left, as shown in Figure 4-8.

2. Click *Timer1* in the drop-down list on the left, and then click the down arrow in the list on the right, as shown in Figure 4-9.

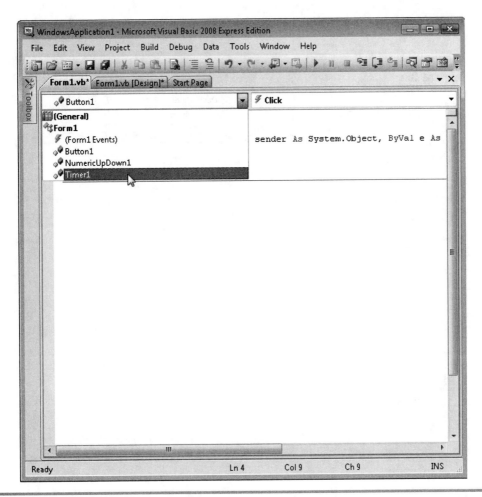

Figure 4-8 Drop this list to see all the controls on your form.

3. Click the `Tick` event in the right drop-down list, and the `Tick` event's `Sub` structure is automatically entered in the code window, ready for you to write your programming between the `Sub` and `End Sub` lines. See this in Figure 4-10.

Also be sure to type in the two `Option` statements (turning off `Strict` and `Explicit`) at the very top of the code window, as shown in Figure 4-10.

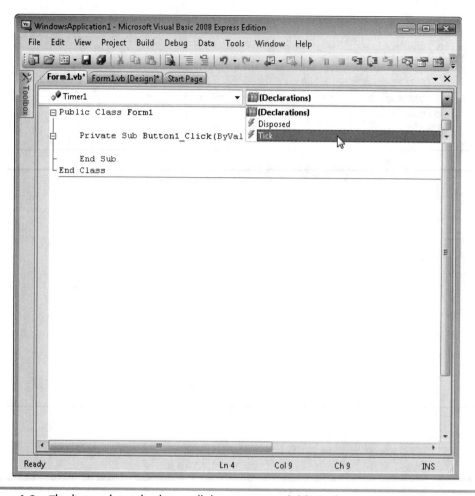

Figure 4-9 The list on the right shows all the events available to the Timer control.

Programming the Tick Event

Complete our Timer program by typing the following lines of code into the Tick event:

```
Private Sub Timer1_Tick(ByVal sender As Object, ByVal e As System.
EventArgs) Handles Timer1.Tick

        Timer1.Stop()

        MsgBox("Time's Up.")
```

```
      End

   End Sub
```

In this `Tick` event code, you stop the Timer control, display a message box to the user, and then end the program. These three lines are fairly self-explanatory.

A Timer control counts down based on its `Interval` property. As soon as the countdown interval has passed, the `Tick` event is triggered (executes its code). However, if you don't employ the `Stop` command, the Timer resets itself *and begins counting down from the interval all over again*!

It's like a strange kind of kitchen timer controlled by a ghost: when it rings its bell, it then automatically rewinds and starts counting down all over again. And it will continue to do this endlessly, unless you intervene and stop it. Why does the Timer do this automatic reset? Because it makes the Timer more flexible.

Since we're using it with our Timer program, it can count down only once, and then we stop it.

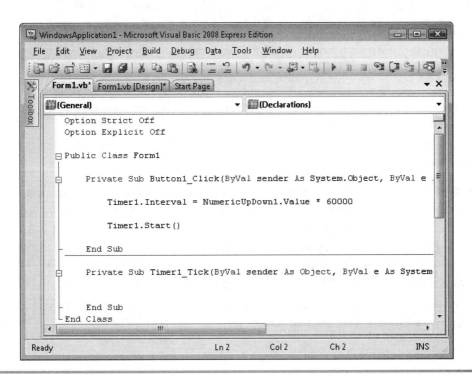

Figure 4-10 VB automatically enters the correct start and end code for an event.

Or, we can use a Timer in a different way: to repeatedly perform a task at a specified interval.

Testing the Program

Press F5 to test the program. Type the number **1** into the NumericUpDown control to set the Timer for one minute. Click the Start button. Nothing seems to happen, but actually the Timer is doing its work behind the scenes. After a minute passes, a message box will pop up.

If you get an error message when you press F5, it's almost certain that you made a mistake while typing or pasting the code from this book's web site. Double-check your typing, or look through the code for any words underlined with a blue sawtooth line. Remember that sawtooth is how VB flags an error. Or just start over and copy and paste the code from this book's web site at www.mhprofessional.com/computingdownload. (Refer to the Introduction for specific instructions on how to download the code.)

NOTE

Even this rather elementary Timer program can be useful. If you want to save it for later use (or give it to others), choose Build | Publish in the editor (click the Build menu, and then choose Publish). A Publish Wizard opens up that will take you through the steps necessary to create a setup program that installs the timer on any computer running Windows. When asked to choose a location for your setup program, the Desktop is convenient. But just follow the instructions and make your own decisions. Once the setup program is created, anyone can run it to install your Timer program on their machine. It will be a normal Windows setup.exe program, (ending in the file extension .exe like all executables).

Improving the Timer

One of the best things about writing your own programs is that you can customize them to suit your preferences. You can modify the Timer program in many different ways. Use the Properties pane to change the BackColor properties of the form and button, if you like. Or put your significant other's photo as wallpaper on the form, as I'll describe next.

Adding Background Textures

You can add wallpaper to a form by changing its BackgroundImage property and displaying a picture there (pictures of textures can look good). Try it.

1. Press SHIFT-F7 to go back to the design window.

2. Click the form's background to select the form.

3. Then click the ellipsis (...) button next to the BackgroundImage property in the Property window. The *Select Resource* dialog box opens, as you can see in Figure 4-11.

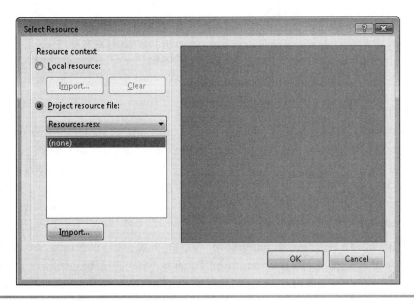

Figure 4-11   Use this dialog box to import a graphic into the background of a form.

4. Click the Local Resource radio button in the Select Resource dialog box (so you can bring in an image from your hard drive).

5. Then click the Import button in the dialog box to open a file browser dialog box. Locate a .jpg or .bmp graphics file on your hard drive and double-click it.

6. Click the OK button to close the Select Resource dialog box.

Figure 4-12 shows how our program looks with a canvas texture imported.

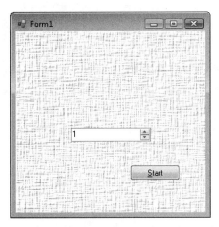

Figure 4-12   Make your programs look less ordinary by adding background textures.

TIP

You can find lots of textures in graphics programs such as Photoshop or Paint Shop Pro, or just Google *background textures*. You'll find zillions of them online—snakeskin, marble, sunsets, or whatever you like.

Adding a Progress Bar

Now let's conclude this chapter by adding visual animation that shows the user the timer's progress as it counts down to the end. Many people get uncomfortable when a program enters a loop and nothing seems to be happening. They rightly worry that maybe the program has crashed. Displaying a progress bar shows them that the program is still operating as it should.

1. If the toolbox isn't visible in the design window, choose View | Toolbox.

2. Drag and drop a ProgressBar control from the toolbox onto your form. See the following image which displays the new, improved Timer program. The progress bar shows how close we are to the end of the countdown.

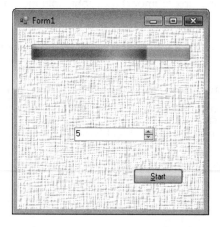

3. Now press F7 or double-click the button control to get to the code window. Replace the existing code with the following code in boldface:

```
Option Strict Off
Option Explicit Off

Public Class Form1

Dim Counter, TotalSeconds
```

```
    Private Sub Button1_Click(ByVal sender As System.Object, ByVal e
As System.EventArgs) Handles Button1.Click

        Timer1.Interval = 1000

        TotalSeconds = NumericUpDown1.Value * 60

        ProgressBar1.Maximum = TotalSeconds

        Timer1.Start()


    End Sub

    Private Sub Timer1_Tick(ByVal sender As Object, ByVal e As
System.EventArgs) Handles Timer1.Tick

        Counter = Counter + 1

        ProgressBar1.Value = Counter


        If Counter >= TotalSeconds Then

            Timer1.Stop()

            MsgBox("Time's up.")

            End

        End If

    End Sub
End Class
```

Tech Tip

We've used a `Dim` command here. It's a new concept. This `Dim` command "declares" (announces the existence of) two variables, `Counter` and `TotalSeconds`. By adding this declaration at the very top of the code window, *above* the various `Sub` procedures, these variables become *global* to this form. When global, variables will always hold their values until the program ends. (*Local* variables, those used only inside individual procedures, hold their values only while the programming is executing the code *in their procedure*.) More on this issue of the "lifetime" of variables' values in Chapter 5.

I won't test your patience by describing all the twists and turns—Internet searches, reading up on the ProgressBar control, and more—that it took me to get this improved version of the Timer program to work. But it did take about an hour and a half.

I had to figure out how to feed the right information to the ProgressBar as the Timer counted down, and that required a whole new way of using the Timer. I had to make it perform its `Tick` event every second, and then count the seconds in the code.

Several times in this book I explain how I got stumped and had to wrestle with bugs or confusing concepts (to me, anyway), such as this interaction between the Timer and ProgressBar controls.

I tell you these things so you'll realize that you're not alone when you have to struggle with code. Sometimes you get lucky and things go smoothly. Other times you have to wrestle the thing to the ground. I find it fun, like solving a puzzle.

Here's how the Timer program now works:

1. We first set the timer interval to 1000, causing the Timer's `Tick` event to trigger once every second. The Timer repeatedly restarts itself every second, so it's now behaving more like a metronome than a kitchen timer.

2. We set the ProgressBar's `Maximum` property to the total number of seconds of our countdown. This means we need to multiply whatever the user typed into the NumericUpDown control (in minutes) by 60. For example, 5 minutes × 60 results in 300 seconds.

3. The `Tick` event executes once every second. Within this event, we raise our counter variable (that I cleverly named `Counter`) by one each time the event executes. We also move the progress bar a little to show where we are in the countdown: `ProgressBar1.Value = Counter`

4. Finally, we compare the counter to see if it's greater than or equal to (`>=`) the total number of seconds we're counting. If `Counter` is greater than or equal to `TotalSeconds`, then we stop the Timer, show the message box, and end the program.

In the next chapter, we'll explore *variables*. Every program uses them, and it's time you got well acquainted with them and everything they can do for you.

Part II

The Elements of Programming

Chapter 5

Mastering Variables

Key Skills & Concepts

- How to name variables

- Operators

- Expressions

- Variables' scope

- Data types

All programs use variables. We'll now focus on how to work with them. They're small, but essential.

To visualize how variables work, imagine a home budget system: a shoebox full of envelopes. You write an identifying name on each envelope: clothing, food, entertainment, medical, and so on. Then you put various amounts of money in each envelope.

A variable is a named container that holds one value at a time (one piece of information, or *datum* at a time). The variable named *food* might hold $200 or $14, or if it's late in the month and times are tough, it might hold nothing. But that envelope can't *simultaneously* hold multiple values, such as holding both $200 and $14 at the same time. A variable holds only one value at any given time.

The data held in variables can, as you might suspect, vary. A variable's name stays the same, but the value held in the variable can change.

Two Ways to Create a Variable

In VB you can create variables in two ways: implicitly or explicitly.

Creating Variables Implicitly

You create a variable implicitly by just using it, like this:

```
MyFoodMoney = 212
```

This statement simultaneously creates a new variable named `MyFoodMoney` and also assigns a value of 212 to it. After a variable is created, you can use its name in other statements, and the value is automatically reported.

Here, for example, you show the value to the user with a message box:

```
MsgBox(MyFoodMoney)
```

The user will see a dialog box displaying the number 212, as shown in Figure 5-1.

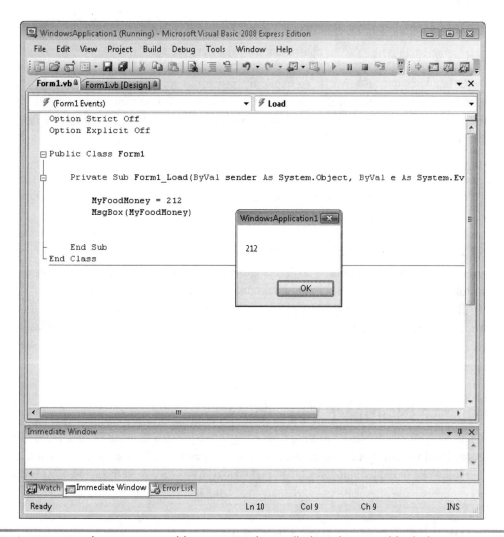

Figure 5-1 Simply using a variable in your code is called *implicit variable declaration*.

Creating Variables Explicitly

Alternatively, instead of creating a new variable by merely using it in your program—as we just did—you can *explicitly* create it with the `Dim` command. This is called *declaring* a variable:

```
Dim MyFoodMoney
```

You can even assign a value to the variable right off the bat, during the declaration:

```
Dim MyFoodMoney = 32
```

Often when declaring variables explicitly, programmers also use the `As` command to specify the *type* of data that the variable holds. For example, the most common data type for numbers is the `Integer`, so you could explicitly declare your food budget variable and its data type like this:

```
Dim MyFoodMoney As Integer
```

Or you could do all three things at once: declare, specify the data type, *and* assign a value all in one statement, like this:

```
Dim MyFoodMoney As Integer = 212
```

From now on in this book, you'll be required to use explicit declaration. In other words, you'll have to use the `Dim` command to announce all your variables.

But you won't need to specify variables' data types (with code like `As String` or `As Integer`). We'll let VB handle that for you automatically. The reasons for insisting on explicit variable declaration, but avoiding variable type specification, will be explained later in this chapter.

Rules for Naming Variables

When naming a variable, you can use most any name you want, even a single letter like *s* or *x*. But for most programmers, it's best to use descriptive names so you can more easily recognize the variable's purpose. That's why `MyFoodMoney` or `MyPartyGuests` are good names—they describe their contents, the value that they hold.

Why Use Descriptive Names?

You see, you or even other programmers will sometimes come back and read a program (*source code* as it's called) later on. Maybe even years after you wrote it.

Why? Perhaps a bug showed up that needs to be fixed, or perhaps you decided to add some new features or otherwise customize the program. Later on, you'll surely have forgotten what *x* represents. But if your program's variables are descriptively named, it's a lot easier to read the source code. `MyFoodMoney = 212` is clearly easier to read than `x = 212`.

And even when you're debugging the program while writing it, descriptive names make your life easier. But I'm not trying to force you to create explanatory variable names. The choice is yours as long as you're not programming with a group of others (they'll probably insist on descriptive variable names).

True, some programmers have a knack for reading programming. It's very clear to them what's going on, no matter how obscure the variable names. These programmers are like some musicians who can effortlessly read music scores and hear the music in their heads. So if you have this knack (I do), you can secretly use quick, easy-to-type variable names such as `g`, `x1`, or whatever, in your private programming.

Understanding the Rules

You do have to follow a few rules when naming a variable (but don't worry, if you violate any of these rules, the VB Editor will tell you loud and clear that you did):

- You can't use special characters such as # * & and so on. The variable name has to contain either normal alphabet characters such as *f* or *j*, or digits (the ten digits are 0 through 9). And the first character must be alphabetic, not numeric. So `9Templates` is illegal, but `Templates9` is fine.

- You can't use spaces. But multiple-word variable names are quite common. (The name `FoodBudget` is more descriptive of its variable's purpose than just `Food`.) You can use a couple of tricks to create multi-word variable names. One approach is to use an underscore character to combine words, like this: `Test_Scores`. But most people don't bother with the underscore, which is hard to type anyway. They simply use capital letters to indicate separate words: `TestScores`. Just remember that you can't use spaces.

- You can't use the commands that BASIC itself already uses, such as `End`, `Dim`, `Stop`, and so on. BASIC's built-in commands are frequently referred to as *reserved words* or *keywords*. See Figure 5-2. Note that VB's help system refers to variable names as *identifiers*.

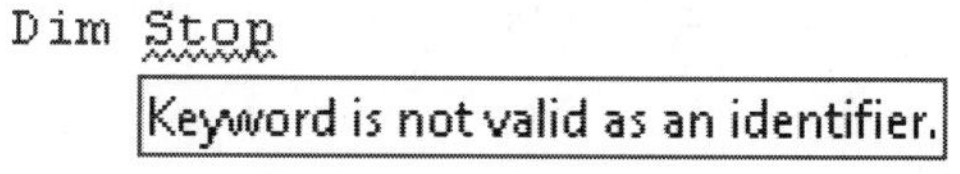

```
Dim Stop
    ┌─────────────────────────────────┐
    │ Keyword is not valid as an identifier. │
    └─────────────────────────────────┘
```

Figure 5-2 VB tells you if you've accidentally used one of its keywords (commands).

- Fortunately, VB ignores case, so if you define a variable named `LandTemperature`, but in other parts of your code you use `landTemperature` or `LANDTEMPERATURE`, and so on, these variations all still refer to the same variable. This case-insensitivity avoids problems if you accidentally capitalize a variable's name in different ways here and there.

NOTE

VB goes one step further in helping you with capitalization. Whatever way you capitalize a variable name when you first declare it in the code, VB will automatically change any future use of this same variable name later on in your code to match the original's case.

Working with Operators

Now let's explore *operators*, which are used frequently with variables.

You often need to examine, test, or modify variables in a program. Operators are used to specify how variables interact.

You're already familiar with several operators if you've ever used a calculator. The + operator means addition, for example:

```
Option Strict Off
Option Explicit Off


Public Class Form1

    Private Sub Form1_Load(ByVal sender As System.Object, ByVal e As
System.EventArgs) Handles MyBase.Load


        Num1 = 14
        Num2 = 7
        MsgBox(Num1 + Num2)

    End Sub
End Class
```

This program displays 21 because the + operator causes the values in these two variables to be added together.

The Arithmetic Operators

Other familiar arithmetic operators include * for multiplication, / for division, and – for subtraction. Here's a complete list of all the arithmetic operators:

- ^   Exponentiation (the number multiplied by itself: 5 ^ 2 is 25 and 5 ^ 3 is 125)
- –   Negation (negative numbers, such as –25)
- *   Multiplication
- /   Division
- \   Integer division (division with no remainder, no fraction); integer division is easier than dividing fractions, and the computer performs it faster than regular division
- **Mod**   Modulo arithmetic (division that provides the remainder only)
- +   Addition
- –   Subtraction

Combining Text

Text variables are also called *strings*. When you want to combine two strings, you use &, the concatenation operator, like this:

```
Str1 = "Sam "
Str2 = "Rockwell"

MsgBox(Str1 & Str2)
```

This results in *Sam Rockwell* because the two strings are concatenated by the & operator. Notice the space character I inserted after *Sam* to avoid getting *SamRockwell* as the result.

Relational Operators

Sometimes you need to compare two variables to find out which holds the larger number, or whether they are equal (hold the same data). Here's an example that tests to see if one variable contains a larger number than the other:

```
Num1 = 14
Num2 = 6

    If Num1 > Num2 Then

        MsgBox("14 wins")

    End If
```

The > symbol is called the *greater-than* operator. You can remember it because the left side of the arrow symbol is larger than the right side. The < symbol tests for *less-than*. Here is a list of all the relational (or *comparison*) operators:

- < Less than
- <= Less than or equal to
- > Greater than
- >= Greater than or equal to
- <> Not equal
- = Equal
- **Is** Do two object variables refer to the same object?
- **IsNot** Opposite of the Is operator
- **Like** Used to match patterns in strings

I wouldn't worry about the last three relational operators for now; just focus on the first six in this list.

The first six, however, are used quite frequently to help a program decide what to do. For example, if the user is heavier than 200 pounds, suggest a diet. Or if the current time is greater than the specified ending time, stop the timer and display a message to the user.

And, as illustrated in the example code (If Num1 > Num2 Then), relational operators are used frequently within an If...Then structure to make a decision. This combination of If...Then and relational operators is quite common in ordinary English, too. For example: *If* the temperature *is lower than* 50 degrees, *then* bring a coat. (If...Then is fully explained in Chapter 8.)

TIP
You can use the relational operators with text as well. When used this way, the operators compare the *alphabetic* qualities of the text, with *Anne* being *less than Heather*, for example.

The Logical Operators
Finally, VB offers a set of six "logical" operators:

- **Not** Negation
- **And** And
- **Or** Or

- **XOR**   Either but not both

- **AndAlso**   Similar to `And` but doesn't pay attention to the second element (operand) if the first element is false

- **OrElse**   Similar to `Or` but doesn't pay attention to the second element (operand) if the first element is true

TIP

The `XOR` operator is handy for encryption—creating secret messages. See the Glossary for more details on this.

You'll likely need to use only `And`, `Or`, and `Not` from among the logical operators. Fortunately, in VB these three operators work pretty much the way they do in English:

```
If 5 + 2 = 4 Or 6 + 6 = 12 Then MsgBox ("One of them is true.")
```

Five plus two does not equal four. However, six plus six *does* equal 12, so the `MsgBox` is displayed. When you use `Or`, *only one of the items needs to be true* for the result to happen. Just as if you said "If Janice *or* Cindy agree to dance with me, I'll have a good time at the party."

But when you use the `And` operator, *both* items must be true. Here's an example:

```
If 5 + 2 = 4 And 6 + 6 = 12 Then MsgBox("Both of them are true.")
```

When you execute this code by pressing F5, nothing happens. The message box isn't displayed because this statement—taken in its *entirety*—is false. Both expressions, the first *and* the second, must be *true* for this `MsgBox` to be displayed. Five plus two does not equal four, so no message box appears. Even though 6 + 6 does equal 12.

That compound expression is *false* (because one part of it is false), so the code following the `Then` command gets ignored. But what do we mean by *true* and *false* in when dealing with operators?

Working with Expressions

When you combine variables (or *literals*, such as the actual numbers *5* or *2*) with operators, you create what's called an *expression*. For example, `5 + 2` is an expression. The 5 and 2 are literal numbers and the + is an operator. Taken together, it's an expression. The expression `5 + 2 = 4 Or 6 + 6 = 12` is longer and more complicated. But it's still an expression (technically, it contains two small expressions, combined by the logical operator `Or`).

Remember that expressions are often used within an `If...Then` structure to find out if the expression is true or false, like this:

```
If Num1 > Num2 Then

    MsgBox("14 wins")

End If
```

Or:

```
If 5 + 2 = 4 And 6 + 6 = 12 Then

MsgBox("Both of them are true.")

End If
```

Notice that the expression in the first example involves variables (`Num1` and `Num2`), but the expression in the second example involves literal numbers 5, 2, 4 and so on. You can mix and match variables and literals in expressions. (You can also use other programming elements in expressions, such as constants or properties that we'll explore later.)

For now, just remember that expressions can be evaluated as either true or false. It's pretty much like English. Here's another weather analogy: "**If** *it's raining* **and** *I want to go out*, **then** I should find my umbrella." The operator here is **and**. The variables are whether *it's raining* and whether *I want to go out*.

This entire expression evaluates to true or false, depending on the weather and your mood. It doesn't matter how complicated an expression is, it can always be evaluated to true or false when used with an `If...Then` structure.

For example, the expression `X < Y` is either true or false, just as is that more complicated umbrella expression above. The `If...Then` structure demands an either/or answer. Either you need to look for your umbrella, or you don't.

Multiple Procedures and Variable Scope

Now we'll turn our attention to an issue known as *scope*. We touched on this topic in Chapter 4 when we declared some variables to be *global* in the Timer program.

Variables behave differently, depending on where in your code you declare them. This phenomenon is called a variable's *scope*. It has to do with procedures. So far, most of our examples (except the Timer program in Chapter 4) have included only a single *procedure* (only one `Sub...End Sub` structure).

NOTE

The term *procedure* is sometimes used instead of *Sub* or *event handler*.

Why Use Procedures

Many programs have two or more procedures, as you'll see in Chapter 9.

Procedures are used to subdivide your program into manageable parts. You aren't *required* to subdivide a program, but unless the program is short, subdividing does help you visualize how the program works, and it helps organize your code into logical sections.

Also, a procedure can be reused in various places throughout the program. You can "call" the procedure from other procedures, rather than repeating the procedure's code in several places.

And, above all, when a program is broken down into small pieces, it's easier to write and test the code.

If you're using controls like we did in Chapter 4's Timer program, each control has its own set of event procedures. This particular kind of procedure—such as the `Click` event of a Button control, or the `Tick` event of the Timer control—is also sometimes called an *event handler*.

Try This See If You Can Guess

Take a look now at the Timer program that we finished in Chapter 4 and see if you can figure out how many procedures this program contains:

```
Option Strict Off
Option Explicit Off

Public Class Form1

Dim Counter, TotalSeconds

    Private Sub Button1_Click(ByVal sender As System.Object, ByVal e
As System.EventArgs) Handles Button1.Click

        Timer1.Interval = 1000

        TotalSeconds = NumericUpDown1.Value * 60

        ProgressBar1.Maximum = TotalSeconds

        Timer1.Start()


    End Sub
```

```
    Private Sub Timer1_Tick(ByVal sender As Object, ByVal e As System
.EventArgs) Handles Timer1.Tick

        Counter = Counter + 1

        ProgressBar1.Value = Counter


        If Counter >= TotalSeconds Then

            Timer1.Stop()

            MsgBox("Time's up.")

            End

        End If

    End Sub
End Class
```

There are two procedures here (namely, two Sub...End Sub structures): the
Button1_Click event and the Timer1_Tick event.

Form-wide Scope

Notice something else interesting in our Timer code example here. Rather than creating
our variables (Counter and TotalSeconds) *inside* one of the procedures, we instead
used the Dim command and declared them up at the top of the code. We did this to make
these variables usable by (visible to) all the procedures in this form. In other words, the
variables become *global* to this form.

Declaring them up at the top puts these two variables outside any particular procedure
and in that way makes them available to *any* procedure in this form. Put another way, these
two variables—because they are declared up at the top like this—have *form-wide scope*.

Local Scope

By contrast, when you declare a variable *inside* a procedure, the variable has only *local
scope*. It can only be used by the code in the procedure where it is declared. Code located
in other procedures simply can't "see" this variable at all. Code in other procedures cannot
"read" (find out the value) or "write" (change the value) of a local variable.

Think of *scope* as a variable's range of influence or visibility. A local variable can be
accessed only within the procedure where it's declared. But a form-wide (global) variable
can be accessed from all the procedures in its form.

It's like getting some expensive chocolates for your birthday. You can either keep them in your bedroom (local scope) or put them in the kitchen (global, house-wide scope). In other words, where you put them determines whether only you, or everybody, can get their hands on them.

Here's some code that uses two procedures to illustrate the idea of scope. Choose File | New Project. Then type this into the new, empty project:

```
Option Strict Off
Option Explicit Off

Public Class Form1

    Private Sub Form1_Load(ByVal sender As System.Object, ByVal e As
System.EventArgs) Handles MyBase.Load

        Dim MyNumber = 3
        AddTwo()

    End Sub


    Sub AddTwo()
        MsgBox(2 + MyNumber)
    End Sub
End Class
```

Notice that we have two procedures here. The `Form_Load` procedure creates (declares) a variable named `MyNumber` and assigns the value 3 to it. Then we "call" (execute) our second procedure by just naming it: `AddTwo()`.

Tech Tip

Technically, when the user clicks a button, *that's* the event (or when the computer clock provides a tick for the timer). The procedure gets notified that the event took place and handles it (responds by executing your code in the event procedure). That's why event procedures such as `Form_Load` or `Button1_Click` have the `Handles` keyword at the end of the procedure declaration. That's also why it's common to call this type of procedure an *event handler*. Technically, the procedures aren't the events, they *handle* the events. But in common usage, people often simply use the words *event* and *event handler* interchangeably to refer to procedures such as a `Button_Click` event.

The `AddTwo` procedure attempts to add the literal *2* to the variable `MyNumber`. However, VB can't accomplish this. The variable `MyNumber` was declared local, up there inside the `Form_Load` procedure. So the `AddTwo` procedure just cannot "see" (view or change) this variable. As far as code in `AddTwo` is concerned, this `MyNumber` variable simply does not exist.

VB responds to this situation in two ways. It puts a sawtooth line under `MyNumber` in the second procedure, alerting you that there's a potential problem. When you hover your mouse pointer over the sawtooth, you see the explanation that this variable contains no value. That should clue you in to what's wrong: you *did* assign the value *3* up in the previous procedure, but down here in this `AddTwo` procedure, *no value* has been assigned. The variable is empty.

Because these are both local variables, VB thinks they are *two entirely different variables*. VB doesn't care that they have the same name. They're both *local*.

Put Form-wide Variables at the Top

How can we fix this "two different variables" problem? How can we permit both the `Form_Load` and `AddTwo` procedures to see and work with our `MyNumber` variable?

The answer is to give `MyNumber` form-wide, global scope by declaring it with `Dim` up near the top of the code window—*outside any particular procedure*. Now all the procedures in this form will be able to access `MyNumber`. It will no longer be *local* to the `Form_Load` procedure because it's no longer declared in there:

```
Option Strict Off
Option Explicit Off

Public Class Form1

    Dim MyNumber = 3

    Private Sub Form1_Load(ByVal sender As System.Object, ByVal e As
System.EventArgs) Handles MyBase.Load

        AddTwo()

    End Sub


    Sub AddTwo()
        MsgBox(2 + MyNumber)

    End Sub
End Class
```

Now the sawtooth error indicator disappears, and when you press F5 to execute the program, a message box appears with the correct result: 5.

Figure 5-3 illustrates the MyNumber variable's local scope because its Dim declaration statement is *within* the first procedure.

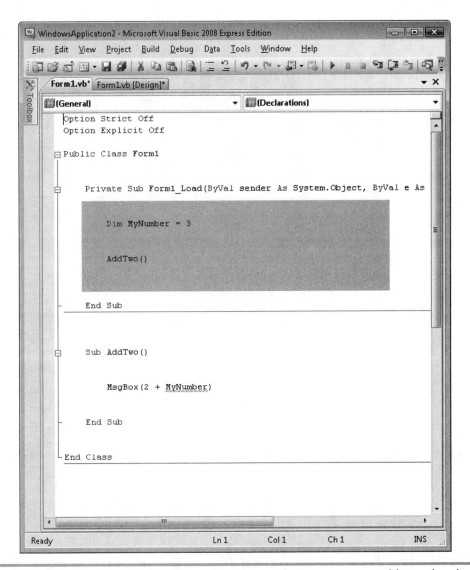

Figure 5-3 The programming that can read or change the MyNumber variable is colored gray.

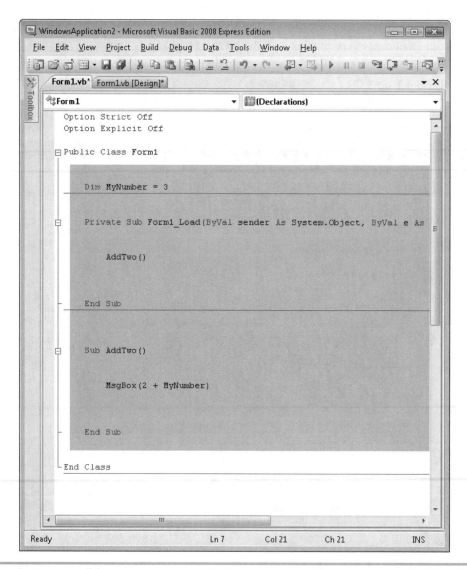

Figure 5-4 Now *all* the programming in this form can access the `MyNumber` variable. The variable's scope (shown in gray) is now form-wide.

But if you move the `Dim` declaration up above the procedures (as shown in Figure 5-4), the variable's scope becomes global to all the procedures in the form.

Why Not Make All Variables Global?

Why not, you might ask, just declare all variables form-wide? Why use local variables at all? Good question.

Expert programmers and programming teachers suggest that you use local variables as much as possible. Local variables eliminate certain kinds of errors and make it easier to debug your program (to test it and fix errors). Local variables are usually more easily managed because they don't affect the entire program—they are only active in their own procedure.

Think of the birthday gift of a box of chocolates. Chocolate is poisonous to dogs. If you leave the chocolates in the kitchen where anybody can get at it, your bumbling cousin Bernie might feed a piece to Fido. But if you keep the box of candy in your room, Fido is more likely to avoid death by chocolate. Locality can reduce the possibility of errors.

Sending Local Variables Between Procedures

We'll fully explore how to subdivide programs into procedures in Chapter 9. But let's now try a brief sample showing how to communicate between procedures.

We'll fix the previous example program so we don't even have to use a global variable. Instead, we'll *pass* local variables between procedures.

Here's how you would rewrite this program to pass a local variable `MyNumber` from the `Form_Load` procedure to the `AddTwo` procedure:

```
Option Strict Off
Option Explicit Off

Public Class Form1

    Private Sub Form1_Load(ByVal sender As System.Object, ByVal e As
System.EventArgs) Handles MyBase.Load

        Dim MyNumber = 3
        AddTwo(MyNumber)


    End Sub


    Sub AddTwo(ByVal WhatTheySent)

        MsgBox(2 + WhatTheySent)

    End Sub
End Class
```

Notice that when we call the `AddTwo` procedure, we put the variable `MyNumber` into the parentheses following `AddTwo`. This causes the variable to be passed to the `AddTwo` procedure: `AddTwo(MyNumber)`.

Remember the discussion in Chapter 3 about *parameters*? The MsgBox command, for example, has a Prompt parameter that you pass in parentheses:

```
MsgBox("Hello")
```

Well, this is the same idea: You're passing the MyNumber variable as a parameter to the AddTwo procedure.

(Ignore the ByVal command that VB sticks in there. You'll probably never need to use this feature, but some members of VB's programming team at Microsoft want it put in there. Just let the editor automatically add it to your code, and pretend it doesn't exist.)

To *receive* the passed variable, we have to provide a new variable name at the AddTwo procedure (in the parentheses).

You can use any name you want for this variable, but I used WhatTheySent. This new variable, which is local to the AddTwo procedure, will contain *3* when this program executes.

In other words, we assigned the value *3* to MyNumber, which gets passed to the AddTwo procedure. So the value *3* in the variable MyNumber is passed to the variable named WhatTheySent in the AddTwo procedure.

Finally, *2* is added to WhatTheySent (now containing the *3*). The message box displays *5*, the correct answer, and you avoid having to use a global variable.

Let's take a look visually at the path taken by the value *3* in this program. The 3 moves four times, as shown in Figures 5-5 through 5-8.

I know, passing variables sounds perplexing. It's really pretty simple, though. You'll get the idea of how to send messages among procedures after a couple of practice examples in Chapter 9.

MyNumber = 3

Figure 5-5   First, the number *3* is stored in (assigned to) the local variable MyNumber.

MyNumber = 3

AddTwo (MyNumber)

Figure 5-6   Then MyNumber is used as a parameter for the procedure call.

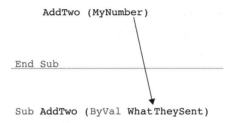

Figure 5-7   The value in `MyNumber` (the *3*) now gets passed to the AddTwo procedure. (The 3 is stored in the `WhatTheySent` variable.)

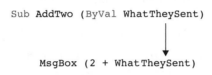

Figure 5-8   Finally, the *3* is added to the *2*.

Understanding Data Types and Data Conversion

You've probably been wondering about those `Option Strict` and `Option Explicit` statements that we've been inserting at the top of our forms in the `example` programs in this book. Both options involve variable declaration and management.

From here to the end of this chapter I explain why for the rest of this book you'll be required to declare all variables explicitly (you'll turn `Option Explicit On`). And I explain why you can *avoid* worrying about strict data type management (you'll turn `Option Strict Off`).

What Option Explicit Does

When you turn off `Option Explicit`, you give yourself the freedom to implicitly create variables. No formal declaration with `Dim` is required. But if you turn on `Option Explicit`, the editor will force you *always declare each variable*.

Using `Dim` isn't much trouble, it's easy to do, and it also provides a handy little list of the variables right at the top of each procedure.

But the major benefit is that declaring variables prevents a common type of programming error. It prevents this bad bug: accidentally creating two different variables when you intended to create only one.

Here's how the bug happens. Typically, variables are used several times in a program. If you accidentally mistype the variable's name, VB will think you're creating a brand new variable. Take a look at this code:

```
MyNumber = 3

AddTwo(MyNmber)
```

You are trying to send the value 3 to the AddTwo procedure. But a zero will be sent instead. VB thinks you're using two different variables here (MyNumber and MyNmber). And it sends the value in the `MyNmber` variable—which is zero—to the `AddTwo` procedure, causing a bug in the program. This kind of bug can be hard to figure out.

`Option Explicit On` prevents this "new variable" typo error by forcing you to declare every single variable explicitly. Therefore, if a new variable appears in the code that VB doesn't see in your list of declared variables, it alerts you to the error and refuses to run the program. For this reason, we'll leave `Option Explicit On` from here forward in this book.

What Option Strict Does

However, the other option, `Option Strict`, we'll leave turned off. This means you won't have to specify variables' *types*, such as As `Integer`, or have to convert variables from one data type to another. VB will do all this for you automatically.

After lots of thought and discussion, I've decided that in this book's programming examples we will always turn off `Option Strict`.

Why? Right now you're learning to program. Later in your programming journey you can decide for yourself whether you want it on or off. But I think that at this point you have enough to learn about without also worrying about declaring, managing, and converting *data types*.

Here's the issue: Some programmers don't worry about data type conversion, and VB allows you to ignore conversion if you want to. So in this book we'll ignore the conversion issue. We'll just let VB handle that problem for you.

However, programming teachers and most programming languages force you to manage data type conversions and also to specify the data type of all your variables.

To be sure, if you go on to study programming academically or become a professional programmer working with a group of other programmers, `Option Strict` will almost certainly be mandatory. In fact, in most programming languages it's not even an option: You *must* manage data type conversions. Most languages have "strong data typing," as it's called.

But this is a book for beginners. I want to steer clear of issues that are not absolutely necessary. Remember that VB permits you to ignore data type conversion issues. So will I.

We'll instead focus on the essentials of programming. Things you unquestionably must master, such as loops and branches, how best to get help, and the other topics explored throughout the rest of this book.

But now let's explore what data types actually are, and why they must sometimes be "converted" at all.

NOTE

If you don't want to bother your pretty head with data types—and my advice is *don't* (at least while you're learning to program)—then perhaps you'll want to skim the rest of this chapter (there *are* a couple of useful tips at the end).

Strict Data Type Management

Specifying data types and managing their conversion is called *strict data type management*. This primarily means two things to a programmer:

- You must specify in advance what kind (type) of data a variable holds (such as `Dim MyNumber` **as Integer**).

- Sometimes you must write extra code to convert a variable's original data type to a different data type. For example, if you turn `Option Strict On`, a message box will display only a string (text) variable type. If you attempt to display an integer type, such as `MyNumber`, VB will refuse. You must first change it into a string type using a conversion command `CStr`, like this:

```
MsgBox(CStr(MyNumber))
```

Programming teachers, and languages, that require data type conversion do have a point. Enforcing *strict data typing* (`Option Strict On` in VB) requires extra effort of the programmer, but it can reduce a particular—if relatively rare—kind of bug. It's debatable, though, how often you'll run into this bug when writing beginner or intermediate programs. Even more debatable is whether it's worth wrestling with all the extra code you need to write to manage data types personally, versus having to fix that particular bug once in a blue moon.

What's the bug? You can lose some of your data when, say, a lengthy number is unintentionally stored in a data type that holds only smaller numbers (this is the rare bug I was talking about). Turning `Option Strict On` prevents this, but it introduces other problems that confuse beginners. We're not going to be writing programs to calculate the national debt, or the orbit of Uranus, where this data conversion bug might come up. So we'll leave `Option Strict Off`. This will make our code less cluttered and our programming simpler—so we can focus on learning the fundamentals of programming without distraction.

Understanding Data Types

The two main types of variables are text (called a *string*) and numeric. Here's the distinction. A string variable contains only characters, such as *k, Bobby,* or *9*. String data is always enclosed in quotation marks, like this: `MyTextVariable = "Susan is happy."`

Why did I say that *9* could be a character, a string data type? The symbols 0 through 9 are *characters* rather than numbers when they're in a string. When used as text, they are called the ten *digits*, rather than actual numbers with which you could do arithmetic. Put some digits in quotes like this, "1341", and they becomes a string of characters, not a number. For example, look at this line of code:

```
MsgBox("9" + "10")
```

This message box displays *910*. You are concatenating two strings into one string here, not adding two numbers.

The Numeric Types

There's only one kind of text data: the *string*. But you may have noticed that more than one kind of number can be used in computing (or indeed in the real world). We can't just say `Dim MyNumber As Number`. There's no such type as a generic *number*. There are several kinds of numbers.

For most programming, the integer data type is used. Integer means *there's no fraction*. In other words, 12, 24000, 1, 0, –88, and 530543 are all integers. But 4.6 or 8.225454 are not integers.

It's true that some special situations require more precision than integers offer (really picky accounting where pennies matter, or calculating shuttle launches, for example). Those kinds of programs do demand fractions. VB has three data types that permit fractions: `Single`, `Double`, and `Decimal`.

Date and time information has a special numeric data type all its own, called `Date`. VB used the `Date` type in the Timer program we wrote earlier in the book. The key phrase here is this: *VB used*. Not you, the programmer.

Leaving `Option Strict Off` means VB will deal with all these data typing and data conversion jobs. You can ignore them. For example, VB knew in the Timer program we wrote earlier that the `Minute(Now)` information had to be managed as `Date` data. You didn't have to define a variable as of the `Date` type: `Dim EndTime As Date`. You were able to declare the variable simply, and leave off the type, like this: `Dim EndTime`.

Frankly, I'm glad that VB is one of those rare languages that offers such options. It makes learning how to program easier for you. Notice that in the preceding code example we left off the `As String` and `As Integer` in these two statements:

```
Dim MyString
Dim MyNumber
```

Ask the Expert

Q: **Should I always declare every variable?**

A: Yes. Declaring is easy to do and isn't the least bit confusing. And remember: using the `Dim` command prevents that common type of bug—the typo variable name.

However, a separate issue—managing data type conversion—can be very puzzling to beginners. Choosing to ignore data typing issues is controversial, and I can appreciate the opinions on the other side of this issue. But I'm convinced that beginners are better off focusing on learning the truly essential elements of programming. And obviously the designers of VB also knew that both sides had valid arguments—they did, after all, make strict data typing *optional* in VB.

But let's experiment a little with data type conversion issues, just so you'll see what conversion involves. Try this program, with `Option Strict` turned On, making the programmer responsible for converting the data types of the variables:

```
Option Strict On
Option Explicit On

Public Class Form1

    Private Sub Form1_Load(ByVal sender As System.Object, ByVal e As
System.EventArgs) Handles MyBase.Load

        MyNumber = InputBox("Please type in a number.")

    End Sub
End Class
```

(continued)

Notice that VB has put a sawtooth line under `MyNumber`, and if you hover your mouse pointer over the sawtooth, a message pops up saying "Name 'MyNumber' is not declared." See Figure 5-9.

To fix this "not declared" problem, add this simple line to your code to declare this variable with the `Dim` command:

```
Private Sub Form1_Load(ByVal sender As System.Object, ByVal e As
System.EventArgs) Handles MyBase.Load

    Dim MyNumber

    MyNumber = InputBox("Please type in a number.")

End Sub
```

Declaring `MyNumber` has fixed *one* of our problems. The `MyNumber` used with the input box is now OK, no sawtooth there. But the sawtooth has now moved up to the `Dim` statement. Is there no rest for the weary?

Because you also have `Option Strict` turned on, the editor is unhappy with that `Dim` statement. What's the beef? Hover your mouse over the sawtooth again. Now the editor is complaining that because of `Option Strict`, all variable declarations must have an `As` clause. In other words, the editor insists that you must specify a *data type*. So modify the `Dim` statement to specify an integer data type for this variable:

```
Dim MyNumber As Integer
```

Oops! Stomp out one bug and another appears. Now there's a sawtooth on the `InputBox`, stating "Option Strict On disallows implicit conversions from 'String' to 'Integer'." Well, glory be! `Option Strict` is like a frowning schoolmarm; it's her way or the highway.

What is this conversion? Why must this integer `MyNumber` be converted into a string?

An input box *returns* (sends back to your program when the user clicks the OK button) a string data type. It always sends back a string. But we've told the input box to store its string in MyNumber, a *numeric* variable. This is the dreaded *data type mismatch*. VB insists that you convert the input box's string into an integer before it can be properly assigned to this integer variable.

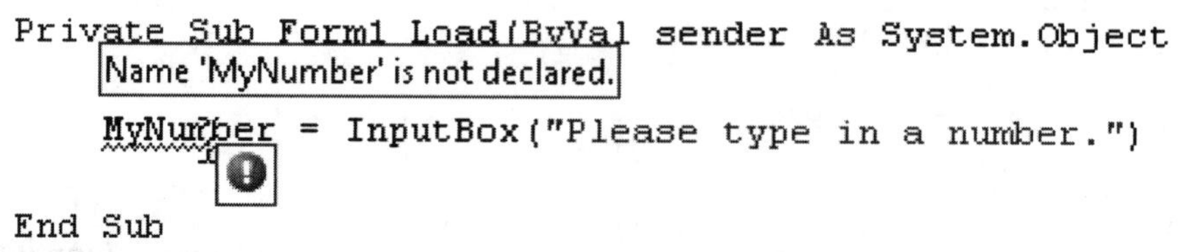

Figure 5-9 With `Option Explicit On`, VB refuses to let you use a variable without first declaring it formally. You must `Dim` that variable.

You've got `Option Strict` turned on, so *you*, the programmer, have to write some extra code to *convert* (also called *coerce* or *cast*) this returned string into an integer. (If you specify `Option Strict Off`, VB will do this and other data conversions for you automatically.)

VB has a set of data conversion commands beginning with *C* (for *convert*). There's `CInt` (convert to an integer), `CStr` (convert to a string), and so on. In this example we need to change a returned string into an integer, so we use `CInt`. Modify the `InputBox` statement so it looks like this:

```
MyNumber = CInt(InputBox("Please type in a number."))
```

Now at last all is well. All the sawtooth error messages have been turned off. The editor likes your code now.

Fortunately, from now on we're going to let VB deal with all these conversion problems for us.

Avoiding Blank Forms

Here's a tip. I'm sure you've noticed this: Visual Basic always displays a form when you execute code. So when you press F5 to execute example code, you always see a form displayed even if it's a blank form and you're not using it. To get rid of the form and return VB to normal editing mode (where VB is not executing your code), just click the close box in the upper-right corner of the form to close it, the same way you'd close any window.

If always having to close a form bothers you (it does me), you can avoid displaying the form by adding the `End` command just above the `End Sub`, like this:

```
Private Sub Form1_Load(ByVal sender As System.Object, ByVal e As
System.EventArgs) Handles MyBase.Load

    Dim MyString
    Dim MyNumber


    MyString = "22"

    MyNumber = 44

    MsgBox(MyString & MyNumber)

    End
End Sub
```

This shuts down the program—no form is displayed.

Automatic Options

Here's another useful tip. If you prefer not to type in the strict and explicit options in the code window, you can instead have VB automatically turn on `Option Explicit` and turn off `Option Strict`. (Remember that these settings will be our defaults for the remainder of the book.) Choose Tools | Options, and click the small arrow next to Projects and Solutions in the left pane of the Options dialog box. Click *VB Defaults* in the left pane. Set Option Strict Off and Option Explicit On. You can see how to do this in Figure 5-10.

Now let's turn our attention to *arrays*. With arrays you can manage large numbers of variables as a single unit. If a variable can be compared to one envelope in a shoebox full of envelopes, an array would be the shoebox.

Arrays are the topic of Chapter 6. And I promise you that arrays will be easier to understand than all this data typing business. Data type management is now behind us, a topic never to be raised again in this book. Mercifully, VB will do that job for us.

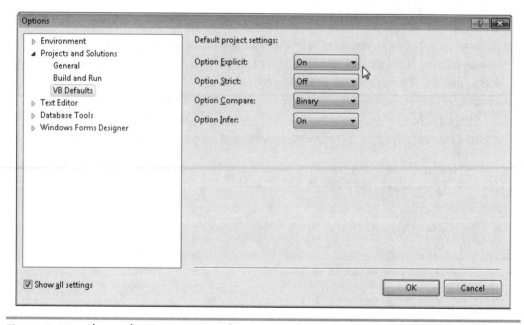

Figure 5-10 Choose these settings to enforce Option Explicit automatically and to turn off Option Strict.

Chapter 6

Using Arrays

Key Skills & Concepts

- The purpose of arrays

- Starting the Quiz program

- Built-in array methods

In this chapter, you start building a useful quiz program that you'll finish in Chapter 8. The quiz displays a list of questions and answers supplied by you, the programmer. It's flexible; it can be used to help with homework, prepare for a civil service test, or quiz anybody on any subject.

And because the Quiz program uses lists, it's more efficient if we go beyond ordinary variables and employ a special kind of storage unit: the *array*. Arrays are perfect for storing lists.

True, you *could* put a list of data in a set of ordinary variables, like this:

```
Dim FirstQuestion = "Who painted the Mona Lisa?"

Dim SecondQuestion = "In what city is the Mona Lisa displayed?"

Dim ThirdQuestion = "Was the Mona Lisa painted before 300 AD?"
```

Each variable of course must have a different name. But that's obviously awkward if a list has dozens of items (and each one must have its own individual name).

Some lists managed by computer programs have hundreds or even hundreds of thousands of items. Providing a separate name for each data item would be a nightmare in these cases.

And as for our Quiz program, later in our code when we're quizzing the user, we'd have to refer to each question by its unique variable name. Why not just use a single name for the whole list, but distinguish the different items in the list by *numbering* them?

Store Lists in Arrays

An *array* has a single name that all members of the array share, but each member has its own unique index number. That way you can then refer to each item of data *numerically* (by the numbers) instead of by a whole pile of different text names. Here's a typical array:

```
Option Strict Off
Option Explicit On
```

```
Public Class Form1
    Private Sub Form1_Load(ByVal sender As System.Object, ByVal e As
System.EventArgs) Handles MyBase.Load

        Dim arrQuestions(3)


        arrQuestions(0) = "Who painted the Mona Lisa?"

        arrQuestions(1) = "In what city is the Mona Lisa displayed?"

        arrQuestions(2) = "Was the Mona Lisa painted before 300 AD?"

        MsgBox(arrQuestions(1))


        End
    End Sub
End Class
```

That list of array elements looks more efficient than using a list of different variable as names, as we did in the first example in this chapter, doesn't it?

Each *element* (item) in an array is similar to a separate ordinary variable. Like an ordinary variable, you can assign a value to the array element or read the value to find out what value the element holds.

But arrays are more efficient when managing a set of related data for the same reason that the post office uses ZIP codes. ZIP codes are *numbers*. Numbers are simply cleaner and easier to work with in a program than all kinds of assorted city and state names.

(You might have noticed that the above list starts with index number 0: arrQuestions(0). Normally, lists start with item #1. We'll explore this quirk later in this chapter.)

Loops Efficiently Manipulate Arrays

Most important, you can manipulate an array's index numbers *arithmetically* in ways you simply can't manipulate text names (ordinary variables), as you'll see later. (You can go through an array by using a loop structure; you can't do that with individually named variables.)

Just remember that the key to the usefulness of arrays is that you can search them, sort them, and otherwise manage the data *using index numbers* to identify each item, instead of using separate text names.

To see the difference between using ordinary variables and using an array, picture a simple food budget. Suppose you want to write a program that calculates your average food bill for the year. You *could* go the cumbersome route, using 12 individual variable names, one for each month, like this:

```
Option Strict Off
Option Explicit On

Public Class Form1
    Private Sub Form1_Load(ByVal sender As System.Object, ByVal e As
System.EventArgs) Handles MyBase.Load

        Dim Total

        Dim JanFood = 90
        Dim FebFood = 122
        Dim MarFood = 125
        Dim AprFood = 78
        Dim MayFood = 144
        Dim JneFood = 89
        Dim JulFood = 90
        Dim AugFood = 140
        Dim SeptFood = 167
        Dim OctFood = 123
        Dim NovFood = 133
        Dim DecFood = 125

        Total = JanFood + FebFood + MarFood + AprFood + MayFood +
JneFood + JulFood + AugFood + SeptFood + OctFood + NovFood + DecFood

        MsgBox(Total)

        End

    End Sub
End Class
```

Or you could simplify your program by putting the same data into an array, like this:

```
Option Strict Off
Option Explicit On

Public Class Form1
    Private Sub Form1_Load(ByVal sender As System.Object, ByVal e As
System.EventArgs) Handles MyBase.Load

        Dim arrMonthFoodBill(11)
        Dim Total
```

```
        arrMonthFoodBill(0)  = 90
        arrMonthFoodBill(1)  = 122
        arrMonthFoodBill(2)  = 125
        arrMonthFoodBill(3)  = 78
        arrMonthFoodBill(4)  = 144
        arrMonthFoodBill(5)  = 89
        arrMonthFoodBill(6)  = 90
        arrMonthFoodBill(7)  = 140
        arrMonthFoodBill(8)  = 167
        arrMonthFoodBill(9)  = 123
        arrMonthFoodBill(10) = 133
        arrMonthFoodBill(11) = 125

        For i = 0 To 11
            Total = Total + arrMonthFoodBill(i)
        Next i

        MsgBox(Total)

    End Sub
End Class
```

As you can see, using an array makes it possible for you to process the array within a loop, as we did in this example.

The loop repeats 12 times, with the loop's counter variable (i) automatically increasing by one each time (*incrementing*) through the loop. This way, you add each arrMonthFoodBill array element, in turn, to the variable Total. Recall that when using individual variables earlier in this chapter, you couldn't use a loop—you had to add each variable to the next using the + operator.

Warnings vs. Errors

Here's a useful tip that will help you distinguish warnings you can ignore from errors you must fix. The editor displays warnings differently from true errors.

If you paste the previous example code into the VB editor, you'll see a sawtooth warning line under the variable name Total (as shown in Figure 6-1). Remember that you need pay no attention when the editor issues a warning about a "null reference" like this. It is *not* a problem. Just ignore it.

Not all sawtooth lines are the same. With a "null reference," the editor is merely pointing out what it thinks a *possible problem*, not an actual error. So when you hover your mouse you see only the message, as shown in Figure 6-1.

(continued)

An actual error message looks different from what's shown in Figure 6-1. Let's cause a real error to see the difference. Remove the line of code that declares the array: (`Dim arrMonthFoodBill(11)`). That causes a true error (because we have `Option Explicit On`, so all variables must be declared, including array variables).

A true error message looks different from a warning in three ways: First, the sawtooth line under a true error is *blue* instead of the warning's green. What's more, a small red box appears at the right end of the sawtooth line. And third, when you hover your mouse over the sawtooth, a red exclamation point symbol is displayed. See Figure 6-2.

There is one more difference between a warning and an error. When you press F5 to run a program that contains an error, the editor will flatly refuse to run the program. Instead, it will display the dialog box shown in Figure 6-3, telling you that build errors were found and asking if you want to try running the most recent error-free version of this program instead. The editor sure isn't going to let you run this current, buggy version.

```
For i = 0 To 11
    Total = Total + arrMonthFoodBill(i)
Next i        Variable 'Total' is used before it has been assigned a value. A null reference exception could result at runtime.
```

Figure 6-1   This sawtooth is *not* an error warning; it's merely notifying you of a possible problem. A warning sawtooth is colored green.

```
' Dim arrMonthFoodBill(11)
Dim Total

            Name 'arrMonthFoodBill' is not declared.
The sawtooth   arrMonthFoodBill(1) = 122
line turns blue  arrMonthFoodB ❶ (2) = 125
            arrMonthFoodBill(3) = 78
```

A red exclamation point appears

A small red box appears at the end of the sawtooth line

Figure 6-2   Three cues let you know this is an error message, not just a warning.

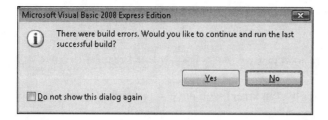

Figure 6-3   If the editor finds a true error in your program, it simply refuses to execute the program.

The Zero Effect

Sharp-eyed readers will have noticed three strange things in the preceding code example:

1. That we declared the array as having 11 elements:

```
Dim MonthFoodBill(11)
```

2. That when assigning values to the various array elements, we started with element 0:

```
MonthFoodBill(0) = 90
```

3. That we repeated the loop in an odd way, from 0 to 11, rather than the way we humans count lists from 1 to 12.

All these oddities are part of the same problem: *Arrays always start with a zero element.* This *zero effect* is a peculiarity that you simply have to remember about arrays.

What makes this quirk a little tricky is that in a loop the upper boundary of an array is *one less* than you would think.

What does that mean? In this example, we have an array with one element for each month. Thus, we have 12 elements, because there are 12 months. But when dealing with this array, our loop must count from: 0 To 11 rather than the expected 1 To 12.

Most people sitting down to write a list of, say, their favorite movies would start with the number 1:

1. Amaracord

2. The Godfather

3. 2001

4. Das Boot

5. The 400 Blows

6. Psycho

7. A Streetcar Named Desire

But in a computer list (an array), you have to remember to start the list with 0.

Use UBound with Loops

There *is* some relief from wrapping your mind around this zero effect. You can avoid bothering with this issue when writing a `For...Next` loop by letting VB figure out the upper index of an array for you. Just use the `UBound` command instead of a literal number.

In fact, I suggest that you always use the `UBound` command in this situation. `UBound` automatically provides an array's upper boundary (its highest index number). You don't have to figure out the counterintuitive fact that the highest index number in an array of months is 11 rather than 12.

How is this done in the code? Instead of specifying the upper boundary with the literal number 11, like this,

```
For i = 0 To 11
```

just replace the 11 with the `UBound` command, like this:

```
For i = 0 To UBound(MonthFoodBill)
```

This works like a charm.

Tech Tip

For decades, BASIC permitted one-based arrays. VB used to have an `Option Base 1` command that allowed you to avoid having to work with zero-based arrays. However, a few years ago, *those who know best* at Microsoft decided to remove this option from VB and force us programmers to make all arrays start with a "zeroth" element. Don't you just love people who want everybody to do things *their* way?

Here's a related question: Why are arrays zero-based in the first place? Originally programming languages, like humans, always used one-based arrays. But then along came the C family of languages (C, C++, Java, and so on). Rumor has it that mathematicians involved in the design of these languages wanted arrays to start with zero because such arrays are easier for them to use in the arcane art of matrix manipulations.

Dynamic Arrays

If you prefer, you can declare an array without even specifying its size, like this:

```
Dim arrQuestions()
```

This is called a *dynamic array*. When are dynamic arrays useful? In some situations, for example, you need to allow the user to specify the size of an array. In such a case, you need a dynamic array. You won't know the size while you're writing your code, so you can't specify the size in the `Dim` command in your code. The size becomes known only after the user types it in while the program is running.

Here's a concrete example. You could write a quiz program that allows the parent to specify the number of questions in the test. But, obviously, you (the programmer) can't know in advance how many quiz questions the parent will request. Thus you can't specify the array's size in your source code.

The following code illustrates how to use a dynamic array. It's a two-step process: first you declare an array without specifying its size, and then later in the code—when the size becomes known—you use the `ReDim` command to specify the size. This example program first declares a dynamic string array named `arrQuestions`. (Notice that some programmers like to add a prefix *arr* to the names of their arrays to identify it as an array.)

```
Option Strict Off
Option Explicit On

Public Class Form1
    Private Sub Form1_Load(ByVal sender As System.Object, ByVal e As
System.EventArgs) Handles MyBase.Load

        Dim arrQuestions()
        Dim Answer

        Answer = Input box("How many questions do you want in this quiz?")

        ReDim arrQuestions(Answer - 1)

        MsgBox(UBound(arrQuestions))

    End Sub
End Class
```

Here an array is declared, but no size is specified—there's no number inside the parentheses following `arrQuestions()`.

Then the user is asked to type in the size of the quiz. The `ReDim` command redimensions (resizes) an array. So after `ReDim` executes, our array has the number of elements the user specified.

Note the zero effect here. We had to subtract 1 from the user's answer, because if the user wants an array with 12 elements, the upper boundary is 11. (Again, this 11 is because of the "zeroth" element. You'll eventually become familiar with the zero effect. If you're like me, you won't always get your arrays correct the first time you write them in your code, but you do get used to taking a close look at your arrays and fixing them as necessary from time to time.)

Starting the Quiz Program

Now that you understand how helpful arrays can be, let's use a couple of them in a real-world Quiz program.

A quiz involves two lists, the questions and the answers, so we'll create two arrays. Why not name them arrQuestions and arrAnswers?

To keep things flexible, yet simple, like Jessica Simpson, you, the programmer, will decide how many questions to ask, and you'll also type the questions directly into the source code. It will be a true-false test, as well. In a later chapter, we'll modify it to ask multiple-choice questions.

To illustrate how the program works, let's create an art quiz with only four questions. You can follow these same steps to create a larger quiz of any size you want. The concepts are the same no matter whether you're asking 4 or 400 questions.

Start a new VB program by pressing CTRL-N and choosing the default Windows-style program. Double-click the form to get to the Form_Load event in the code window. Then type this code, or copy and paste it from this book's web site at www.mhprofessional.com/computingdownload. Refer to the Introduction for specific instructions on how to download the code.

```
Option Strict Off
Option Explicit On

Public Class Form1
    Private Sub Form1_Load(ByVal sender As System.Object, ByVal e As System
.EventArgs) Handles MyBase.Load

        Dim arrQuestions(3)
        Dim arrAnswers(3)

        Dim Response

        Dim Counter   'Holds the number of correct answers

        arrQuestions(0) = "Was the Mona Lisa painted by Leonardo?"
        arrAnswers(0) = 1

        arrQuestions(1) = "Is the Mona Lisa displayed in a museum in Rome?"
        arrAnswers(1) = 0
```

```
    arrQuestions(2) = "Was the Mona Lisa painted before 300 AD?"
    arrAnswers(2) = 0

    arrQuestions(3) = "Is the Mona Lisa also known as La Gioconda?"
    arrAnswers(3) = 1

    For i = 0 To UBound(arrQuestions)

        Response = MsgBox(arrQuestions(i), MsgBoxStyle.YesNo, "Question " & (i))

        'THEY CLICKED THE YES BUTTON (6 = Yes button):

        ' Answer = 1 means True (yes) so they are correct:
        If Response = vbYes And arrAnswers(i) = 1 Then

            MsgBox("Correct")
            Counter = Counter + 1

        End If


        ' answer = 0 False, so they are wrong:
        If Response = vbYes And arrAnswers(i) = 0 Then

            MsgBox("Wrong")

        End If

        'THEY CLICKED THE NO BUTTON (7 = No button):

        ' Answer = 0 means False (no) so they are correct:
        If Response = vbNo And arrAnswers(i) = 0 Then

            MsgBox("Correct")
            Counter = Counter + 1

        End If


        ' Answer = 1 (True) so they are wrong:
        If Response = vbNo And arrAnswers(i) = 1 Then

            MsgBox("Wrong")

        End If

    Next

        MsgBox("You got " & Counter & " correct out of " & UBound(arrAnswers) + 1 &
" questions.")


        End


    End Sub
End Class
```

How This Code Works

Here's how this source code works. First we declare two arrays. Each is defined as having an index that goes up to 3. One array holds the questions, and the other holds the answers.

We also declare a variable named `Response` to hold the user's input, and another variable named `Counter` to keep track of the number of right answers so we can score the test at the end.

```
Dim arrQuestions(3)
Dim arrAnswers(3)

Dim Response

Dim Counter  'Holds the number of correct answers
```

Then, we assign the questions and answers to the individual elements in the arrays, starting as always with element 0.

```
arrQuestions(0) = "Was the Mona Lisa painted by Leonardo?"
arrAnswers(0) = 1

arrQuestions(1) = "Is the Mona Lisa displayed in a museum in Rome?"
arrAnswers(1) = 0

arrQuestions(2) = "Was the Mona Lisa painted before 300 AD?"
arrAnswers(2) = 0

arrQuestions(3) = "Is the Mona Lisa also known as La Gioconda?"
arrAnswers(3) = 1
```

A Loop to UBound

Now we create a `For...Next` loop that will repeat four times (`0 to UBound`). Recall that the `UBound` command automatically supplies the upper boundary (the highest index number) in an array. You don't have to bother specifying a literal number for the loop's end condition.

Another good reason for using `UBound` with loops is that when you reuse the quiz later and have a different number of questions, you don't have to bother changing this loop. You're not saying loop four times from `0 To 3` (this specificity is called *hard coding*).

Instead, you're saying this: loop from 0 to the highest element in the array, whatever it currently is.

```
For i = 0 To UBound(arrQuestions)
```

The first thing that happens within the loop is that we display a message box:

```
Response = MsgBox(arrQuestions(i), MsgBoxStyle.YesNo, "Question " & (i + 1))
```

We use the loop's i variable to indicate which array element we want to display. Each time a loop repeats, it automatically increases i by one. So, the first time through the loop, i = 0 and the question in the array element zero, arrQuestions(0), is displayed in the message box. The second time through the loop, i will have been incremented to 1, so the next question (array element 1) will be displayed to the user. And so on until the loop finishes when it reaches the upper boundary, the UBound, of our array.

A Special Message Box

Remember that you can choose from a variety of message box styles, but here we selected to display a Yes and a No button on the message box. The IntelliSense help system (described in Chapter 2) told me that one of the options for a message box's buttons is to display the two buttons Yes and No, so I selected MsgBoxStyle.YesNo from the list that IntelliSense displayed.

Figure 6-4 illustrates how IntelliSense provides a list of the available message box styles. As soon as you reach the button style parameter's location in the MsgBox command's parameter list, by typing that comma after (i), IntelliSense kicks in as shown in Figure 6-4.

Finally, we come to the optional title bar argument for a message box. I decided to display *Question 1*, *Question 2*, and so on. This is a nice touch that tells the user where he or she is in the quiz.

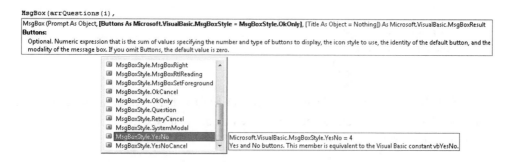

Figure 6-4   IntelliSense shows you all the possible message box styles. Just click your choice in this drop-down list.

You could get even more fancy by displaying *Question 1 of 4* in the title bar, like this:

```
Response = MsgBox(arrQuestions(i), MsgBoxStyle.YesNo, "Question " & (i
+ 1) & " of " & UBound(arrQuestions) + 1)
```

NOTE
Including + 1 is necessary here; the zero effect again. When I wrote this program I originally left out these + 1 adjustments. Then I pressed F5 and saw this: *Question 0 of 3*. Oops! So I went back into the code and added those adjustments to deal with the zero effect. Believe me, it's much easier to press F5 and see what's happening than it is to try to get your code perfect before testing it. If I, even I, who have written dozens of books on programming, made the mistake of leaving out + 1 when I first wrote this line of code, why should you expect to get things right all the time? The "one-off" issue (zero effect) will come up over and over again when you work with arrays. Don't fret about it. Just press F5, and then go back and add or subtract 1 in your code as required to get the result you're after.

Our final job within the loop is to figure out whether the user's answer is right or not. Four outcomes are possible when the user answers a question:

1. The user clicks Yes, and the answer is yes.

2. The user clicks Yes, but the answer is no.

3. The user clicks No, and the answer is no.

4. The user clicks No, but the answer is yes.

To check the user's response, we employ four If...Then structures. Each of them looks pretty much the same, but they represent the four possibilities in the list.

```
If Response = vbYes And arrAnswers(i) = 1 Then

    MsgBox("Correct")
    Counter = Counter + 1

End If
```

VB has built-in "constants" named vbYes and vbNo that you can use when figuring out which button the user clicked in a message box or input box. To see the IntelliSense list of these constants, type this:

```
If Response = vb
```

As soon as you type vb, IntelliSense knows you're looking for one of the constants, so it opens a list of options from which you can choose (see Figure 6-5). Constants are available for other button-click results as well, such as vbCancel or vbOK.

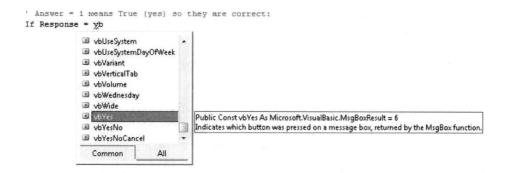

```
' Answer = 1 means True (yes) so they are correct:
If Response = vb
```

vbUseSystem
vbUseSystemDayOfWeek
vbVariant
vbVerticalTab
vbVolume
vbWednesday
vbWide
vbYes
vbYesNo
vbYesNoCancel

Common   All

Public Const vbYes As Microsoft.VisualBasic.MsgBoxResult = 6
Indicates which button was pressed on a message box, returned by the MsgBox function.

Figure 6-5   Type the letters *vb* and IntelliSense intelligently senses that you want to see a list of the built-in constants that start with *vb*.

Once the program has the user's response to a question, we look at each of the four possible combinations of button clicks and answers. The first test finds out if the user clicked Yes and the answer *was* yes (we used the number 1 in the answer array to mean *true* and the number 0 to mean *false*).

If it turns out the user clicked Yes in response to a question whose answer is true, we display a message to him or her saying *correct* and we also add 1 to the `Counter` variable, increasing the user's score. At the end, the `Counter` will contain the total number of correct answers.

Ask the Expert

Q: What are those lines of descriptive text in the Quiz program code? The lines that start with a single-quotation mark? And the words are all colored *green*?

A: You doubtless noticed some additional lines, that I added to the code lines that aren't actually programming but instead describe the programming. These are called *comments* or *remarks*.

Whenever you use a single-quotation mark in a line of code, the following words in that line are *ignored* by VB.

Put another way, VB understands that you're making a note to yourself (or other programmers who might later work with your code).

(continued)

You can "comment out" part of a line, like this:

```
Dim Counter 'Holds the number of correct answers
```

Or you can make a whole line into a comment by putting the single quotation mark at the start, like this:

```
' Answer = 1 means True (yes) so they are correct:
    If Response = vbYes And arrAnswers(i) = 1 Then
```

Comments can be helpful because they make your code more understandable while you're fixing a bug or improving the program by modifying it later.

How many comments you use is up to you. Some programmers comment almost every line of code; others rarely use comments.

The Visual Basic language is in some ways self-commenting because so much of it is English-like and therefore pretty easy to read and understand. Other programming languages, however, can be much harder to read.

But it never hurts to add comments in your programs, even in VB, particularly where something complicated or obscure is going on. That's why I added comments to each of these If...Then analyses in our quiz. The comments clarify what each section of code is doing. This helps me keep things straight while I'm writing the program, and also describes what's going on here if I come back and modify the program at a later date.

TIP

By default, the editor displays comments in green to distinguish them from ordinary code (black), commands (blue), strings (brown), and so on. You can, however, change these color cues, and even change their typefaces if you wish. Just choose Tools | Options, and then open the Environment area in the Options dialog box and select the Fonts and Colors option.

Array Techniques and Methods

I'll conclude this chapter with a look at some of the things you can do with arrays.

First, here's a shortcut way to assign values to an array. Type this code into the editor:

```
Option Strict Off
Option Explicit On

Public Class Form1
    Private Sub Form1_Load(ByVal sender As System.Object, ByVal e As
System.EventArgs) Handles MyBase.Load
```

```
Dim arrTest() = {1, 5, 6, 2, 66}

For i = 0 To UBound(arrTest)

    Debug.WriteLine(arrTest(i))

Next

End
    End Sub
End Class
```

The line in boldface in this example illustrates one way to assign values to arrays.

Remember that in the Quiz program earlier in this chapter, we assigned each value on a separate line, like this:

```
arrQuestions(0) = "Was the Mona Lisa painted by Leonardo?"
arrAnswers(0) = 1

arrQuestions(1) = "Is the Mona Lisa displayed in a museum in
Rome?"
arrAnswers(1) = 0
```

But if you're working with only a small number of elements in an array, and the data itself is short (as opposed to lengthy strings), you can enclose the data in braces { } and separate each individual datum with commas.

Notice that the size of this kind of array isn't specified in the code. VB counts the number of data you assign and automatically figures out the array size. VB also automatically numbers these array elements: 0, 1, 2 … and so on.

OK, but what does this line in our example do? Read on.

```
Debug.WriteLine(arrTest(i))
```

Multiple Values with Debug.WriteLine

The `Debug.WriteLine` command is useful when you're testing a program. It allows you to view several values at once. The previous example code in the book tested only a single variable's value. If you want to see a single value, you can temporarily add a message box in your code to show you what value was returned when the user clicked a Yes or No button, for example: `MsgBox(Response)`. Then you can remove the message box line from the code after you press F5 and see what the value is.

However, in this current example program, we want to see what happens to *five* values in an array. You could insert several message boxes in the code to display each value in turn, but that's clumsy and you have to click each message box's close button to close it before you can see the next box. Wastes time. Instead, using `Debug.WriteLine` is a good way to see the entire array at once.

`Debug.WriteLine` prints information in the Editor's *Immediate Window,* so press CTRL-G to display the Immediate Window, as shown in Figure 6-6.

Press F5 to run the example program. You should see results similar to those shown in Figure 6-6, with the output of the program (the five values from the array) listed in the Immediate Window.

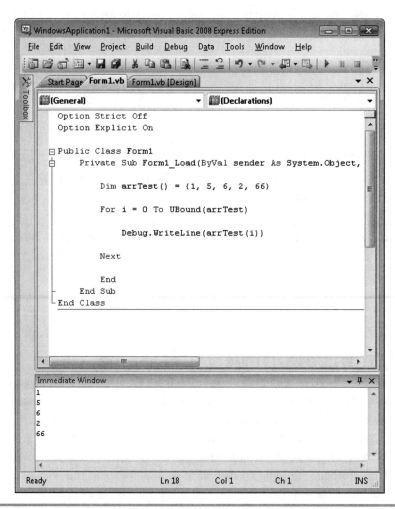

Figure 6-6 The Immediate Window can display multiple values.

To clean the Immediate Window so the next time you execute a program the current results won't still be there, right-click in the Immediate Window and choose Clear All.

Methods to Sort and Reverse Arrays

Methods are tasks that an object can perform—built-in capabilities. Like many other commands in VB, arrays are objects. (More on *objects* in Chapter 13.)

VB's arrays have some useful methods that you might want to know about in case you ever need to use them in your programming. Let's experiment with some methods that the `Array` command makes available to you.

NOTE

As you've doubtless observed, I always refer to VB's elements as *commands* (words recognized as part of the VB language). *Commands* is a generic term for the elements of a programming language. However, people use synonyms for the word *command*, such as *keyword*, *instruction*, and so on. But in this book, any word that is *reserved* (you can't use it to name a variable because it's used already by VB) is referred to as a *command*.

Now go to the VB code window. To see the methods (and properties) of the `Array` object, just below the array declaration in your code example, type in **Array.** (including the period) as shown here in boldface:

```
Dim arrTest() = {1, 5, 6, 2, 66}

    Array.

    For i = 0 To UBound(arrTest)
```

As soon as you type a period following the word `Array`, a list box pops open, showing you all the methods and properties available for use with an array. See Figure 6-7.

TIP

One way to tell whether a command is an *object* (with built-in methods and properties) is to type a period following the command, and then see whether a list box opens. If you don't see a list box, the command isn't an object. But if a list box does open, you can scroll through it to see what built-in methods and properties the object provides for your use when programming.

Now scroll the `Array` list box so you can see the various properties and methods of the `Array` object. The methods have purple diamond icons next to them. Scroll until you find the `Sort` method, and then press ENTER to add it to the `Array` command in the editor.

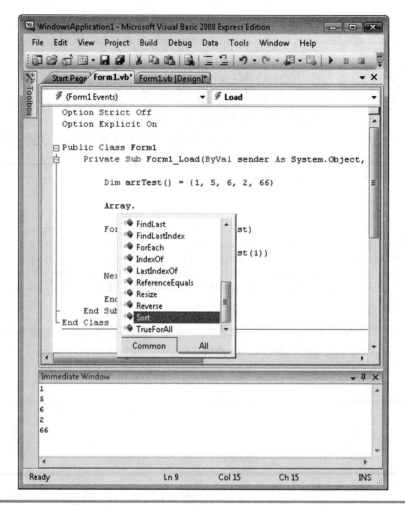

Figure 6-7   This list displays all the methods you can use with an array.

Notice the sawtooth underline. If you hover your mouse pointer over `Array.Sort()` in the editor, you'll see an error message informing you that no version of the `Sort` method accepts this number of arguments (see Figure 6-8). In other words, you currently have zero arguments between the parentheses, and you need at least one argument for this method to work.

What's the problem? The `Sort` method expects you to supply the name of the array you want to sort. So, change the line to this:

```
Array.Sort(arrTest)
```

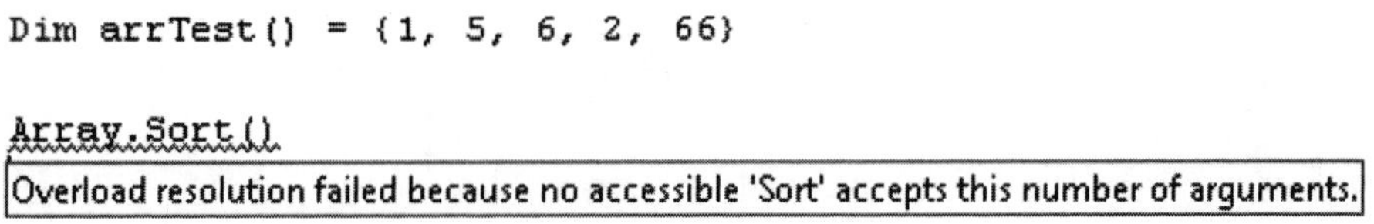

```
Dim arrTest() = {1, 5, 6, 2, 66}

Array.Sort()
```
Overload resolution failed because no accessible 'Sort' accepts this number of arguments.

Figure 6-8   You don't have enough arguments between these parentheses. In fact, you have none.

Now the sawtooth warning line disappears. Press F5 to execute this program and look in the Immediate Window. You'll see that the array has indeed been sorted. The array members are now listed in this order: 1, 2, 5, 6, 66.

OK, try one more thing. Change the line again so you can experiment with the `Reverse` method:

```
Array.Reverse(arrTest)
```

Press F5 again and notice that the array elements are now in reverse order—66, 2, 6, 5, 1—from their original order in the `Dim` statement.

Although we've used For...Next structures already a few times in this book, in the next chapter we'll go into detail about this very important tool in computer programming: *loops.*

Chapter 7

Looping for Repetitive Tasks

Key Skills & Concepts

● The two main types of loops

● For...Next loops

● Nesting loops

● Do...Loop structures

*L*ooping, or repeating, is a cornerstone of programming. In fact, when you think about it, loops are common in everyday life. To *loop* merely means to continue doing something until a task is finished—like addressing 150 invitations or tightening a screw.

VB has three kinds of loop structures: For...Next, For...Each, and Do...Loop. (The For...Each structure is covered in Chapter 10.)

If you find a place in your code that looks repetitious, you can probably create a loop and eliminate the repetitions. For example, this code

```
Debug.Write(1)
Debug.Write(2)
Debug.Write(3)
Debug.Write(4)
```

can be simplified by putting it into a loop:

```
For i = 1 To 4
    Debug.Write(i)
Next
```

The For...Next loop structure uses a *counter variable* that keeps track of the number of times the loop repeats. The counter variable in the For...Next loop in our example code is the i. Counter variables are automatically incremented (increased by 1) each time a loop repeats. So when you execute this example, you get the result 1234 in the editor's Immediate Window. (Recall that the Debug.Write command displays its output in the Immediate Window.)

Whatever code statements are inside a loop structure are repeatedly executed. The Debug.Print command writes the value of i four times, because I specified that this loop should execute four times: 1 To 4.

The Two Types of Loops

There are two main kinds of loops. One kind, the For...Next loop, specifies the number of *iterations* (repetitions). The preceding example specified 1 To 4.

When You Know the Number

In the For...Next type of loop, you often know while writing the program how many times you want to execute the loop. Therefore, you can just type that literal number into your code. In the preceding example, we knew while coding that we wanted to print four times, so we created a For...Next loop that specified *4* as the end point (also called the *exit condition*) of the loop:

```
For i = 1 to 4

Next i
```

Or, if you're inviting 150 people to your wedding, then envelopes have to be addressed 150 times. With a For...Next loop, you know in advance how many times you want the loop to repeat: For i = 1 to 150.

Looping Based on True or False

There is also a different type of loop. It repeats based on a true/false condition, rather than a specific number of times. You, the programmer, don't know in advance the specific number of times the loop should repeat. So you can't write 1 To 4 or 1 To 150 in your source code. You just don't know while writing the code exactly how many times to loop.

The most common form of this true/false loop is the Do...Loop structure. This loop repeats as long as a *condition* remains true. Here's an example:

```
Do While you can still turn the screwdriver (this is the condition)
     Turn the screwdriver once
Loop back up to the start of the loop structure
```

A Do...Loop starts off without knowing the exact number of times it will loop.

This distinction between the two main types of loops is easy to remember if you consider the difference between addressing 150 envelopes and tightening a screw. You know in advance that you'll stop writing addresses after you've done it 150 times. You *don't* know in advance how many times you'll need to turn the screw: you repeat twisting the screwdriver until it won't turn anymore.

For another example, recall the Timer program in Chapter 2. You, the programmer, don't know how many minutes the user will set the timer to count down. In fact, this countdown will be different when the user sets the timer for different purposes. Clearly, you won't use a For...Next loop. You'll use a Do...Loop.

In a Do...Loop, an expression usually specifies the exit condition for the loop, like this:

```
Do While CurrentTime < EndTime

    CurrentTime = Minute(Now)

Loop
```

Here the exit condition is the expression `CurrentTime < EndTime`—current time is less than end time.

In this code, the user specifies the duration (in minutes), and that value is held in the variable `EndTime`. Then the loop keeps updating the value in the variable `CurrentTime` by assigning the current minute as reported by the computer's built-in clock.

Each time the loop executes, these two variables are compared, using the less-than (<) comparison operator. Eventually, the current minute becomes less than (<) the user's specified end time and the loop is finished with its work. The exit condition is *satisfied* (it changes from *true* to *false*). The program then exits the loop structure and moves on to execute the code that follows the loop.

The point to remember is that this second type of loop repeatedly tests the exit condition while the loop is executing. It keeps testing to determine whether it's time to exit. And, equally important, something *inside the loop* (usually the value of a variable) must keep changing to allow the loop to eventually satisfy the exit condition. In the preceding example, the value in the variable `CurrentTime` keeps getting updated.

If nothing were to change within this type of loop, it would be an *endless loop* (also called an *infinite loop*). It could never stop looping!

Avoiding Endless Loops

Let's briefly review the two types of loops. It's typical to employ a For...Next loop structure when you know in advance the number of times the loop should repeat. But when you don't know in advance how many times the loop should repeat, you use a Do...Loop structure (or one of the Do...Loop variations, such as Do...While and Do...Until, that I'll discuss later in this chapter).

Recall that the key difference for a programmer between For...Next and Do...Loop structures is that when using a Do...Loop, you must ensure that some change occurs *inside the loop*. You must be able to eventually satisfy the loop's exit condition, so the loop stops looping.

Notice the important difference between these two example loops:

```
Option Strict Off
Option Explicit On

Public Class Form1
    Private Sub Form1_Load(ByVal sender As System.Object, ByVal e As
System.EventArgs) Handles MyBase.Load


        Dim Countdown

        For i = 1 To 4
            Debug.Write(i & ",")
        Next

        Debug.WriteLine(" ")

        Countdown = InputBox("Please enter the number of times you
want to do this task")

        Do While Countdown > 0
            Debug.Write("Looping" & ",")
            Countdown -= 1
        Loop

        End
    End Sub
End Class
```

In the second loop, the variable Countdown is *inside the loop* and *keeps changing as the loop repeats.* If this variable is not changed while inside the loop, the exit condition (CountDown reaching zero) will never be met.

NOTE

Did you notice that somewhat strange —= operator? It means "Lower this variable's value by 1." It's just a shorthand for this code:

```
Countdown = Countdown - 1
```

The += operator raises a variable's value. In fact, a whole slew of similar operators are available, such as &= to concatenate text, *= for multiplication, and so on. Use them if you like the shorthand.

A loop that can never exit is known as an *endless loop* or *infinite loop.* The program will continue looping, never getting out of the loop. The program will keep churning away with nothing happening other than the mindless looping.

This is a classic bug in computer programming. It's the equivalent of screwing into cardboard. You never reach a point where the condition (can't screw anymore) is satisfied: it just turns and turns without end. But this isn't usually a tough bug to figure out. You're sitting there a long time and nothing is happening—that's your clue that maybe you have an endless loop.

TIP

Did you notice the `Debug.WriteLine(" ")` statement in the example program? Inside the loops, we used the familiar `Debug.Write` command to display the loop's results on the *same* line in the Immediate Window. But we wanted to move down a line in the Immediate Window before showing the `Do...While` loop's results. So we used `Debug.WriteLine(" ")`. `WriteLine` moves you down one line in the Immediate Window; the `Write` command doesn't. See Figure 7-1.

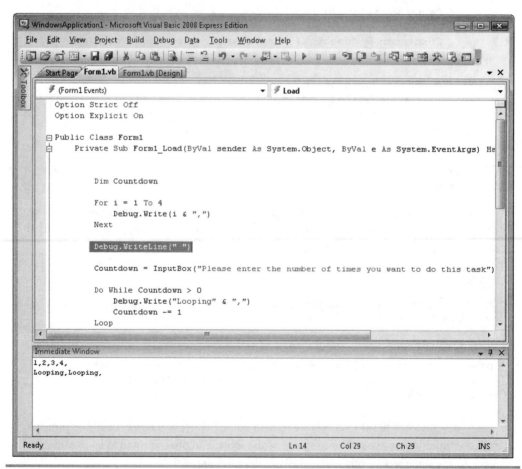

Figure 7-1 Notice that the `Debug.Writeline (" ")` statement moved the output down one line in the Immediate Window at the bottom of the code window.

The Main Idea

In any loop, the program repeatedly executes the code within the loop structure (or *block*) until the loop condition is satisfied. Then the program continues on to execute whatever code is below the loop structure.

For...Next loop structures end with the Next command. Do...Loop structures end with the Loop command.

Counter, Start, and End

Let's take a look now at some of the finer points of the For...Next loop structure.

```
For i = 1 To 4
```

This structure starts with a counter variable, which by tradition is named i. You can think of i as standing for *increment* or *iterate*. Then you specify the start and end values. In this case, we're saying start with *1* and end with *4*.

Stepping Through Loops

However, you can use any numbers you want. You can start with *22* and end with *27*, or start with *1* and end with *4932*.

Ask the Expert

Q: Can you iterate *backward* through a loop?

A: Yes, you can go backward (from a higher to a lower number) using the optional Step command, like this:

```
For i = 4 To 1 Step -1

    Debug.Write(i)

Next
```

This results in: 4321

You can also use Step to skip through the count. Normally, the counter variable (i) always counts up by 1. But what if you want to count up by, say, 3? The following code shows how.

(continued)

```
For i = 12 To 24 Step 3

        Debug.Write(i & ", ")

Next
```

This results in: 12, 15, 18, 21, 24,

The Step command is optional, but use it if you want to count by intervals (Step 2, for example, to count every other number) or to count down backwards.

Optional Early Exit

If you want, you can optionally exit a loop early (before the counter reaches the exit condition). Sometimes this comes in handy, but as you'll see shortly, it's frowned upon by programming teachers.

Let's assume you are looping through an array of 200 items, searching for the name *Clovis*. Once you find *Clovis*, there's no point in continuing the search, so you can employ the Exit For command to exit the loop. Exit For forces an early exit from the loop, and the program continues executing whatever code follows the Next command at the end of the loop:

```
Option Strict Off
Option Explicit On

Public Class Form1
    Private Sub Form1_Load(ByVal sender As System.Object, ByVal e As
System.EventArgs) Handles MyBase.Load

        Dim MyArray(200)

        MyArray(72) = "Clovis"

        For i = 0 To UBound(MyArray)

            If MyArray(i) = "Clovis" Then
                Debug.Write("Clovis found at index number: " & i)
                Exit For
            End If

        Next i

        End

    End Sub
End Class
```

If you execute this example, you'll see in the Immediate Window that, in fact, *Clovis* was located in the 72nd element of the array.

Best practices alert: Even though this Exit For approach works, most programming teachers want you to avoid using the Exit For command entirely. They argue that using Exit For makes the program a bit harder to read and understand, and that only one exit condition from a loop should exist. See Figure 7-2.

Programming teachers would prefer that you instead replace this For...Next structure with a Do...Loop structure, like this:

```
Option Strict Off
Option Explicit On

Public Class Form1
    Private Sub Form1_Load(ByVal sender As System.Object, ByVal e As
System.EventArgs) Handles MyBase.Load

        Dim s, i
        Dim MyArray(200)

        MyArray(72) = "Clovis"

        Do While s <> "Clovis"

            s = MyArray(i)

            If MyArray(i) = "Clovis" Then
                Debug.Write("Clovis found at index number: " & i)
            End If

            i += 1
        Loop

        End

    End Sub
End Class
```

```
For i = 0 To UBound(MyArray)

    If MyArray(i) = "Clovis" Then
        Debug.Write("Clovis found at index number: " & i)
        Exit For
    End If

Next i
```

Figure 7-2 Most programming teachers prefer that you avoid this kind of code (employing two exit conditions in a loop).

In this version, we have moved the exit condition from *within* the loop structure, as shown here,

```
For i = 0 To UBound(MyArray)

    If MyArray(i) = "Clovis" Then
        Debug.Write("Clovis found at index number: " & i)
        Exit For
    End If

Next i
```

to the very top of the loop structure, as shown here:

```
Do While s <> "Clovis"
```

Programming teachers also prefer that the exit condition of all loops appear at the top of the loop structure (for readability). In the case of Do...Loop structures, the exit condition can also be placed at the bottom of the loop. Just avoid putting it *inside* the loop. See Figure 7-3.

When at the top or bottom of the loop, and when it's the only exit, you can always see right off the bat what the exit condition is. You don't have to search around within the loop to see if there's a second exit condition somewhere in there.

I'm somewhat torn on this issue. Most languages offer an Exit command for a reason. I actually find the For...Next...Exit For version in this example program a bit *more* readable. And to me, it also has the added advantage that it can't become an endless loop—even if the loop never finds *Clovis* in the array, it will end after 201 iterations. But the Do...Loop version *will* be endless if *Clovis* isn't found. Its exit condition assumes that *Clovis* is in that array.

(I can hear someone say "But Clovis *is* in that array in the code example!" This code is just an example. If you're searching for something in a database in the real world,

```
Do While s <> "Clovis"

    s = MyArray(i)

    If MyArray(i) = "Clovis" Then
        Debug.Write("Clovis found at index number: " & i)
    End If

    i += 1
Loop
```

Figure 7-3 Best practices call for using only one exit condition and locating it at the top of the loop structure, not within it.

you are looking through a collection of data the contents of which you usually *don't* know. Clovis might well not be in the database anymore because he didn't pay his bills or moved to Des Moines.)

One further point: As this example illustrates, some overlap exists between the `For...Next` and `Do...Loop` approaches. Sometimes, which loop structure you choose to employ in a given situation is a matter of your personal programming style.

And whether you use the `Exit For` command is also, ultimately, a personal choice (unless you become a teacher or professional programmer—in which case you have to follow the rules, whatever they might be at the school or company where you work).

Loops Within Loops

`For...Next` loops can be *nested*, meaning that a loop can be placed inside another loop. This technique, however, is a bit tough to grasp. And depending on the kinds of programs you write, you might never use nested loops, especially if you remain an amateur programmer. So if you want, you can just skip down to the final section in this chapter, titled "Do Loops, While and Until."

Nested loops can be confusing, because you add a new dimension when you put one loop inside another. It's like that ride at Disneyland, the Mad Tea Party, where you're sitting in a spinning teacup—but at the same time all the teacups are also revolving on a large plate. So two loops are involved, a fast small loop and a slower, larger loop.

When nesting, you use two loops, the inner and the outer. (You can even nest more than two loops, but let's not go there.) The inner loop interacts with the outer loop in ways that are immediately clear only to the mathematically gifted. Essentially, the inner loop executes its code the number of times specified by its own counter variable *multiplied* by the counter variable of the outer loop.

For example, here a `j` loop is nested inside an `i` loop:

```
For i = 1 To 3

    For j = 1 To 10
    Next j

Next i
```

The `j` loop will execute a total of 30 times. Can you see why?

Nested loops are most often used when working with *tables* of data. In the Quiz program we worked with a *one-dimensional array*. That works great when you're working only with a *list* of information. But a table is like two lists in one: it goes, both down vertically (like a regular list), and it also has a horizontal dimension, too.

Two-dimensional arrays are like spreadsheets. Spreadsheets or other tables (crossword puzzles and so on) have *two* indexes—down and across. A table is a list on steroids. It goes down (1, 2, 3, 4) like a list, and also across (a1, b1, c1, d1). A list only has rows; a table has both rows and columns.

So if you want to search through all the elements in a table, a two-dimensional array, the easiest way to do it is by using a nested loop. (In Chapter 8, we'll improve the Quiz program and discover how to work with two-dimensional arrays.)

Here's an example that illustrates visually how nested loops work. We'll count from 1 to 5 in the outer loop and from 1 to 10 in the inner loop:

```
Option Strict Off
Option Explicit On

Public Class Form1
    Private Sub Form1_Load(ByVal sender As System.Object, ByVal e As
System.EventArgs) Handles MyBase.Load

        Dim i, j

        For i = 1 To 5

            For j = 1 To 10
                Debug.Write(j)
            Next j

            Debug.WriteLine(" ")

        Next i

        End
    End Sub
End Class
```

Execute this example and you'll see this result in the Immediate Window:

```
12345678910
12345678910
12345678910
12345678910
12345678910
```

Here you have five rows of ten digits each.

The outer loop does two things: it executes the inner loop five times, and it also writes an empty line (Debug.WriteLine) in the Immediate Window five times. The inner loop counts from 1 to 10 and displays its results in the Immediate Window. (It's traditional to use the counter variable name j for an inner loop.)

When working with a nested loop, just *hack* away, as programmers say, substituting counter numbers (and maybe moving commands from one loop to the other) until things work the way they should.

Recall that *hacking* to a programmer means essentially the same thing as carving means to a sculptor—chipping away until the desired result emerges. You probably won't write the correct code on the first try. And you almost certainly won't get it right initially when hacking away to create a nested loop or when employing other puzzling programming techniques.

Do Loops, While and Until

Do Loops come in a variety of flavors.

You can place the exit condition at the beginning of the loop, as we've done so far in this chapter's examples:

```
Do While CurrentTime < EndTime

    CurrentTime = Minute(Now)

Loop
```

Or you can move the exit condition down to the end of the loop, like this:

```
Do

    CurrentTime = Minute(Now)

Loop While CurrentTime < EndTime
```

Executing at Least Once

Moving the exit condition test to the end of the loop structure ensures that the loop structure *will always execute its inner code at least once*. And sometimes you want it to execute at least once.

Put another way, if the test is at the start of the loop and the test fails as soon as the loop structure is first reached, the code within the loop will never execute (VB will just skip past the loop).

It's Only Semantics

A Do...Loop also permits you to use two kinds of exit condition tests: While or Until. You can say Do...While or Do...Until. So far, we've always said While, and it is the more common usage. But you can use either one, interchangeably.

The distinction between *while* and *until* is only a matter of how you want to express things. It's like the difference between "Mop *until* the floor is clean" versus "Mop *while* the floor is dirty." In both cases, you're performing the same task and ending at the same time—but you're just describing the end point using different wording.

This While versus Until is just another readability issue. The way you express the exit condition can sometimes make your meaning clearer to you and other programmers who might read your program. For example, you could reword the previous example to replace While with Until.

Here's a While version:

```
Do While CurrentTime < EndTime

        CurrentTime = Minute(Now)

   Loop
```

And here's the Until version of the same thing:

```
Do Until CurrentTime = EndTime

    CurrentTime = Minute(Now)

Loop
```

Which wording you prefer is, well, your preference.

Chapter 8

Making Decisions

Key Skills & Concepts

● Intelligent behavior through branching

● `If...Then...ElseIf...Else` structure

● `Select Case` structure

● Finishing the Quiz program

> *Two roads diverged in a wood, and I—*
> *I took the one less traveled by,*
> *And that has made all the difference.*
> —Robert Frost

Making accurate decisions is fundamental to intelligent behavior. A flooding river makes no decisions; it merely follows a path of least resistance. But if you're a cat chasing a mouse, you make decisions continually: If the mouse turns left, you must turn left; if the mouse freezes in panic, you pounce; if the mouse runs into his hole, don't try to follow him or you'll crash into the wall like last time.

Computer programs can also behave intelligently because they can *branch*—taking different courses of action depending on circumstances. This is quite similar to the behavior of the cat. The primary difference is that you, the programmer, specify in your code the branching rules that the computer will follow when the program executes. You tell it, "If this happens, do that."

Understanding Decision Structures

VB offers two different branching structures: `If...Then` and `Select Case`.

You've seen branching behaviors already in various example programs in earlier chapters. In the Timer program, the `If...Then` structure demonstrates branching:

```
If Counter >= TotalSeconds Then

    Timer1.Stop()

    MsgBox("Time's up.")

    End

End If
```

Two Possible Paths

The preceding code uses If...Then to check whether the time is up and, if it is, stops the timer, displays a message to the user, and ends the program.

On the other hand, if the time is not yet up, execution *skips over* the If...Then structure and continues with whatever code lies below the structure. The timer continues executing, no message is displayed, and the program doesn't yet end.

Thus, when a program reaches an If...Then structure, it can take more than one potential execution path. In programming terminology, this is called *branching*. In living animals, it's called *making a decision*. A section of code that branches is also sometimes called a *decision structure*.

If...Then structures are quite common in computer programs, often branching between only two possible paths (as in the Timer program).

Many Paths

But branches can also have multiple paths. In the Quiz program in Chapter 6, we created a stack of four If...Then structures, one after the other. In this case, four paths of execution are possible—four branches:

```
If Response = vbYes And arrAnswers(i) = 1 Then

    MsgBox("Correct")
    Counter = Counter + 1

End If


' answer = 0 False, so they are wrong:
If Response = vbYes And arrAnswers(i) = 0 Then

    MsgBox("Wrong")

End If

'THEY CLICKED THE NO BUTTON (7 = No button):

' Answer = 0 means False (no) so they are correct:
If Response = vbNo And arrAnswers(i) = 0 Then

    MsgBox("Correct")
    Counter = Counter + 1

End If
```

```
' Answer = 1 (True) so they are wrong:
If Response = vbNo And arrAnswers(i) = 1 Then

    MsgBox("Wrong")

End If
```

We stacked these If...Then structures because code like that is easiest for beginners to understand. However, more experienced programmers rarely use a stack of If...Then structures in this situation. There's nothing *wrong* with stacking If...Then blocks. The code works fine that way. But it can be simplified and made a bit easier to read.

As you'll see later in this chapter, a multiple-branch decision structure usually employs a variation on If...Then called an If...ElseIf structure, or the famous Select Case structure.

TIP

Always remember that you can usually accomplish a given programming task in several different ways. So if you are writing programs merely for your own enjoyment, and you find stacked If...Then structures easier to read, go ahead and use them. That's one of the advantages of being an amateur. Nobody will smirk if you're not using the official "approved" techniques or if your code isn't as *elegant* as it could be. You have the freedom to be yourself. One more point: Some of the official rules are sensible, some are important only if you gang-program as a group, and others are merely current fads that have no more utility than pet rocks or beanie babies.

The Simplest Branch

You can use a shorthand version of an If...Then structure by putting the whole structure on a single line. A single-line If...Then is the simplest branch structure.

Here's an example that ends the program if the value in the variable *X* is greater than 12:

```
If X > 12 Then End
```

As this example illustrates, when your branch involves something short and simple (like merely executing the End command, or not), you can use this shorthand version of If... Then. Write the whole structure on a single line of code and leave out the End If. It's implied.

Usually, though, If...Then structures are written so they take up several lines of code, with the statements inside the structure indented, like this:

```
If X > 12 Then
    End
End If
```

The editor automatically indents the lines inside a multi-line `If...Then` structure. This makes it easy for you to see what statements are executed if the trigger expression is true. (In this code, the trigger expression is *X is greater than 12.*)

Multiple Lines of Code

Sometimes you need to do several things inside a decision structure. You can write as many code statements as you need within the `If...Then` structure. Consider the `If...Then` structures in our Quiz program, for example. Here, two lines of code are contained inside the structure:

```
If Response = 7 And arrQuiz(i, 2) = "0" Then

        MsgBox("Correct")
        Counter = Counter + 1

End If
```

Using the Else Command

Another common version of branching involves listing two possible responses to the trigger expression: what to do if the expression is true, or `Else` what to do if it isn't true. An expression is either true or false in computer programming—there are no shades of gray here.

In the examples so far in this chapter, we looked at simple branches: the branch either executed the code *inside* the structure or continued executing the code *below* the structure. Only two possible paths.

But what if you want the program to take one of several paths? Here's an example of how to specify multiple paths. We want to display different message boxes, depending on what the user claims to weigh:

```
Option Strict Off
Option Explicit On

Public Class Form1
    Private Sub Form1_Load(ByVal sender As System.Object, ByVal e As
System.EventArgs) Handles MyBase.Load

        Dim X

        X = Input box("What's your weight?")

        If x > 200 Then
```

```
        MsgBox("Maybe it's time to diet?")

    Else

        MsgBox("Have another cookie!")

    End If

        End
    End Sub
End Class
```

In this example, the statements between the `Then` and `Else` commands specify what to do if the trigger expression is true.

Statements between the `Else` and `End If` commands specify what to do if the trigger expression is false.

Using ElseIf

Yet another kind of multiple branching allows you to use multiple trigger expressions. This is an alternative to the stacked `If...Then` structures I described earlier in this chapter.

For example, let's say you want to display several different message boxes depending on which of several possible weight ranges the user claims.

To use multiple trigger expressions, you can employ the `ElseIf` command, like this:

```
Option Strict Off
Option Explicit On

Public Class Form1
    Private Sub Form1_Load(ByVal sender As System.Object, ByVal e As
System.EventArgs) Handles MyBase.Load

        Dim X

        X = Input box("What's your weight?")

        If X > 200 Then

            MsgBox("Maybe it's time to diet")

        ElseIf X > 100 Then

            MsgBox("Have another cookie!")

        ElseIf X > 60 Then
```

```
        MsgBox("Please eat something!")

    End If

      End
  End Sub
End Class
```

CAUTION

You can use as many `ElseIf` commands as you want, but sometimes the order in which you list them is important. The following discussion explains why.

Avoiding a Bug

Notice that the order in which you put `ElseIf` expressions does matter in the preceding example. What would happen if you *reversed* the order of the `If` and `ElseIf` tests in the example code, like this?

```
If X > 60 Then


ElseIf X > 100 Then


ElseIf X > 200 Then
```

Do you see the problem here? This code is buggy.

Visual Basic always moves down through a set of `ElseIf` statements, looking for the first true statement. After it handles that first true statement, VB *exits the entire decision structure.* In other words, as soon as VB finds a true `ElseIf` statement, it does not look at any other `ElseIf` statements located below the first true one.

The order in which we've listed these expressions means that the second and third expressions here can *never trigger.* They will never execute.

The first expression (> 60) will always be true before VB can even reach the second and third expressions. Any weight the user types in that's above 60 pounds always triggers the first branch. Lower branches will *always* be ignored, even if the user types in 500 pounds.

Put another way, the expression *greater than 60* includes the values 100 and 200 or even 5000 tons, or the total weight of the universe. The first trigger *precludes* all possible triggers greater than 60.

Do you see that if the user answers any weight above 60, the first expression (greater than 60) will always be triggered and the structure exited? VB will not even test to see if the following triggers are valid. Remember that as soon as one of the expressions is true, the entire If...Then structure is exited.

The lesson here is to pay attention to the relationship between the order of the expressions in an If...Then structure. Ensure that one of them doesn't prevent others below it from ever executing, as happens in the preceding example.

TIP

This is an example of a *logic bug*—the hardest type of bug to track down and fix. However, if you do forget to see if a branch is inclusive of lower branches, and your program acts funny as a result, you can use some debugging strategies to discover the problem. I'll cover debugging in Chapter 11.

Using Ranges to Solve the "Precludes Problem"

Fortunately, there is a good solution to this "precludes problem." If you don't want to worry about the order of your expressions, just specify *ranges*, like this:

```
If X > 59 And < 100 Then


ElseIf X > 99 And < 200 Then
```

These statements specify ranges (between 60 and 99, between 100 and 199). When you specify ranges, the precludes problem goes away. We'll revisit using ranges later in this chapter.

Including All Possible Cases with the Else Command

In addition to the precludes problem, there's a second bug in our original ElseIf example code. It's bugs-a-go-go.

What happens if some waif user types in *55*? Nothing happens. None of our three conditions is triggered. We're testing for 60, 100, or 200, and 55 is not greater than any of our tests. So nothing at all happens. No messages are displayed. VB slides right through this decision structure, taking no branches at all.

We forgot to deal with the fact that some people actually do weigh less than 60.

Usually you want to ensure that you've made provisions for *any possible* user input. Not just some answers but any answer. Users expect a program to respond in some way when they provide input.

To deal with these "none of the above" situations, you add an `Else` command. `Else` means *anything else other than what I've already listed.* In our example, `Else` can handle any weight that the user types in that is not already covered by the other three expressions:

```
Private Sub Form1_Load(ByVal sender As System.Object, ByVal e As
System.EventArgs) Handles MyBase.Load

    Dim X

    X = Input box("What's your weight?")

    If X > 200 Then

        MsgBox("Maybe it's time to diet")

    ElseIf X > 100 Then

        MsgBox("Have another cookie!")

    ElseIf X > 60 Then

        MsgBox("Please eat something!")

    Else

        MsgBox("Your weight suggests that you're under the age of
12.")

    End If

    End

End Sub
```

Multiple Branches Using the Select Case Structure

The `Select Case` decision structure is an alternative to the `If...ElseIf` structure. `Select Case` is generally easier to read—it's often simpler and clearer than a stack of multiple `ElseIf` statements, or a stack of `If...Then` structures.

Here's how you would rewrite the example we used earlier in this chapter as a `Select Case` decision structure rather than a set of `ElseIf` statements:

```
Option Strict Off
Option Explicit On

Public Class Form1
```

```
Private Sub Form1_Load(ByVal sender As System.Object, ByVal e As
System.EventArgs) Handles MyBase.Load

    Dim X

    X = Input box("What's your weight?")

    Select Case X

        Case Is > 200

            MsgBox("Maybe it's time to diet")

        Case Is > 100

            MsgBox("Have another cookie!")

        Case Is > 60

            MsgBox("Please eat something!")

    End Select

    End
End Sub
```

Note that If...Then decision structures end with End If, and Select Case structures end with End Select.

Using the To Command for Ranges

Another way to program this same Select Case example is to use the To command, which allows you to specify a range, like this:

```
Public Class Form1
Private Sub Form1_Load(ByVal sender As System.Object, ByVal e As
System.EventArgs) Handles MyBase.Load

    Dim X

    X = Input box("What's your weight?")

    Select Case X

        Case 200 To 1000

            MsgBox("Maybe it's time to diet")
```

```
        Case 100 To 200

            MsgBox("Have another cookie!")

        Case 0 To 60

            MsgBox("Please eat something!")

    End Select

        End
    End Sub
End Class
```

This example is merely another way of writing the preceding example, but here we use ranges like `200 To 1000` rather than `> 200`.

TIP

Recall that using ranges like this is usually the preferred approach. Ranges eliminate the need to worry about listing `Case` statements (or `ElseIf` statements) in any particular order. Also, my friend John Mueller pointed out a bug in this example program. I should probably change the first `Case` to read, `Case 201 To 1000` to prevent the possibility of someone typing *200* and receiving an incorrect message. What's more, I have no range for 61 to 99 pounds. The lesson here (for you and me) is to study your list of cases carefully to ensure that none of your ranges overlap, and take into account all possible cases (leaving no gaps).

All Other Possibilities with Case Else

Is there command you can use in a `Select Case` structure to respond if "none of the above" cases is true (the same way that the `Else` command works in an `If...Then` structure)?

Indeed there is. You can use `Case Else`, like this:

```
Private Sub Form1_Load(ByVal sender As System.Object, ByVal e As
System.EventArgs) Handles MyBase.Load

Private Sub Form1_Load(ByVal sender As System.Object, ByVal e As
System.EventArgs) Handles MyBase.Load

    Dim X

    X = Input box("What's your weight?")

    Select Case X
```

```
        Case Is > 200

            MsgBox("Maybe it's time to diet?")

        Case Else

            MsgBox("Have another cookie!")

    End Select

    End
End Sub
```

Omitting the Is Command

Notice in the preceding examples that we used the greater-than comparison operator, >. Whenever you use comparison operators, you use the `Case Is` command as we did.

However, if you are merely listing specific individual values, leave out the `Is`, like this:

```
Private Sub Form1_Load(ByVal sender As System.Object, ByVal e As
System.EventArgs) Handles MyBase.Load

    Dim Name = "Ashley"

    Select Case Name

        Case "Bob"
            MsgBox("Hi Bob!")
        Case "Nancy"
            MsgBox("Hi Nancy!")
        Case "Ashley"
            MsgBox("Hi Ashley!")
        Case Else
            MsgBox("I don't recognize that name.")

    End Select

    End
End Sub
```

Finishing the Quiz Program

When last we worked in the Quiz program in Chapter 6, it was rather elementary. It just displayed a series of message boxes and it worked only with true/false questions.

To conclude this chapter, we'll flesh out the Quiz program by creating a window (form) the user can interact with rather than the simple message boxes. We'll also upgrade it from a true/false quiz to the more advanced multiple-choice format. In the process, you'll learn a little more about using multidimensional arrays.

Designing the Form

How do you change the Quiz program from the earlier true/false version to a multiple-choice quiz? We'll display three possible answers to each question. One good way to do that is to use three radio button controls—one for each answer.

The user will be able to select only one of these controls at a time; that's how radio buttons work if they're grouped together on a form. Just like the preset station buttons on a car radio, if the user clicks one of the radio buttons, the others will be deselected. Users will make their selection from among the multiple choices we'll offer by selecting one of the radio buttons.

A radio button control includes a Text property that displays a caption to the right of the button. We'll display the quiz answers as captions to the radio buttons.

We'll place a label control at the top of the form to display each quiz question.

Finally, we'll put two buttons on the bottom of the form, captioned *Submit* and *Next*. When users are satisfied that they've selected the right answer, they click the Submit button to see if they were correct. Then they click the Next button when they're ready to move on to the next question.

OK, now that we've visualized what controls the form should contain, let's build the form. (Remember that you can design a user interface in many different ways. The design we're using here is just my idea of a good approach, but it's certainly not the only good approach.)

1. Press CTRL-N to start a new project.

2. In the New Project dialog box, type the name **MultiQuiz**. Then double-click the Windows Forms Application icon.

3. Drag the lower-right corner of the form to make it somewhat larger than the default size (see Figure 8-1). If your Properties window isn't visible, press F4. A size of 490,550 is good, but it's not a major issue. To see or modify the size, look at the Size property in the Properties window.

4. From the Toolbox, drag and drop three radio buttons and stack them one on top of the other.

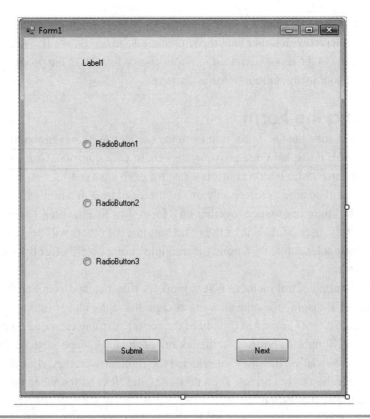

Figure 8-1 Here's my suggestion about how your multiple-choice Quiz program should look.

5. Next, drag and drop a label onto the top of the form.

6. Finally, drag and drop two buttons near the bottom of the form.

7. In the Properties window, change the first button's Text property to *Submit* and the second button's Text property to *Next*.

8. In the Properties window, change the Submit button's Name property to *btnSubmit* and the Next button's name to *btnNext*. The finished form is shown in Figure 8-1.

Ask the Expert

Q: **Can you modify several controls all at once? For example, can you increase the font size of a group of controls in one fell swoop without having to change the size for each control individually?**

A: Yes. You do this by temporarily *grouping* a set of controls. Grouping controls is an efficient way to modify them as if they were a single unit. You can group all the controls on your form by dragging your mouse around all the controls (drag on the background of the form), as shown in the following image. This selects the controls.

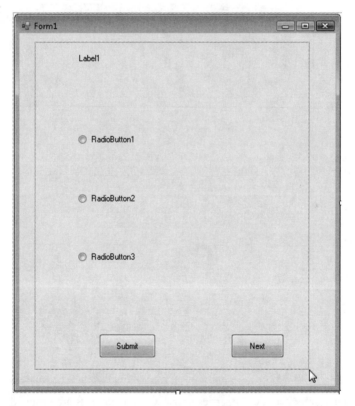

When you group a set of controls like this, the Properties window automatically hides some properties—displaying only those properties that the group of controls has in common. At this point, you can modify a property in the Properties window, and the entire group will be modified as a unit.

The group can also be repositioned all at the same time (you can drag them as a unit), or you can change any property that the group has in common by changing its value in the Properties window.

(continued)

Let's experiment by changing the font size of all the controls on the form. For some reason, Visual Basic, since its beginning 15 years ago, has employed a default font size of 8.5, which is too small for most purposes. Let's change the font size for all the controls to 11, which is more readable. You'll probably want to boost the font size for pretty much any program you create in VB, so you might as well learn to do it as efficiently as possible.

Drag a frame around all the controls on the form, as shown previously. When you release the left mouse button after dragging, each control will have a selection frame drawn around it and will also display small drag handles, as you can see next. This indicates that the controls are now grouped. If you resize one of them, all will be similarly resized. If you drag one, they all move to a new position on the form.

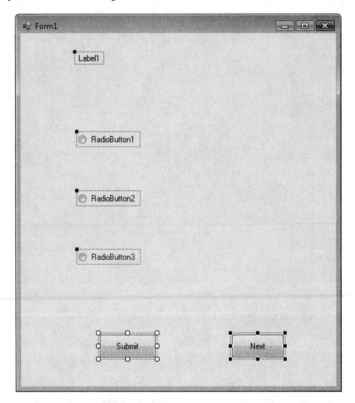

And if you look at the Properties window while controls are grouped, you'll see that it now displays only those properties that the group has in common. For example, forms, buttons, and radio buttons all have a BackGroundImage property you can use to display .jpg, .bmp, and other graphics files as a kind of wallpaper. But, because the Label control doesn't have this property, and you've selected all the controls on this form (including the Label), the Properties window temporarily hides the BackGroundImage property.

However, the Font property is still visible in the Properties window because all these grouped controls have that property.

We want to change the font property of this group to 11, up from the default 8.25 size. So double-click the Font property in the Properties window to display all the font-related properties, and then change the 8.25 to 11.

Notice that immediately all the characters increase in size in all the controls on the form, as shown next. Finally, click anywhere on the form's background to deselect the controls, thus ungrouping them and returning to normal design mode. (You might also want to enlarge the buttons so their newly enlarged text fits comfortably on them.)

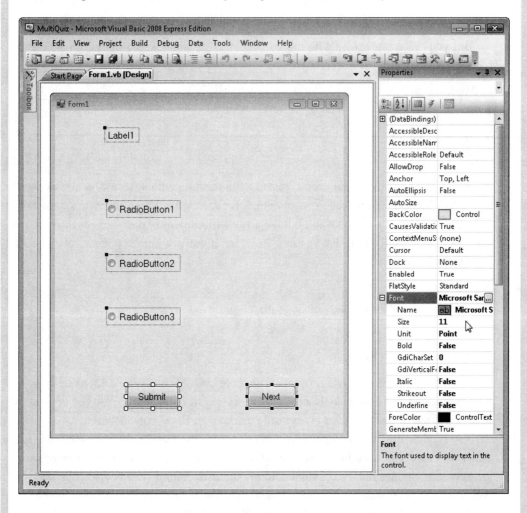

Writing the Code

So far in this book, we've used only *one*-dimensional arrays (like those we explored in Chapter 6). Recall that a one-dimensional array resembles a simple list, with one item of data on each line:

0. Apples

1. Oranges

2. Bananas

3. Cherries

But you can create arrays with more than one dimension. A two-dimensional array could look like this:

0. Apples, Red

1. Oranges, Orange

2. Bananas, Yellow

3. Cherries, Red

When you have two dimensions, you're really dealing with a table structure rather than a list. You can extend each row of data as far as you want. In other words, you can add as many columns as you want, but the array still remains two-dimensional. Here's an example: This is still a two-dimensional array, but it now has three columns (Name, Color, and Price Per Pound):

0. Apples,	Red,	1.75
1. Oranges,	Orange,	1.60
2. Bananas,	Yellow,	.55
3. Cherries,	Red,	3.12

For a multiple-choice Quiz program with three possible answers to each question, a tabular, two-dimensional array is an excellent way to store the data. This type of array is best visualized as a table, like a crossword puzzle or an Excel spreadsheet.

To visualize how we're organizing this array, imagine that the quiz questions are listed down the first column, and then we'll use three additional columns for the three possible answers to each question. And a final column, the fifth column, can be used to specify which answer is correct. Such a table would look like Figure 8-2.

An array that mirrors the tabular (table-like) organization shown in Figure 8-2 is declared like this:

```
Dim arrQuiz (3,4)
```

	A	B	C	D	E
1	Question #1	Answer 1	Answer 2	Answer 3	Correct Answer to Question #1
2	Question #2	Answer 1	Answer 2	Answer 3	Correct Answer to Question #2
3	Question #3	Answer 1	Answer 2	Answer 3	Correct Answer to Question #3
4	Question #4	Answer 1	Answer 2	Answer 3	Correct Answer to Question #4

Figure 8-2   A set of questions with three possible answers can be visualized like this spreadsheet table.

Dimensioning this array using (3,4) allows you to store four questions, with three answers each, plus the correct answer. (Remember the zero-effect. Arrays always have a zero element, so array specifications are always off by one. In an ideal world, you would dimension this array as 4, 5.) But here's what our array declaration looks like, thanks to the zero-effect:

```
Dim arrQuiz(3, 4)
```

The *3* represents the number of questions we are going to ask (think of these as *rows* going down the left side of our table, and the rows are labeled *0, 1, 2,* and *3*).

The *4* represents the number of data we need to store for each question (think of these as five *columns* labeled *0, 1, 2, 3, 4* going across the top of the table).

Remember that we need a total of five columns, because each question involves these five items of data:

- The question itself
- The three possible answers
- A key specifying the correct answer

Now let's type in the code for this program. Double-click the form to open the Form_ Load event. Type this source code (or copy and paste it from this book's web site at www .mhprofessional.com/computingdownload):

```
Option Strict Off
Option Explicit On

Public Class Form1

    Dim arrQuiz(3, 4)
    Dim QuestionNumber
```

```
    Private Sub Form1_Load(ByVal sender As System.Object, ByVal e As
System.EventArgs) Handles MyBase.Load

        arrQuiz(0, 0) = "Manet"
        arrQuiz(0, 1) = "Monet"
        arrQuiz(0, 2) = "Van Gogh"
        arrQuiz(0, 3) = "Who famously painted water lilies?"
        arrQuiz(0, 4) = "2"

        arrQuiz(1, 0) = "A painting by Van Gogh"
        arrQuiz(1, 1) = "A well-known planetarium in New York"
        arrQuiz(1, 2) = "A cereal"
        arrQuiz(1, 3) = "What is Starry Night?"
        arrQuiz(1, 4) = "1"

        arrQuiz(2, 0) = "love"
        arrQuiz(2, 1) = "war"
        arrQuiz(2, 2) = "Both of the above"
        arrQuiz(2, 3) = "What is the subject of Picasso's Guernica?"
        arrQuiz(2, 4) = "2"

        arrQuiz(3, 0) = "Sophisticated use of perspective."
        arrQuiz(3, 1) = "Complete lack of color."
        arrQuiz(3, 2) = "No use of perspective at all."
        arrQuiz(3, 3) = "Name one important quality of Egyptian art."
        arrQuiz(3, 4) = "3"

        'display first question

        RadioButton1.Text = arrQuiz(0, 0)
        RadioButton2.Text = arrQuiz(0, 1)
        RadioButton3.Text = arrQuiz(0, 2)
        Label1.Text = arrQuiz(0, 3)



    End Sub

    Private Sub btnSubmit_Click(ByVal sender As System.Object, ByVal e
As System.EventArgs) Handles btnSubmit.Click
        ' The Submit button was clicked
        ' Check their answer, report the result, update the counter


        Static Counter 'Holds the number of correct answers
```

```
        'find out which radio button is clicked
        If RadioButton1.Checked = True And arrQuiz(QuestionNumber, 4)
= "1" Then

            Label1.Text = Label1.Text & "  CORRECT!"
            Counter = Counter + 1

        ElseIf RadioButton2.Checked = True And arrQuiz(QuestionNumber,
4) = "2" Then

            Label1.Text = Label1.Text & "  CORRECT!"
            Counter = Counter + 1

        ElseIf RadioButton3.Checked = True And arrQuiz(QuestionNumber,
4) = "3" Then

            Label1.Text = Label1.Text & "  CORRECT!"
            Counter = Counter + 1

        Else

            Label1.Text = Label1.Text & "  INCORRECT."

        End If

        Me.Text = Counter & " correct answers so far."


        ' raise the question number variable, redraw the question/
answers or exit if finished
        QuestionNumber = QuestionNumber + 1

        If QuestionNumber > UBound(arrQuiz) Then 'we're finished with
the quiz
            MsgBox("You got " & Counter & " correct out of " &
UBound(arrQuiz) + 1 & " questions.")
            End
        End If

    End Sub

    Private Sub btnNextQuestion_Click(ByVal sender As System.Object,
ByVal e As System.EventArgs) Handles btnNextQuestion.Click
        'the Next Question button was clicked

        'redraw the form:
```

```
      RadioButton1.Checked = False
      RadioButton2.Checked = False
      RadioButton3.Checked = False

      RadioButton1.Text = arrQuiz(QuestionNumber, 0)
      RadioButton2.Text = arrQuiz(QuestionNumber, 1)
      RadioButton3.Text = arrQuiz(QuestionNumber, 2)
      Label1.Text = arrQuiz(QuestionNumber, 3)

   End Sub
End Class
```

Notice that we declare the `arrQuiz` array and the `QuestionNumber` variable up above the `Form_Load` event:

```
Public Class Form1

   Dim arrQuiz(3, 4)
   Dim QuestionNumber


   Private Sub Form1_Load(ByVal sender As System.Object, ByVal e As
System.EventArgs) Handles MyBase.Load
```

Recall that when you declare something outside any procedure like this, it then has form-wide scope. In other words, it's available to all the procedures (subs or functions) in the form.

In this program, several procedures need to access the `QuestionNumber` variable and `arrQuiz` array. Using form-wide scope like this is generally considered undesirable by programming teachers, but for small, simple programs like this quiz you can go ahead and employ this techinque. Even in larger programs, global scope is sometimes the easiest way to allow multiple procedures access to a variable or an array. Such wide scope is also called *global scope*.

NOTE

Remember from Chapter 5 that most programming professors consider using global variables sleazy. They prefer that you always pass data back and forth between procedures, a technique you'll explore in the next chapter. This kind of rule is called *best practices*, in the same sense that never eating a fast-food burger is a best nutritional practice. But, once in a while, what's the harm? Plus, you usually write less code and your program is simpler when you employ global variables. Just be judicious in their use, and do use local variables (declared inside procedures) whenever possible. That's my advice, sleazy as it may be.

Exploring What the Code Does

OK. Let me describe how this code works. When the program first executes, the code in the `Form_Load` event fills the array with all the necessary data for the quiz. At the end of the `Form_Load` event, the first question and its three possible answers are displayed on the form to the user. In other words, the `Text` properties of the three radio buttons and the label are assigned strings from the first question (row zero) in the array:

```
'display first question

        RadioButton1.Text = arrQuiz(0, 0)
        RadioButton2.Text = arrQuiz(0, 1)
        RadioButton3.Text = arrQuiz(0, 2)
        Label1.Text = arrQuiz(0, 3)
```

The variable named `QuestionNumber` keeps track of which question is currently displayed on the form. This variable is used to point to the correct data within the array (`QuestionNumber` provides the index number).

When a numeric variable is first declared, it automatically contains a zero by default. Similarly, a text variable initially contains nothing—empty text, "", or what amounts to the same thing: *vbNullString*.

For this reason, we did not need to adjust the `QuestionNumber` variable at this time (raise it to 1) in the `Form_Load` event. The first question in our quiz is the question with the zero index in the array (once again, I must stress that arrays always start with a zero element).

So, the fact that the `QuestionNumber` variable contains that default zero is just fine. It will point to the zeroth element in the quiz array. And that's what we want it to point to, until it's told otherwise later in the program.

The `btnSubmit_Click` event is where most of the action happens in this program. That's the button captioned *Submit*. When the user clicks it after answering the question, the code in this event must check to see what radio button the user has selected (which answer the user chose).

We use a large `If...Then` structure to go through the possible radio button selections—from RadioButton1 through RadioButton3. In each case, we check array item 4, where we've stored the correct answer to the questions.

A *1* in array item 4 indicates that RadioButton1 (the first answer) is the correct answer, a *2* indicates that RadioButton2 is correct, and a *3* indicates that RadioButton3 is correct:

```
If RadioButton1.Checked = True And arrQuiz(QuestionNumber, 4) = "1" Then

        Label1.Text = Label1.Text & "  CORRECT!"
        Counter = Counter + 1
```

This code sample tests to see whether the user has selected the first radio button *and* whether the correct answer is the first answer. If so, we append the word *CORRECT!* to the label at the top of the form to let the user know he got it right (see Figure 8-3). Then we raise the counter variable by 1. This variable named `Counter` keeps track of the number of correct answers the user has so far achieved.

After all three possible answers (radio buttons) are explored using a couple of `ElseIf` commands, the program reaches an `Else` command that displays the word *INCORRECT*, if necessary. In other words, if the user hasn't selected the correct radio button (the one that matches the correct answer in array item #5), the user is told he made a mistake.

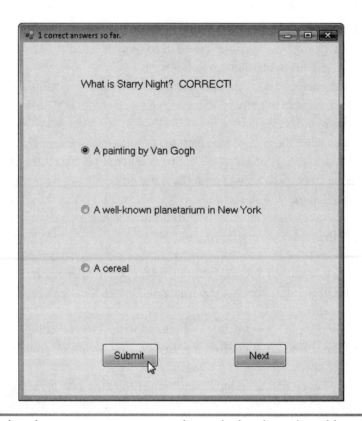

Figure 8-3 When the user gets an answer right, we let him know by adding the word *CORRECT!* to the label at the top of the window.

Try This   Communicating via the Title Bar

Sometimes you want to provide information to the user, but in a more subtle, unobtrusive way than halting execution with a message box. To improve this program, we can show the user how many questions she has answered correctly so far and also how many total questions are in the quiz.

You could use a label on the form for this purpose, but a form's title bar is also a good place to quietly show information.

In the Quiz program, the form's title bar is already employed to display the current score:

```
        QuestionNumber = QuestionNumber + 1


        If QuestionNumber > UBound(arrQuiz) Then 'we're finished with
the quiz
            MsgBox("You got " & Counter & " correct out of " &
UBound(arrQuiz) + 1 & " questions.")
                End
        End If
```

If you want to provide both the current score and the total number of questions, replace the preceding code with this (this borrowed from code I used for a message box displayed after the quiz is over):

```
Me.Text = Counter & " correct out of " & UBound(arrQuiz) + 1 & "
questions. "
```

By the way, you might think you can refer to Form1 as *Form1* in your code. Nope. For reasons that are obscure and not worth worrying about, you must use the format Me.Text to modify the form's title bar. You always employ the Me object to refer to the current form.

When the quiz is over, the btnSubmit_Click event displays a message box with the final score:

```
Me.Text = Counter & " correct answers so far."

        ' raise the question number variable, redraw the question/
answers or exit if finished
        QuestionNumber = QuestionNumber + 1
```

Here we increment (raise by 1) the variable QuestionNumber. This moves us to the next question in the quiz. The UBound command tells us the highest index number in the array. So if the `QuestionNumber` variable has increased past the number of array items, we know the quiz is over, display the final results to the user, then end the program.

The `btnNextQuestion_Click` event is triggered when the user clicks the Next button on the form. What our code needs to do in this event is deselect all the radio buttons to give the user a fresh start with the next question:

```
'redraw the form:

        RadioButton1.Checked = False
        RadioButton2.Checked = False
        RadioButton3.Checked = False
```

Then we fetch the next question and its three possible answers from the array and display them to the user:

```
        RadioButton1.Text = arrQuiz(QuestionNumber, 0)
        RadioButton2.Text = arrQuiz(QuestionNumber, 1)
        RadioButton3.Text = arrQuiz(QuestionNumber, 2)
        Label1.Text = arrQuiz(QuestionNumber, 3)
```

The Quiz program has become fairly sophisticated. But in the final chapters of the book we'll undertake an even bigger and more advanced project: a personal diary program. We'll begin in Chapter 9 by seeing how to employ procedures to help organize large programs.

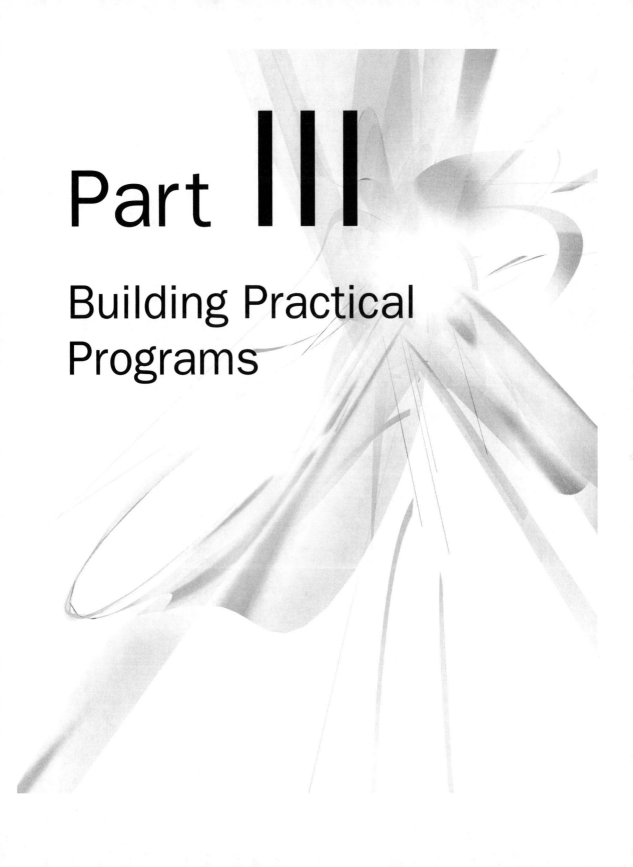

Part III

Building Practical Programs

Chapter 9

Organizing a Large Program

Key Skills & Concepts

● Subdividing programs

● Procedure-oriented programming

● Starting the Diary program

As you become more comfortable with programming, you're likely to write some increasingly large programs. And although you'll usually work on small sections of a program at a time, combining these sections into one big, harmonious whole requires some new tactics. You'll run into a few clerical and organizational issues that aren't usually a problem in simpler programs.

To help you break down larger programs into manageably small units, programming languages offer *procedures*. By far the most common procedures are subroutines (Sub... End Sub) and functions (Function...End Function).

You've already worked with subs: An event handler, such as a Button1_Click event, is a procedure. It starts with Sub and finishes with an End Sub. But these built-in events aren't the only possible kinds of subroutines. You can also write your own.

Functions Offer Two-way Communication

A second type of procedure, the *function,* differs from a subroutine because a function permits two-way communication with other procedures. You can *send* data to a subroutine, but typically no data is sent *back* from a subroutine. Subs ordinarily allow one-way communication only. But you send data to, and get data back from, a function. We'll explore functions a bit later in this chapter.

Tech Tip

You *can* send data back from a subroutine by employing the ByRef command—but most VB programmers ignore this capability. It's rather confusing and obscure, and functions handle two-way communications just fine.

Most of the examples so far in this book have contained their code within subs (or *event handlers*, which are simply subs that specialize in handling the activities of a control, such as a button).

In a few cases, we've declared a form-wide variable, and we always put the two `Option` features (`Strict` and `Explicit`) up at the very top of the code window. But code outside procedures is relatively rare and is limited primarily to declaring form-wide variables and specifying those options.

Use Procedures to Subdivide Programs

As you've already seen in several examples in this book—particularly the multiple-choice Quiz program you built in Chapter 8—procedures are an excellent way to subdivide a program into various specific tasks.

In the Quiz program you used three procedures. Each procedure had its own job, or set of closely related jobs, to carry out.

In the `Form_Load` event procedure, you filled the quiz array with questions and answers. Remember that `Form_Load` automatically executes before the form is even displayed to the user, so it's an excellent place to put housekeeping code that needs to be completed before the program is presented to the user.

Second, you used a `Button_Click` event to house code that executes whenever the user clicks that button (in this case, a button captioned *Submit*). The user triggers this code after selecting an answer to a question. The code in this Submit button procedure checks to see whether the user got the right answer, reports the result to the user, and updates a counter that keeps track of the total number of right answers.

Finally, a third procedure—another `Button_Click` event named `btnNextQuestion`—refreshes the window by replacing the question and all three answer with a new set so the user can respond to the next question in the quiz. This procedure executes when the user clicks the button captioned *Next*.

As you can see, putting controls on a form automatically makes available a variety of event handler procedures in which you can write code to respond to various events. Almost without realizing it, as you add controls to a form you are subdividing your program into several small, easily managed sections that each perform a specific task.

Visualizing Procedure-oriented Programming

Programming that divides code into procedures is called *procedure-oriented programming*. To visualize how procedure-oriented programming organizes a program, imagine pulling the roof off a typical doctor's office. You would be able to see how the building is subdivided into zones devoted to various specific tasks: storing patient data, waiting for the doctor, taking samples, weighing the patient, examining patients, and so on. Think of procedures in this same way: procedures divide your program into various specialized zones.

The User Interface Helps Design a Program

In this chapter, we'll start designing a useful Diary program—a place to write your private thoughts. We'll also protect your diary entries from prying eyes by using a secret password to open the diary and by encrypting the entries before storing them in a file on the hard drive.

We'll begin as usual by designing the form, adding the necessary controls that the user interacts with. In a way, designing the user interface on a form is similar to drawing a blueprint for a doctor's office—you're forced to think of the various tasks that the program will need to perform.

Starting the Diary Program

Start a new VB program by pressing CTRL-N. When the New Project dialog box opens, you can type a name for your new program. So far in this book, we've mostly just used the default name *WindowsProgram1*. But now it's time to start getting used to saving your programs in their own folders and giving them recognizable names.

Saving and Loading .sln Files

Type **MyDiary** into the New Project dialog box, as shown in Figure 9-1.

Click the OK button to close the New Project dialog box. You see your new project—a new, blank form. Now choose File | Save All, or click the Save All icon shown in Figure 9-2.

When you click the Save All button the first time in a new project, you'll see the Save Project dialog box shown in Figure 9-3. Be sure that the *Create directory for solution* check box is checked. Directories (folders) are a good place to keep all the elements of your program together, and they can be moved easily if necessary.

Click the Browse button to specify a directory on the hard drive where you want to store your project's folder. Finally, click the Save button to close the Save Project dialog box.

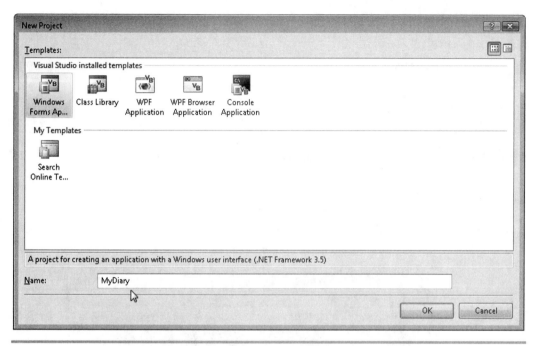

Figure 9-1 Type a descriptive name for your new program.

Later on, if you want to modify the program, you can double-click your program's *solution* (.sln) file in Windows Explorer (such as *MyDiary.sln*) to load your program into VB. Or you can choose File | Open Project in the VB editor and then browse your hard drive to locate the MyDiary folder and, inside, MyDiary.sln. See Figure 9-4.

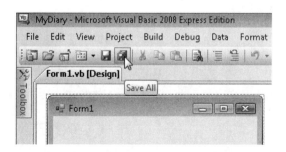

Figure 9-2 Click the Save All icon from time to time while writing a program to save your work on the forms and code in case of power failure.

Figure 9-3 Specify a location and create a directory for your new project.

Figure 9-4 Load a program into the VB editor by double-clicking its .sln file.

Building the Interface

Now back to our regular programming. Stretch the form so it resembles a notepad—the same shape (though not as large) as a typical 8.5 × 11 sheet of typing paper. If the Properties window is closed, press F4 to open it. Then change the form's Size property from the default 300,300 to something like 440,560. You can do this by stretching the form or by just typing in the new *width,height* numbers in the Properties window.

From the Toolbox, drag-and-drop a text box control onto the form. The text box control always defaults to a single-line mode, so double-click the text box's Multiline property in the Properties window to change that property from False to True.

Now drag the textbox so it fills most of the form, as you can see in Figure 9-5.

Put a button on the bottom of the form, and change its Text property in the Properties window to *Save*. When the user clicks this button, the diary contents will be saved and the program will close. Using the Properties window, change the font size for the button and text box to 11.

Figure 9-5   The user will write on the "pages" in the diary using a text box control.

Providing Descriptive Control Names

While we're at it, you might also get used to another good programming habit: Change the Name property of *Button1* to *btnSave*. (The Name property is up at the top of the Properties window.)

TIP

Many programmers find that their code is easier to read if they replace the default names that VB gives controls (such as *Button1, Button2,* and so on) with more descriptive names. It's also common practice to identify the control as a button by prepending *btn* to the descriptive name. Hence, *btnSave*. (Appendix B contains a list of commonly used prefixes for other controls, such as *txt* for text box.)

OK, on the form we've now placed the components of the simplest possible diary program—a text box and a button. The user types something into the text box (passwords, confidential notes, descriptions of other people's personality defects, and whatever). Then the user clicks the Save button and the diary is saved to the hard drive.

Obviously, we'll have to add one additional task: loading the previously saved diary from the hard drive. But no user involvement is required for this: we can just load in the diary each time the program starts up.

However, let's just take this programming one step at a time. First, we'll write the code necessary to save the contents of the text box to a file. Then we'll test that code by using Windows Explorer to look at the disk file and see if the contents were, in fact, saved. Remember that this is the usual way to write a program: Write the code for a procedure, then press F5 to see if that task is working as it should. Then code the next task, and test it. Write, test, write, test.

Double-click the Save button to open its Click event in the code window. Now add the usual two `Option` statements:

```
Option Strict Off
Option Explicit On
```

Then add a line just below those statements that "imports" a code library. This `System.IO` library contains the commands necessary to access the hard drive (shown in boldface):

```
Imports System.IO


Public Class Form1

    Private Sub btnSave_Click(ByVal sender As System.Object, ByVal e
As System.EventArgs) Handles btnSave.Click

    End Sub
End Class
```

Ask the Expert

Q: Why do I have to *import* libraries of commands to load or save disk files? Why aren't these disk I/O programming commands simply built into the VB language? So far in this book, we've not had to import any special code libraries for other common tasks, like displaying a message box. Why now? Why me?

A: Any time you write a program that employs I/O (input/output to peripherals such as hard drives or printers), you will need to add this `Imports System.IO` line at the very top of the code window. Adding libraries is just sometimes necessary. It's just one of those things, one of those crazy things.

Technically, you can avoid adding libraries by spelling out the whole library path in your code for each command that requires the library. For example, when saving a file to the hard drive, you use the `StreamWriter` command. But unless you import the IO library, you must always write the command this way: `System.IO.StreamWriter`. Adding that library reference becomes tedious if you are writing a long program. The `Imports` command allows you to use the abbreviated command `StreamWriter` in your code, without specifying its library.

If you try to use a command that requires a special library, VB will alert you that something is wrong by underlining the command with the usual sawtooth line. When you pause your mouse pointer on the command to see the error message, it will say something like this: *Type 'StreamWriter' is not defined.* This alerts you that you need to import a library by adding an `Imports` statement. VB Help or online help resources will also let you know when importing a library is required. (Click the command, such as *StreamWriter*, then press F1.)

You must frequently import the System.IO library in your VB programs because you often need to employ commands to access the hard drive.

Some libraries are "built-in" to VB, so you need not explicitly import them. For example, the library that handles variable declarations is built-in, so you can employ commands such as `Dim` or `Private` without importing that library.

But why is it sometimes necessary to import libraries? Actually, for most of its history, VB did not employ libraries at all. *All* the commands (including disk I/O) were simply available to the programmer inside one, large, built-in library. But now the sheer number of commands available to VB programmers has grown immense (with many thousands of commands versus the 350 or so commands available in 1990 in VB version 1).

For convenience, sets of related commands are now gathered in code libraries, technically called *namespaces* (among other names such as *DLL* or *assembly*). The first two projects we wrote in this book—the Timer and Quiz programs—required no imported libraries. So you can sometimes ignore this importation issue.

But other programs with more specialized behaviors (drawing, I/O, data management, multimedia, web programming, and security, for example) usually require that you import

(continued)

a library. After you import the `System.Drawing` library, for instance, you can then write `Rectangle` in your code instead of having to write the command's full path: `System.Drawing.Rectangle`.

As time goes on, you'll get used to the few common libraries, and you'll find plenty of guidance about this issue online. Try searching for "vb namespaces" or "vb imports" in Google.

Now type the following code in the `btnSave_Click` event:

```
Option Strict Off
Option Explicit On

Imports System.IO


Public Class Form1

    Private Sub btnSave_Click(ByVal sender As System.Object, ByVal e
As System.EventArgs) Handles btnSave.Click

        Dim strFilePath = "C:\temp\MyDiary.txt"

        SaveText(strFilePath)

        End

    End Sub
End Class
```

When you type this in, the editor displays a sawtooth underline beneath the word `SaveText` and tells you that it's not declared.

Soon we will add a new procedure named `SaveText`, and that sawtooth error underline will go away. Just ignore it for now. The editor is merely warning you that it's confused about what you're up to. The editor thinks this word `SaveText` might refer to an undeclared variable. Actually, it's an unwritten procedure that we'll create shortly.

When the user clicks this `btnSave` button, we create a string variable named `strFilePath` that specifies the location on our hard drive where we want to save the diary. Be sure that you have a C:\temp subdirectory. If not, create one for our Diary program to use when storing its data file.

TIP

If you're using Microsoft Vista, avoid trying to save directly into your boot directory (C:\). Use a subdirectory (such as C:\temp\) instead. The reason is that Vista, for security purposes, guards the root directory like a lion and will resist any efforts to programmatically (from inside a program) save to this root location. In other words, you'll get an error message and the program will not be allowed to save to root C:\. (see Figure 9-6). The error message says: *A required privilege is not held by the client.*

And also, to avoid other kinds of security issues when programming, be sure you have administrative-level permissions on your computer. Search Google or your computer's local help system for information about how to grant yourself administrative rights and privileges.

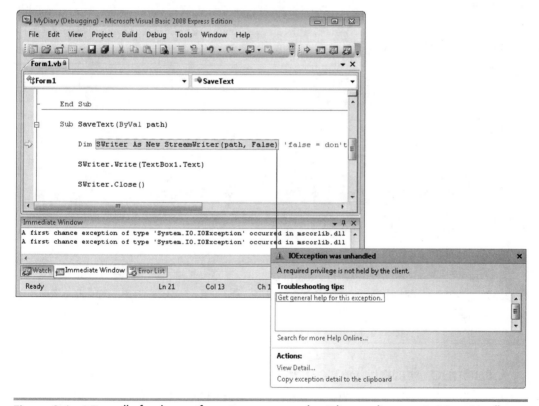

Figure 9-6   VB totally freaks out if you try to save to the C:\ root directory in Vista. You'll set off all kinds of security alarms.

Tech Tip

In this book, we're specifying ("hard-coding" as it's called) the file path (C:\temp\) where the Diary file will be stored. We're doing this because it's simple and quick. But it's usually a better idea to let the computer tell you where default data files can be safely stored on that particular machine. This avoids problems if you're planning to give this program to others (they might not have your hard-coded file path on their computer), or you might buy a new machine later and run into the same problem. To avoid hard-coding paths in your programming, you can request a safe, usable path with this command (shown in boldface):

```
Dim path

path = Environment.GetFolderPath(Environment.SpecialFolder
.MyDocuments)

path = path & "\MyDiary.txt"

MsgBox(path)
```

Or with this command:

```
Dim path

path = Application.UserAppDataPath

path = path & "\MyDiary.txt"

MsgBox(path)
```

This way, your program will save the file in a location that you're *sure* the user can access. The operating system always reserves these two locations as accessible for everyone.

Creating Your Own Subs

The next line in our code, `SaveText`, is not a built-in command, like `Dim` or `End`. Instead, it's a word I made up—a custom "command" that we're going to create.

You're going to write a Sub of your own—a procedure named `SaveText` that will save the contents of TextBox1 to the specified path using the specified filename, *MyDiary.txt*. And all we have to do to *call* (execute) a procedure is to name it and provide it with whatever *arguments* data it needs to do its work.

Here in the `Form_Load` event we call the `SaveText` procedure and pass it the necessary argument: `strFilePath`, the variable that contains the file path information:

```
SaveText(strFilePath)
```

To review: When you call a procedure (which is done simply by using its name, remember), you must pass to it any necessary data by putting the data in parentheses after the procedure's name.

Some procedures require no data, but others need data. Our `SaveText` procedure needs to know where you want the text saved, so you must pass that one piece of information—the file path—when calling `SaveText`.

TIP

You can pass multiple arguments if necessary; just separate them with commas in the call's parentheses and also in the target procedure's parentheses. And be sure the arguments are in the same order in both the call (that sends the data) and the target procedure (that gets the data).

Just as when naming variables, you can give your procedures whatever names suit you. But, as usual, you must avoid using the names of VB's commands, such as `Stop` or `Dim`. These built-in keywords are *reserved* words.

Type this new `SaveText` procedure just below the `btnSave` event procedure (just following the `End Sub`):

```
Option Strict Off
Option Explicit On

Imports System.IO


Public Class Form1

    Private Sub btnSave_Click(ByVal sender As System.Object, ByVal e
As System.EventArgs) Handles btnSave.Click

        Dim strFilePath = "C:\temp\MyDiary.txt"

        SaveText(strFilePath)

        End

    End Sub
```

```
Sub SaveText(ByVal path)

        Dim SWriter As New StreamWriter(path, False) 'false = don't
append to an existing file

        SWriter.Write(TextBox1.Text)

        SWriter.Close()

    End Sub

End Class
```

Using a StreamWriter to Save a File

Here's what our `SaveText` procedure does. When the procedure is called (executed), the file path is passed to it. This passed data is assigned to a variable we named `path` in the `SaveText` procedure:

```
Sub SaveText(ByVal path)
```

As with any variable, you can use whatever name you wish for the variables in a procedure's argument list. Just ignore the `ByVal` command; it's always in argument lists, but you don't need to worry about it.

In fact, if you just type `Sub SaveText (path)` and press ENTER, VB will automatically insert a `ByVal` command. VB's supervisors insist on including this command, though you'll likely always ignore it even if you write programs for 30 years.

After the `SaveText` procedure receives the path information, you create a `StreamWriter` object named `SWriter`. The `As New` command creates an *object variable*. Here you're declaring (`Dim`) that this new object variable is of the `StreamWriter` object type. But the `As New` alerts the editor that this is a special kind of variable, the object type. As usual, with any kind of variable, choose some descriptive name for it. I chose `SWriter`.

The `StreamWriter` object specializes in sending data (usually to a hard drive file). A `StreamWriter` object can accept various optional arguments, but its *path* argument is required. We specify `False` for the `StreamWriter`'s *append* argument. We will not be adding data to an existing file. Every time the user clicks the Save button, we'll replace the existing file with the new version of the diary.

So now we have a `StreamWriter` that knows the path where the file is to be saved, and knows to replace rather than append if a file by the name *MyDiary* already exists in that path on the hard drive.

Next we write the contents of the text box to the *MyDiary* file on the hard drive, with this statement:

```
SWriter.Write(TextBox1.Text)
```

And then close (destroy) the no longer needed `StreamWriter` object:

```
SWriter.Close()
```

Ask the Expert

Q: Why *pass* the file path data to the `SaveText` procedure? Couldn't you just specify the file path information right in the `SaveText` procedure itself, thus avoiding having to pass it from the caller?

A: You could take that approach; it's another kind of *hard-coding*. But it's considered a bad idea for a couple of reasons. First, if you specify the file path within the procedure, you greatly narrow the usefulness of the procedure. It becomes inflexible. It would be able to open and load only that one specific file.

By contrast, as written, this sub is more general-purpose—it can save data to *any* file whose path is passed to it. Therefore, you could call this sub from other locations in your program to save to different files for different purposes.

Or you could perhaps reuse the procedure in other programs. However, in my experience, you rarely end up reusing your own code. I always start a new project from scratch rather than trying to play Dr. Frankenstein and cobble together a new program out of parts pulled out of old programs. I just find it simpler to start from scratch.

Programs aren't transformer toys that can easily be manipulated into entirely different shapes. You certainly can and will modify and improve existing programs, but you're unlikely to play mix-and-match by plugging in legacy procedures when building a brand-new program. Professional group-programming, on the other hand, often requires cobbling code pieces together-if only because programming from multiple programmers must be merged.

The second reason to pass data back and forth between procedures is that it allows you to avoid having to use form-wide or global variables, which is something you should avoid whenever practical. Using local variables as much as possible can prevent some types of bugs, and also makes it easier to locate and fix whatever bugs do crop up.

Normally when communicating with the hard drive or other peripherals, you'd enclose your code within a `Try...End Try` structure. But we'll deal with error-handling topics in Chapter 11.

TIP

We've finished writing this procedure that saves the diary to the disk. Now it's testing time. Let's see if the diary text is in fact being saved to the file. (Some people *do* write a whole program before testing it, but that doesn't work well for me. It's easier, I think, to test each procedure right after you've finished writing it and it's still fresh in your mind. Also, by testing small pieces of code—individual procedures mostly—it's usually easier to figure out where a bug is located.)

To test the `SaveText` procedure, press F5, type some lines of text into the text box, and then click the Save button. Then use Windows Explorer to look at your C:\temp subdirectory. Look for the *MyDiary.txt* file, and then double-click it. It opens in Notepad and displays whatever you typed into the text box. *We hope!*

If there's a problem, go back and find the code at this book's web site and replace your current code. See if that fixes it. Or look for sawtooth lines in the code. If all else fails, read Chapter 11 to learn how to fix errors.

Loading a File from the Hard Drive with a StreamReader

When the user starts our Diary program running, the diary must be loaded from the hard drive file. Whether the user wants to add to the diary, modify what's already there, or just read it—it has to be loaded into the text box. That's our program's first job.

Loading is accomplished by a `StreamReader` object—a close relative of the `StreamWriter`. Just below the `SaveText` sub, (between the `End Sub` and `End Class` statements), type in this new procedure that will load the diary text from the disk file:

```
Function LoadText(ByVal path As String)

    If Not File.Exists(path) Then

        MsgBox("The diary file was not found in " & path)

    End If
```

```
    Dim SReader As New StreamReader(path), strDiary

    strDiary = SReader.ReadToEnd()

    SReader.Close()

    Return strDiary

  End Function
```

Since loading the diary from the hard drive file is the first thing we need to do in this program, it makes sense to call our `LoadText` function from the `Form_Load` event. Remember that `Form_Load` automatically executes its code when the program starts.

TIP

Here's a quick way to have the editor create a `Form_Load` event for you. Click the Form1.vb[Design] tab at the top of the code window to switch back to the design window (or press SHIFT-F7). Then double-click anywhere on the form background—not on the button or text box, but on the form itself. The code window appears, with your blinking insertion cursor ready to type in the source code for the `Load` event.

Now type this into the `Form_Load` event:

```
Private Sub Form1_Load(ByVal sender As System.Object, ByVal e As
System.EventArgs) Handles MyBase.Load

    Dim FilePath = "C:\temp\MyDiary.txt"

    TextBox1.Text = LoadText(FilePath)

End Sub
```

Remember that you *call* (execute) a function or sub simply by typing in the procedure's name and then typing in any required argument data in parentheses. If you forget to type in a required argument when calling a procedure, the editor will alert you with a blue sawtooth underline and the error message shown in Figure 9-7.

```
TextBox1.Text = LoadText()
              ┌─────────────────────────────────────────────────────────────────────┐
              │Argument not specified for parameter 'path' of 'Public Function LoadText(path As String) As Object'.│
              └─────────────────────────────────────────────────────────────────────┘
```

Figure 9-7 This error message tells you that you're not providing a needed argument.

The editor tends to be a bit verbose at times when describing an error, and this is no exception. The editor says

Argument not specified for parameter 'path' of 'Public Function LoadText (path as string) As Object.'

This can be translated like so:

You need to provide an argument that the LoadText function requires.

Now let's take a closer look at this function call. Our `LoadText` function is called by this statement in the `Form_Load` event:

```
TextBox1.Text = LoadText(FilePath)
```

This one line does quite a few things. It calls the `LoadText` function, simultaneously passing the file path data to that function. When the function finishes doing its job, it returns data (the contents of our diary file in this case). And that data is assigned (put into) the text box. All this happens in this single line of code!

NOTE
The = command tells you that some data is being assigned to a variable or, in this case, a property.

Earlier in this chapter, in the section titled "Using a StreamWriter to Save a File" we stored some sample text in this disk file when testing the `SaveText` procedure. Now we can test the `LoadText` function to see if this new function can do its job and retrieve the sample text. Press F5 and you should see your sample text displayed in the text box, as shown in Figure 9-8.

We now have the essentials of a diary program. Sure, it's pretty elementary at this point, but we've got some of the main mechanisms tested and working.

Functions vs. Subroutines

Notice that I made the `LoadText` procedure a *function* rather than a *sub* procedure. Remember that the difference between these two types of procedures is that a function uses the `Return` command to send data back to its caller. A function carries out two-way communication with the caller. A sub normally employs only one-way communication— sending data from the caller, but not passing any data back.

What Is a Caller?

A *caller* is the statement in your code that triggers (executes) a procedure. In this example, we're calling the `LoadText` function. Here's the call (in boldface):

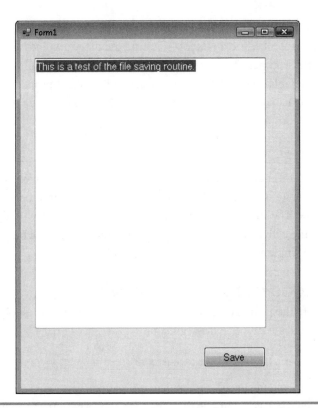

Figure 9-8   If your `LoadText` function is working correctly, you should see your sample text displayed in the text box.

```
Private Sub Form1_Load(ByVal sender As System.Object, ByVal e As
System.EventArgs) Handles MyBase.Load

        Dim FilePath = "C:\temp\MyDiary.txt"

        TextBox1.Text = LoadText(FilePath)

End Sub
```

So the *caller* here is the `Form_Load` procedure. And the *call* is this statement that executes the `LoadText` function: `TextBox1.Text = LoadText(FilePath)`.

Let's review: Earlier in this chapter we *passed* data (the file path) to the `SaveText` sub, but no data was passed back to the caller. Subs just do some job such as saving a file or whatever—but there's a need to pass data back to the caller.

The `btnSave` event calls the `SaveText` procedure, and notice that no = command is used in this statement (no data is assigned to a variable or a text box):

```
SaveText(FilePath)
```

This call statement merely passes the `FilePath` information, and then sits back and lets the `SaveText` procedure do its job—storing the diary text into a file. No need for anything to be passed back. Therefore, a call to a sub does not employ an = assignment command or a variable (or a property such as a text box's text property) to receive data.

But a function usually sends data back, so you do need to assign that data to *something* (usually a variable, or as in this case, to a text property):

```
TextBox1.Text = LoadText(FilePath)
```

The `LoadText` function opens a disk file and extracts data. After the data is extracted, it can't just evaporate into the air. It has to go back to the caller to be stored, displayed, or used somehow. The function passes a datum back to the caller with the `Return` statement. And the caller must receive that datum. Note that the `Return` command can pass back only a single variable, not multiple variables.

How the LoadText Function Works

Now let's explore the `LoadText` function's code to see how it does its job. Notice that we've specified the data type in the argument list `As String`:

```
Function LoadText(ByVal path As String)
```

In this book I've avoided specifying the data type of our variables, allowing the editor to manage this task for us automatically. The `Option Strict Off` statement tells the editor that data typing and conversion are its responsibility.

However, for some reason, the `StreamReader` object requires that the data type be specified for the path information. If you leave out `As String`, VB responds with error messages about *narrowing conversion* and *path narrows from object to string*.

This is probably a bug in VB itself. Yes, languages themselves can have bugs. `Option Strict Off` is supposed to prevent this kind of error message. But once in a while you just have to deal with the unexpected. So, after mumbling to yourself "Why me! Why now?" just remember that if you ever run into error messages about *conversion*, that's your clue to be more specific about a variable's data type. (See Chapter 5 if you need more information about this data typing issue.) Just insert `As String` here, even though it makes no sense, and even though you don't have to specify the exact same data type for the `StreamWriter` object.

OK. What's the first job of the `LoadText` function? If this is the first time that the user has used the Diary program (or the *MyDiary.txt* file has been deleted or moved), then no file exists on the hard drive. So we test for this possibility and if necessary display a message to the user.

We'll alert the user that the file doesn't exist by displaying a message box:

```
If Not File.Exists(path) Then

    MsgBox("The diary file was not found in " & path)

End If
```

But if the file *is* found, we read the entire contents of the diary using the convenient ReadToEnd method of a StreamReader object:

```
Function LoadText(ByVal path As String)

    If Not File.Exists(path) Then

        MsgBox("The diary file was not found in " & path)

    End If

    Dim SReader As New StreamReader(path), strDiary

    strDiary = SReader.ReadToEnd()

    SReader.Close()

    Return strDiary

End Function
```

At this point, the string variable strDiary contains the entire contents of the file named myDiary.txt. So we Close (dispose of) the StreamReader object and then return the string variable to the caller:

```
Return strDiary
```

As you can see, you return data to the caller by using the Return command.

Testing the Completed Diary Program

Here's the complete Diary program code so you can see it as a unit:

```
Option Strict Off
Option Explicit On

Imports System.IO
```

```
Public Class Form1

    Private Sub btnSave_Click(ByVal sender As System.Object, ByVal e
As System.EventArgs) Handles btnSave.Click

        Dim strFilePath = "C:\temp\MyDiary.txt"

        SaveText(strFilePath)

        End

    End Sub


    Sub SaveText(ByVal path)


        Dim SWriter As New StreamWriter(path, False) 'false = don't
append to an existing file

        SWriter.Write(TextBox1.Text)

        SWriter.Close()

    End Sub


    Private Sub Form1_Load(ByVal sender As System.Object, ByVal e As
System.EventArgs) Handles MyBase.Load

        Dim FilePath = "C:\temp\MyDiary.txt"

        TextBox1.Text = LoadText(FilePath)

    End Sub

    Function LoadText(ByVal path As String)

        If Not File.Exists(path) Then

            MsgBox("The diary file was not found in " & path)

        End If

        Dim SReader As New StreamReader(path), strDiary

        strDiary = SReader.ReadToEnd()
```

```
     SReader.Close()

     Return strDiary

   End Function


End Class
```

We now have a simple, but usable, Diary program. Try it out. Press F5. Remember that if you see a *Not Found* message, it means you've not yet created that file by saving anything. This will happen the first time you run the Diary program. (That message will startle unprepared users, so we'll fix it later in his book. It's not good to scare users.)

But if the file *MyDiary.txt* does exist, you'll see its contents displayed in the text box where you can edit it or add to it. Type a few new words into the text box to modify the existing sample text, and then click the Save button. The End command shuts down the program after the text is saved to the hard drive.

Now restart the program by pressing F5 again. You should see the exact text you previously saved.

You could use this program as is. It saves your diary as one large text variable. But the standard text box has a limit of 64K, or approximately 64,000 characters, which is about 10,500 words. So that's a problem, too.

Though our Diary program is usable, we can certainly improve it. In the next chapter, we'll store the diary as an array of "pages" rather than a single, large text variable as we did in this chapter. This approach will overcome the character limit of the text box. The diary can then grow as large as you wish. We'll also add some functions to allow the user to move back and forth through the pages.

Finally, we'll build in a security feature. After all, people will probably write about their most terrible secret needs in this diary. But at this point, it's being saved as an ordinary .txt file that anybody can double-click and then easily read in Notepad! To avoid this potentially disastrous situation, we'll encrypt the text. The public should never be privy to terrible secret needs.

Chapter 10

Adding Features to Programs

Key Skills & Concepts

- Understanding the `ArrayList` object

- Improving the Diary program

- Adding a security feature

Large programs are never really finished. You can always find ways to improve them, and you'll even find new bugs you never noticed while writing and testing the program. That's why when you buy a commercial program, you're later offered "updates" and new versions. And the bigger the program, the more "updates" or "service packs" you can expect.

The Diary program we started in Chapter 9 is no exception. It's not that large yet, but we're going to add some new procedures to it in this chapter. In the process, your understanding of how to communicate between procedures will deepen. And you'll get a better idea about how useful it is to subdivide a program into separate procedures, each carrying out its individual task.

Here are the improvements we'll make to the Diary program in this chapter, as we change it from storing data in a text variable as in the previous version, to employing an array:

- Close down the program when the user clicks a button captioned *Exit*.

- Move up one element in the array (one page in the diary) when the user clicks a button captioned *Forward*.

- Move back down one element in the array (one page in the diary) when the user clicks a button captioned *Back*.

- Encrypt the entire diary when it is saved to the disk file.

- Decrypt the diary when it is loaded in from the disk file.

You can subdivide and organize a program in several ways, but for me the most sensible approach is to use a separate procedure for each job the program does. It should therefore come as no surprise that this chapter's new version of the Diary program will be made up of the following procedures (which parallel the list of jobs we accomplished in Chapter 9 and the new jobs that we're now adding to the program):

- `Private Sub Form1_Load`

- `Function LoadArray`

- `Sub SaveArray`

- `Private Sub btnExit_Click`

- `Private Sub btnBack_Click`

- `Private Sub btnForward_Click`

- `Function Encrypt`

- `Function Decrypt`

Ask the Expert

Q: What do those `Private` commands mean that are often used when declaring sub and function procedures?

A: `Private` specifies a procedure's scope. This is very similar to the way variables have scope. Recall the discussion in Chapter 5 of how variables have various ranges of influence (scope), depending on where you declare them. Declare them up at the top of a form and they have form-wide scope, but declare them within a procedure and they have only local scope—they can be accessed only by code in that same procedure.

Scope is sometimes called *visibility* because scope determines whether or not code in one location can "see" (communicate with) code in another location. Procedures have scope, too. Declare a procedure `Private` and only other procedures within its own form can communicate with it. Declare it `Public`, however, and it becomes accessible to any form in an entire project.

A VB program is called a *project* by the editor, and some projects have more than one form (in other words, multiple windows with which the user can interact).

In the Diary program, we're using only one form so far. Therefore, the scope of our procedures doesn't matter. They're all visible to each other, whether labeled `Public` or `Private`. You can also just write `Sub` or `Function` without specifying the scope at all, as we do in the Diary program. If you don't specify its scope, a procedure defaults to `Public` scope.

Large programs often involve multiple forms. In that case, the scope you give a procedure determines whether other forms can communicate with (call) that procedure. Remember that a `Public` procedure can be seen from other forms, and a `Private` procedure is visible only to the other procedures in its own form.

Using an ArrayList

We've already worked with arrays in this book, but a handy and relatively new type of array is available to VB programmers: the `ArrayList`.

An `ArrayList` is similar to a traditional array, but an `ArrayList` simplifies and streamlines some tasks. Most important, you need not worry about resizing an `ArrayList` (using a `Redim` command as you would with an ordinary array). Dynamic resizing is handled automatically by an `ArrayList` while your program executes. You just add new items to the `ArrayList` with the `Add` method, like this:

```
myArrayList.Add("New piece of data")
```

When you use the `Add` method, the `ArrayList` automatically resizes itself to accommodate the new item.

In addition to its `Add` method, an `ArrayList` includes other useful capabilities such as `AddRange`, `Insert`, and `InsertRange` methods. And deleting items in the array is easy with methods such as `Remove` and `RemoveAt`.

These methods are handy. You have to write extra code to add or delete an item from a traditional array. To delete, for example, the 12th item in a traditional array, you must write a loop that goes through the array to re-index it (to make the 13th item now the 12th, the 14th now the 13th, and so on). This gets complicated. An `ArrayList`, however, resizes and re-indexes for you when you add or remove an item, or a range of items.

Using an ArrayList in the Diary Program

An `ArrayList` is ideal for our Diary program and indeed works well in any program that mimics a traditional book (such as a cookbook program). Each item in the `ArrayList` can represent an individual page in the book. Each page can be displayed in a text box. And each page can also be edited as much as the user wishes, and then saved back from the text box into the `ArrayList`.

Redoing the Diary Program from Scratch

Now we'll redo the Diary program. Start a new VB program by pressing ALT-N. Name this project *Diary*, and then double-click the Windows Forms Application icon in the New Project dialog box. If you wish, you can avoid future confusion by deleting the folder containing the MyDiary project that we wrote in Chapter 9.

Use the Toolbox to add a text box control to the form. Change the text box's **MultiLine** property to True and resize the text box so it looks good for use as a page in a diary (refer to Figure 9-1).

Then add a button at the bottom of the form. Name the button *btnExit* and change its Text property to *Exit*. Finally, change the font size properties for both the text box and button to 11 point. (You'll probably have to resize the button a little bit to make the now-larger caption *Exit* look centered in the button.)

Double-click somewhere on the form background to open the `Form_Load` event. When the user starts the Diary program running, we want it to load the diary data automatically. So the `Form_Load` event is a good place to put the code that fetches the diary data.

Importing Libraries

First you need to add the usual `Option` statements, import the System.IO library, and define a couple of variables with form-wide scope. Type in this code (or copy it from this book's web site at www.mhprofessional.com/computingdownload, see the instructions at the end of this book's Introduction).

```
Option Strict Off
Option Explicit On

Imports System.IO

Public Class Form1

    Dim arrlistDiary As New ArrayList 'an array to store the pages of
the diary
    Dim IndexPointer ' current element's index number
```

Now type in this code that loads the diary from the hard drive:

```
Private Sub Form1_Load(ByVal sender As System.Object, ByVal e As
System.EventArgs) Handles MyBase.Load

        Dim FilePath = "C:\temp\arrDiary.txt"

        If File.Exists(FilePath) Then   ' they're not using the diary
program for the first time
            ' so load the array from the hard drive.

            arrlistDiary = LoadArray(FilePath)

        Else 'no file exists yet, so create an empty ArrayList "page"
element for them to start with

            arrlistDiary.Add("")

        End If
```

```
        TextBox1.Text = arrlistDiary(arrlistDiary.Count - 1)
        IndexPointer = arrlistDiary.Count - 1 'set the array pointer
(index number) to the currently displayed array element.

    End Sub
```

Here's how this code works. First the `Imports` statement adds the necessary input/ output library of commands. Recall that this library contains commands to load data from or save data to the hard drive.

Then we declare the `ArrayList`, but declare it up at the top (outside any function). This way the `ArrayList` will have form-wide scope: it will be accessible to all the functions in this form.

The `Form_Load` event's job in this program is to fetch the diary from the hard drive and display it in the text box. First we specify the file path where the diary is stored on the hard drive, and then we use the `Exists` method of the file object to see whether this file already exists. If so, execution jumps to the `LoadArray` function (that we'll write in a moment); if not, we create a new, blank page (array element) by using the `Add` method of the `ArrayList` object.

Finally, a diary page is displayed to the user in the text box. Because this is the page with the highest index number in the `ArrayList`, it will be the page most recently added to the diary:

```
TextBox1.Text = arrlistDiary(arrlistDiary.Count - 1)
```

Count vs. the Highest Index Number

The `Count` property does the same thing for an `ArrayList` as the `UBound` property does for an ordinary array. It tells you the total number of elements in the array.

But why subtract 1 from the `Count` property? It's the zero effect again. Always remember that with arrays and other collections of data, you must not confuse the *total number* of elements with the *index number* of the highest element. They're never the same. They're always off by one.

`ArrayLists`, like arrays, start with element *zero*. For example, if our `ArrayList` has four elements, they are

- `item(0)`
- `item(1)`
- `item(2)`
- `item(3)`

In this example, the Count property will return a *4* because there are actually four items in the ArrayList. Nonetheless, as you see, the highest item's *index* is only *3*—item(3). This is why you always have to subtract 1 from the Count property to get the proper index number of the highest item.

IndexPointer is the variable we created that will always contain the index number of the currently displayed diary page. So IndexPointer is now set to contain the diary page displayed in the text box:

```
IndexPointer = arrlistDiary.Count - 1
```

Understanding How to Load Data

To fetch the diary data from the hard drive, the Form_Load event relies on a function we will write named LoadArray. This function accepts the file path information, opens the specified file, extracts the ArrayList data, and returns the ArrayList to the caller (in this case, the caller is the Form_Load event).

When the Form_Load procedure gets the ArrayList data back from the function, that data is stored in our array named arrlistDiary:

```
arrlistDiary = LoadArray(FilePath)
```

Type in the LoadArray function now, being sure not to put it inside another procedure (between some other Sub...End Sub or Function...End Function structure). Instead, type this new function just below the End Sub line that concludes the Form_Load procedure (and just above the End Class line):

```
Function LoadArray(ByVal path As String)

        Dim ArrReader As New StreamReader(path), tempArrayList As New
ArrayList, s

        Do
            s = ArrReader.ReadLine
            tempArrayList.Add(s)
        Loop Until ArrReader.EndOfStream

        ArrReader.Close()

        Return tempArrayList

End Function
```

This `LoadArray` function first declares three items:

- A `StreamReader` object to read the data from the hard drive.

- An `ArrayList` that will receive the data from the `StreamReader` (and later in this function to be passed back to the caller via the `Return` command). Notice that you can pass an entire array, not just a variable, between procedures.

- A string variable `s` that will hold each line of data as the `StreamReader` moves through the disk file, plucking one line at a time using its `ReadLine` method.

Next, a `Do...Loop` structure employs the `ReadLine` method (of the `StreamReader` object) to fetch each line of text in the diary, one at a time, and then uses the `Add` method (of our `ArrayList` object) to insert it into the `ArrayList`.

Recall that with `ArrayLists`, you, the programmer, don't need to keep track of the index numbers; the `Add` method automatically appends a new element to the `ArrayList` each time the method is used.

The `StreamReader`'s `EndOfStream` property lets the program know when we've reached the end of the data in the file. No more lines of text to pull in. So we loop *until* this property changes to *true*, and then leave the `Do...Loop` structure and continue on executing the code below the loop:

```
Loop Until ArrReader.EndOfStream
```

Then the `StreamReader` is closed and the `ArrayList` is returned to the caller.

Saving Data to the Hard Drive

To finish the I/O operations of our diary program, we need to write code that will save the `ArrayList` of diary pages to the hard drive. Because we don't need to return any data to the caller when simply saving data to the hard drive, we can use a sub procedure rather than a function. Recall that functions return data to the caller, but subs normally don't. So type in this sub, just above the `End Class` line in the code window:

```
Sub SaveArray(ByVal path, ByVal arrayList)

    Dim Arrwriter As New StreamWriter(path, False) 'false = don't
append to an existing file

    For Each s In arrayList
        Arrwriter.WriteLine(s)
    Next
```

```
        Arrwriter.Close()

End Sub
```

Streaming Data Out to a File

To save data, you create a `StreamWriter` object and provide it with a file path. Recall from Chapter 9 that the second argument for a `StreamWriter` object has to do with appending, and this argument can be specified as either `True` or `False`. If `True`, the data stored by the `StreamWriter` will be *appended* to the file. However, we don't want that. We want to replace the entire existing file with whatever changes the user might have made (editing old pages or adding new pages to the diary). So we specify that this appending option is `False`.

Introducing the For…Each Loop Structure

Next we use a variation on the `For…Next` loop structure called a `For…Each` structure. Objects such as an `ArrayList` can maintain information about themselves. In this way, they have some limited intelligence. So you, the programmer, don't have to specify everything about them when manipulating them in your code.

An `ArrayList` is a collection of data, and most collections in VB allow you to use the `For…Each` loop structure. What's useful about this structure is that you don't have to specify how many times this loop executes. `For…Each` knows when to stop because an `ArrayList` "knows" how many items it contains. The `For…Each` structure is automatically exited when the final item is reached.

By contrast, other loop structures (`Do…Loop` or `For…Next`) always requires that the programmer supply an exit condition from the loop.

Each time through this `For…Each` loop, the `WriteLine` property of the `StreamWriter` object sends the next element in the `ArrayList` to the hard drive file.

Programming the Exit Button

When the user clicks the Exit button, we want to save the diary text (the `ArrayList`) and end the program. You can create the code for the `btnExit_Click` event in one of two ways. Click the *Form1.vb(Design)* tab at the top of the code window. This returns you to the form design window. Then double-click the button to return to the code window and you'll see that the editor automatically created the necessary `Sub…End Sub` code lines for this button's `Click` event.

Using Code Window List Boxes to Create an Event Handler

The second way to create an event's Sub...End Sub code lines is to remain in the code window, but click the down arrow in the "class name" list box at the top-left of the code window. Currently this list box displays *Form1*, but you want to select *btnExit* from the drop-down list. Then also drop the adjacent "method name" list box (currently displaying *Declarations*). Select Click from the long list of events (methods) available to a button control.

Final Housekeeping Details Are Handled in the btnExit Event Handler

Now type in this code that stores the text currently in the text box into the ArrayList, calls the SaveArray sub to save the ArrayList to the hard drive, and then shuts down the program:

```
Private Sub btnExit_Click(ByVal sender As System.Object, ByVal e As
System.EventArgs) Handles btnExit.Click

        'first store the current page in the ArrayList, in case the
user modified it:
        arrlistDiary(IndexPointer) = TextBox1.Text

        Dim FilePath = "C:\temp\arrDiary.txt"
        SaveArray(FilePath, arrlistDiary)
        End


End Sub
```

Testing the Program

At this point, we have built the primary procedures needed to store and load data. This is a good time to test the program to see if these features work as they should. (We couldn't really test the individual procedures earlier because they depend on each other. The LoadArray function, for example, can't be tested until the SaveArray function has been created and stores some data on the hard drive.)

Press the F8 key to "walk" through the program, executing it one line at a time. Each time you press F8, the next line is triggered. If you see any error messages, you have a typo in your code, so copy and paste the code again from this book's web site.

This walking line-by-line through code is called *single-stepping*. It's a very valuable testing and debugging technique that I'll have more to say about in Chapter 11.

Press F8 repeatedly as you watch the yellow highlight move down from line to line, as shown in Figure 10-1. As you step from statement to statement, a yellow arrow points to the currently highlighted line of code, as you can see in Figure 10-1.

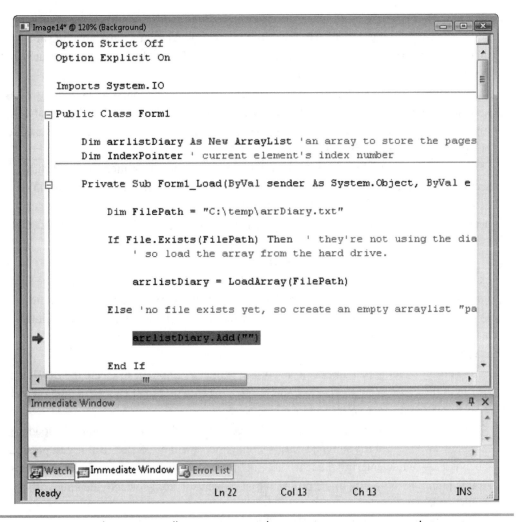

Figure 10-1   Single-stepping allows you to watch your program execute in slow motion.

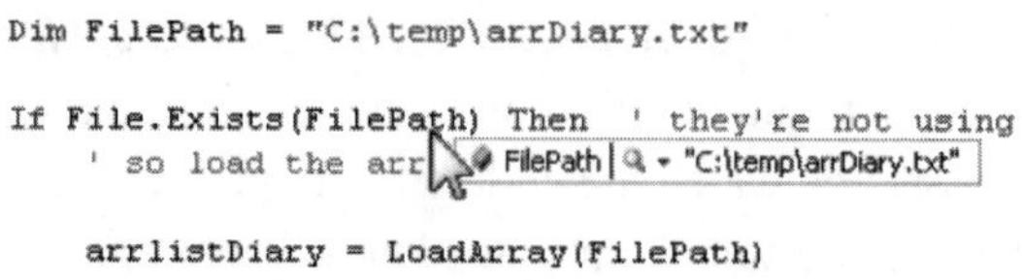

```
Dim FilePath = "C:\temp\arrDiary.txt"

If File.Exists(FilePath) Then  ' they're not using
      ' so load the arr    FilePath  Q ▾ "C:\temp\arrDiary.txt"

arrlistDiary = LoadArray(FilePath)
```

Figure 10-2 While single-stepping, you can view the contents of any variable.

While single-stepping, you can hover the mouse pointer over a variable name at any time to see that variable's current contents (as shown in Figure 10-2). This is a great way to track down errors, as you'll see in the next chapter.

After the code in the `Form_Load` event finishes executing, pressing F8 no longer has an effect. No further code execution will take place until you click the Exit button and trigger the `btnExit` event. At that point, there's again more code to execute, so the editor resumes single-stepping if you press F8.

Now type some text into the text box, and then click the Exit button. Nothing may seem to happen, but the single-stepping *has* actually resumed. If necessary, press ALT-TAB to switch between whatever programs are currently running in Windows until you get back to the VB code window. Now you can see that VB has highlighted the `btnExit_ Click` event's first line of code, as shown in Figure 10-3.

Press F8 repeatedly to watch VB save the `ArrayList` to the hard drive; then execution stops with the `End` command. Notice that when you single-step into the line `SaveArray(FilePath, arrlistDiary)`, you'll see execution jump from the `btn_Exit` event down to the `SaveArray` function. Single-stepping is an excellent learning tool. Here you can see how execution proceeds down whatever path you've specified for it.

To ensure that the data has been saved, use Windows Explorer to locate the *arrDiary. txt* file in the C:\temp subdirectory. Double-click *arrDiary.txt* to open the file in Notepad. You should see the text you typed in. Close Notepad.

Press F5 to rerun the Diary program. The text you typed previously should be loaded into the text box. And if you typed only a single line, it will be loaded. But if you pressed the ENTER key while entering the text, creating more than one line, there will be problems. At this point, there's a bug in the program that prevents it from correctly dealing with multi-line text.

Now close the program again. We still have a bit of work to do.

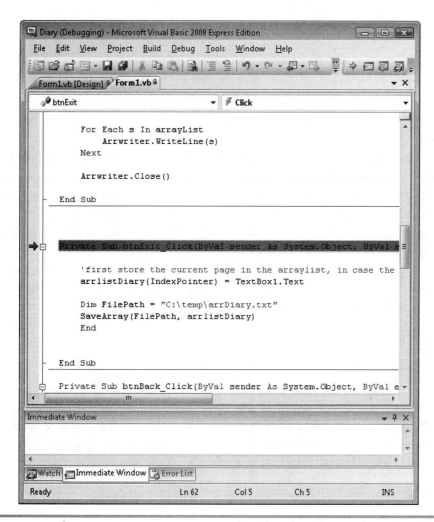

```
For Each s In arrayList
    Arrwriter.WriteLine(s)
Next

Arrwriter.Close()

End Sub


Private Sub btnExit_Click(ByVal sender As System.Object, ByVal e

    'first store the current page in the arraylist, in case the
    arrlistDiary(IndexPointer) = TextBox1.Text

    Dim FilePath = "C:\temp\arrDiary.txt"
    SaveArray(FilePath, arrlistDiary)
    End

End Sub


Private Sub btnBack_Click(ByVal sender As System.Object, ByVal e
```

Figure 10-3   Single-stepping resumes at an event handler when that event is triggered.

Managing the Array

We'll track down the multi-line bug later. We already know that it resides somewhere in the saving or loading functions, so we'll return to them when we work on this bug. And it's not really a simple bug to solve.

There's no sawtooth in the code alerting us to an easily fixed typo bug; there's no error message when we execute alerting us to a simple run-time error. Instead, this is the worst kind of bug—a *logic* bug. We'll need to roll out our heavy debugging guns, so we'll postpone solving this problem until the next chapter.

For now, let's add a couple of procedures that will allow the user to "turn the pages" of the diary.

The Diary program has to permit the user to move among the pages. Just as in a real book, the user must be able to turn back to previous pages or forward to subsequent pages. This means that we must include a variable that always contains the index number of the array element currently displayed in the array (in other words, the diary page that's currently visible in the text box).

That way, if the user clicks a button captioned *Back,* the program can look at the index number variable, subtract 1 from that index number, and then display the array element with that lower index number. The same concept applies to another button captioned *Forward*, except we add 1.

Our index number variable must be visible to (accessible by) several procedures in this form, so we made it form-wide in scope. You can see the `IndexPointer` variable declared at the top of the code window:

```
Public Class Form1

    Dim arrlistDiary As New ArrayList
    Dim IndexPointer ' current element's index number
```

For this pointer to work correctly, we have to ensure that it never goes out of bounds—neither lower than the lowest index number, which is zero, or higher than whatever is currently the highest index number. We can always calculate the highest index number using this code: `arrlistDiary.Count - 1`.

We must also raise or lower the `IndexPointer` variable's value by 1 whenever the user moves forward a page or back a page through the array (when the user clicks the btnForward or btnBack button).

Now we'll add to the form these two buttons that let the user maneuver through the diary pages. Click the tab at the top of the code window labeled Form1.vb(Design) to return to the design window, and then add two buttons to the form. Change the name of one button to *btnBack* and its text property to *Back*. Change the name of the other button to *btnForward* and its text property to *Forward*.

At this point, your diary program should look like Figure 10-4. Actually, you can put the text box and buttons wherever you wish and make them any size you wish. My design for this form is fairly conventional, but it pleases me. At the very least, it's traditional in many programs to put the Exit button (or OK button or whatever closes the program) in the lower-right corner. But please yourself.

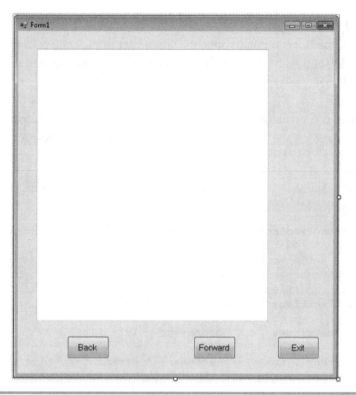

Figure 10-4   Your program should now display a text box, two navigation buttons, and an Exit button.

And above all, never apologize for being a novice, or later, choosing to stay an amateur programmer. Talented amateurs can be vastly superior to professionals. Remember the saying, "Noah's ark was built by one man working alone, but a committee of professionals built the *Titanic*."

Try This Copying and Pasting Controls

Try this shortcut: Recall that you can save time by copying and pasting controls. For example, you can create these two new forward and backward buttons without having to resize them or adjust their font properties to match the existing Exit button. Just click the Exit button to select it, press CTRL-C to copy it, and then press CTRL-V twice to paste two new buttons on the form. They'll automatically be the same size, employ the same font size, and share other properties (except their Location and Name properties) as the Exit button you cloned. All you have to do now is drag them into position, and change their Name and Text properties.

Moving Back

Double-click the Back button to open its click event in the code editor. When the user clicks this button, he or she will want to move back one page in the diary. So we need to fetch and display the page that's one index number lower than the currently displayed page.

If the user is now viewing page 12 in the diary, for example, the program needs to move back and display page 11. Type in this code for the move-back-one-page feature:

```
Private Sub btnBack_Click(ByVal sender As System.Object, ByVal e As
System.EventArgs) Handles btnBack.Click

        If IndexPointer = 0 Then Exit Sub 'avoid going down out of
bounds to a non-existent element(-1)

        ' save the current page by replacing it in the diary (in case
the user has modified it)
        arrlistDiary(IndexPointer) = TextBox1.Text

        IndexPointer -= 1 'decrement pointer

        TextBox1.Text = arrlistDiary(IndexPointer) 'display the page
that's down one in the array


End Sub
```

At the start of this procedure, we check to see if we're currently displaying the very first page in the diary. If so, the `IndexPointer` variable will contain `0`. We'll simply exit the procedure and do nothing. There is no element in an `ArrayList` with a -1 index number. Attempting to use this index number would trigger an error message from VB complaining that you are "out of bounds," as indeed you would be.

But if the `IndexPointer` *can* be decremented (lowered by 1), we first save the currently displayed page into the array, in case the user has made any changes to it. Then we lower the `IndexPointer` by 1 and display in the text box the new, lower page.

Moving Forward

Similarly, we have a button that, when clicked, displays the next higher page in the diary. Press SHIFT-F7 to return to the design window, and double-click the Forward button to create its event handler in the code.

Then type this code into the `btnForward` event:

```
Private Sub btnForward_Click(ByVal sender As System.Object, ByVal e As
System.EventArgs) Handles btnForward.Click

        ' save the current page by replacing it in the diary (in case
the user modified it)
        arrlistDiary(IndexPointer) = TextBox1.Text

        IndexPointer += 1 'increment the pointer

        If IndexPointer = arrlistDiary.Count Then 'they want a new,
blank page to write on because there is no higher page

                'create new, empty ArrayList element
                arrlistDiary.Add(vbNullString)

                TextBox1.Text = arrlistDiary(IndexPointer)

        Else 'this page already exists

                TextBox1.Text = arrlistDiary(IndexPointer) 'display the
page that's up one in the array

        End If

End Sub
```

This `btnForward` code is similar to the `btnBack` code. However, here we need not test to see if this is an impossible –1 index number. When moving forward, two things could happen. Either there's an existing page, in which case we show it to the user. Or the user has moved past the highest page in the array, so we'll create a new, blank page for the user to write in.

First we save the current page to the `ArrayList` in case it's been modified by the user. Then we raise the value in the `IndexPointer` variable by 1. Finally, we see if the requested page already exists.

If not, we add a new, empty array element and display that blank page in the text box. But if the page *does* exist already in the array, we display it in the text box.

Now test the program again. Press F5, type in some sample text, click the Forward button, and type in some sample text on the new blank page that's displayed. Do this for a few pages. Remember that at this point you can't yet use the ENTER key to create multi-line pages. We'll solve that problem in the next chapter. So avoid pressing the ENTER key for now.

After you've added a few new pages, click Exit.

Now press F5 again to restart the program and use the Back and Forward buttons to navigate through the diary to lower and higher pages, and see if your entries are all accounted for.

Thwarting Prying Eyes

Let's complete this chapter by adding a security feature.

Recall that you *or anyone else* can double-click the *arrDiary.txt* file in Windows Explorer to open the file and view its contents in Notepad. That's great for testing the program while you're writing it. Not so great when you're actually using the Diary program later on to store your explosive secrets.

Your sister, friend, father-in-law, or pretty much *anybody* could get a look at your most personal information—that incident in Puerto Vallarta, for example. Of course, it might help a little if you change the name of the file to something boring like *PhoneBills*, but still.

Adding Encryption and Decryption

Let's add a quick little encryption feature that automatically messes up the text when it's stored, and then restores it back to normal when the text is loaded into the program. The text will thus be unreadable in the .txt file, but will be normal when you're viewing it in the program.

Long ago, a numeric code named the *ASCII code* was created for computing purposes. A number was assigned to each of the letters of the alphabet, the various punctuation marks, digits, and so on. The ASCII code for the lowercase *n*, for example, is *110*, the code for the lowercase *o* is *111*, and so on. The ASCII codes are listed in Appendix D of this book.

We can make use of this code to scramble the letters in the diary. We'll simply add 1 to the code number for each letter in the diary. Thus, *n* will become *o*, *t* will become *u*, and so on. When stored in the hard drive file, the word *ace* becomes *bdf*. You get the idea.

When we load the text back into the Diary program, we'll subtract 1 from the code of each character to restore the text to the original version, or *plaintext,* as code-breakers call it.

A Warning and a Solution

Do be warned: Our little encryption scheme is admittedly not going to fool a determined cryptanalyst (or even a bright 12-year-old) for more than a few minutes. It's the simplest kind of shift-substitution. But it will at least temporarily baffle and maybe discourage ordinary intruders.

You can improve this encryption considerably by employing the XOR command. See the entry titled "*Logical operators*" in the Glossary.

If you want to add heavy-duty, bank-quality, encryption to the Diary program (the same system used by financial institutions and some governments), take a look at an article I wrote describing how to do this in VB at http://archive.devx.com/security/articles/rm0802/rm0802.asp.

Managing Characters with the Len, Asc, Mid, and Chr Commands

At the bottom of the code window, just above the `End Class` line, type in this simple encryption function:

```
Function Encrypt(ByVal s)

        Dim tempString = vbNullString
        Dim n


        For i = 1 To Len(s)
            n = Asc(Mid(s, i))
            n = n + 1
            tempString = tempString & Chr(n)
        Next

        Return tempString

End Function
```

This function illustrates how to use several built-in that manipulate characters in a text string:

- **Len** Returns (tells you) the length of a string
- **Asc** Returns the ASCII code number of a character
- **Mid** Fetches a particular character from within a string
- **Chr** Returns the character that is equivalent to an ASCII code number (the opposite of `Asc`)

When a string is passed to this function, a `For...Next` loop examines each character in the string, one-by-one.

The `Len` command reports the length (number of characters) in a string. So this loop will execute from 1 up to the string's length:

```
For i = 1 To Len(s)
```

Inside the loop, we start off by using the `Mid` command to extract a character from the string. The `Mid` command uses two arguments: the string itself (`s` here) and the position within the string where the character is located.

In this loop, the position moves forward one character each time through the loop (as the value of the variable i automatically increments each time the loop executes). This is how we can pick off each character in turn using the Mid command.

The actual encryption occurs in the line n = n + 1. Here we're increasing the code number by one, thereby changing an *s* to a *t*, or an *f* to a *g*. For example, if your diary contains these three words,

```
one
two
three
```

The Encrypt function will change them to this:

```
pof
uxp
uisff
```

Our encryption function concludes its work by translating the ASCII code held in the variable n back into a character, by using the Chr command: Chr(n). Each time through the loop, a local string named tempString is built up until it contains the completely encrypted string. Then that string is returned to the caller.

TIP

Don't worry about that *VBNullString*. It just means an empty string (""). You could alternatively use this code:

```
Dim tempString = ""
```

I assigned the built-in constant VBNullString to the variable tempString, just to calm the editor. If you don't assign anything in this situation (as you've seen several times in this book), the editor complains that the variable is being used before being assigned a value. The code runs fine without the assignment, but just to satisfy the editor, we'll assign an initial value to it.

As I've mentioned previously, you can just ignore these "Null reference" objections that the editor displays from time to time as sawtooth warnings. They're not errors. Or to get rid of the sawtooth, you can do what I did here and assign *nothing* to the variable in the statement where you declare it. Similarly, you can optionally assign a 0 to a numeric variable declaration, like this:

```
Dim n = 0
```

One Tiny Change

Of course, you later need to *decrypt* the text strings when they are loaded back into the Diary program from the hard drive. You need to restore the text to its readable form.

One of the interesting aspects of cryptology (to me at least) is how encryption and decryption are sometimes totally symmetrical. The process you use to encrypt (to mess up) the original text is sometimes simply reversed to decrypt (transform the mangled, encrypted text back to the original). It's as if you could run hamburger backward through the grinder to restore the original chuck steak. Spooky.

Type this function just below the `Encrypt` function:

```
Function Decrypt(ByVal s)

        Dim tempString = vbNullString
        Dim n

        For i = 1 To Len(s)
            n = Asc(Mid(s, i))
            n = n - 1
            tempString = tempString & Chr(n)
        Next

        Return tempString

End Function
```

The only change we have to make to the earlier `Encrypt` function to transform it into a decryption process is shown in boldface. We change the `+1` that added 1 to the ASCII code (earlier in the `Encrypt` function) to a `-1` here to restore the original character code value.

Calling the Encrypt and Decrypt Procedures

Now we need to add a line to the `LoadArray` function to make it call the decrypt procedure. And a similar call must be added to the `SaveArray` procedure to encrypt the data before it's sent to the file.

Add the line shown in boldface to call the decryption procedure:

```
Function LoadArray(ByVal path As String)

        Dim ArrReader As New StreamReader(path), tempArrayList As New
ArrayList, s

        Do
            s = ArrReader.ReadLine
            s = Decrypt(s)
            tempArrayList.Add(s)
        Loop Until ArrReader.EndOfStream
```

```
        ArrReader.Close()

        Return tempArrayList

    End Function
```

Add the line shown in boldface to call the encryption procedure:

```
Sub SaveArray(ByVal path, ByVal arrayList)

        Dim Arrwriter As New StreamWriter(path, False) 'false = don't
append to an existing file

        For Each s In arrayList
            s = Encrypt(s)
            Arrwriter.WriteLine(s)
        Next

        Arrwriter.Close()

End Sub
```

Our encryption will probably discourage most prying eyes who would open the *arrDiary.txt* file in Windows Explorer. But there's yet another security concern. What if some busybody runs the Diary program itself? When our program executes, the text file is loaded in, decrypted, and displayed in all its glory in the text box.

To solve this problem, we'll need to add password protection so they can't even open the Diary program unless they know the secret word. Fortunately, adding a password system is easy to do. We'll add that feature in Chapter 11.

The Complete Diary Program

Here is the complete Diary program shown as a single listing:

```
Option Strict Off
Option Explicit On

Imports System.IO

Public Class Form1

    Dim arrlistDiary As New ArrayList 'an array to store the pages of
the diary
    Dim IndexPointer ' current element's index number
```

```
    Private Sub Form1_Load(ByVal sender As System.Object, ByVal e As
System.EventArgs) Handles MyBase.Load

        Dim FilePath = "C:\temp\arrDiary.txt"

        If File.Exists(FilePath) Then   ' they're not using the diary
program for the first time
                ' so load the array from the hard drive.

            arrlistDiary = LoadArray(FilePath)

        Else 'no file exists yet, so create an empty ArrayList "page"
element for them to start with

            arrlistDiary.Add("")

        End If


        TextBox1.Text = arrlistDiary(arrlistDiary.Count - 1)
        IndexPointer = arrlistDiary.Count - 1 'set the array pointer
(index number) to the currently displayed array element.

    End Sub

    Function LoadArray(ByVal path As String)

        Dim ArrReader As New StreamReader(path), tempArrayList As New
ArrayList, s

        Do
            s = ArrReader.ReadLine
            s = Decrypt(s)
            tempArrayList.Add(s)
        Loop Until ArrReader.EndOfStream

        ArrReader.Close()

        Return tempArrayList

    End Function


    Sub SaveArray(ByVal path, ByVal arrayList)

        Dim Arrwriter As New StreamWriter(path, False) 'false = don't
append to an existing file
```

```vb
      For Each s In arrayList
          s = Encrypt(s)
          Arrwriter.WriteLine(s)
      Next

      Arrwriter.Close()

  End Sub



  Private Sub btnExit_Click(ByVal sender As System.Object, ByVal e
As System.EventArgs) Handles btnExit.Click

      'first store the current page in the ArrayList, in case the
user modified it:
      arrlistDiary(IndexPointer) = TextBox1.Text

      Dim FilePath = "C:\temp\arrDiary.txt"
      SaveArray(FilePath, arrlistDiary)
      End


  End Sub

  Private Sub btnBack_Click(ByVal sender As System.Object, ByVal e
As System.EventArgs) Handles btnBack.Click

      If IndexPointer = 0 Then Exit Sub 'avoid going down out of
bounds to a non-existent element(-1)

      ' save the current page by replacing it in the diary (in case
the user has modified it)
      arrlistDiary(IndexPointer) = TextBox1.Text

      IndexPointer -= 1 'decrement pointer

      TextBox1.Text = arrlistDiary(IndexPointer) 'display the page
that's down one in the array


  End Sub

  Private Sub btnForward_Click(ByVal sender As System.Object, ByVal
e As System.EventArgs) Handles btnForward.Click

      ' save the current page by replacing it in the diary (in case
the user modified it)
```

```
        arrlistDiary(IndexPointer) = TextBox1.Text

        IndexPointer += 1 'increment the pointer

        If IndexPointer = arrlistDiary.Count Then 'they want a new,
blank page to write on because there is no higher page

            'create new, empty ArrayList element
            arrlistDiary.Add(vbNullString)

            TextBox1.Text = arrlistDiary(IndexPointer)

        Else 'this page already exists

            TextBox1.Text = arrlistDiary(IndexPointer) 'display the
page that's up one in the array

        End If

    End Sub

    Function Encrypt(ByVal s)

        Dim tempString = vbNullString
        Dim n

        For i = 1 To Len(s)
            n = Asc(Mid(s, i))
            n = n + 1
            tempString = tempString & Chr(n)
        Next

        Return tempString

    End Function

    Function Decrypt(ByVal s)

        Dim tempString = vbNullString
        Dim n

        For i = 1 To Len(s)
            n = Asc(Mid(s, i))
            n = n - 1
            tempString = tempString & Chr(n)
        Next

        Return tempString
```

```
        End Function


    End Class
```

It's time to test this entire program. First delete the existing *arrDiary.txt* file from your hard drive. (That file is no longer compatible with the changes we've made to the program. You need to start fresh.)

Press F5 and type a line of text into the first page of the diary. Click the Forward button and type another line of text, this time into page two. Then click Exit.

Press F5 again to restart the Diary program. You should see the page you most recently added to the diary (page two). Click the Back button to see the first page.

To see the encrypted text, double-click the *arrDiary.txt* file in the C:\temp subdirectory to open it in Notepad.

Moving On

Chapter 11 is all about handling errors and bugs, so we'll wait until then to reveal the nasty bug that hides within the Diary program. We will track that bug down, explain how it happened, where it's located, and reveal the solution.

Chapter 11

Tracking Down Errors

Key Skills & Concepts

- Handling syntax errors

- Catching runtime errors

- Using the `Try...End Try` structure

- Tracking down logic errors

- Debugging tools and techniques

- Finding the bug in the Diary program

- Adding password protection

This chapter focuses on how to track down and fix the three primary types of programming errors: syntax errors, runtime errors, and logic errors.

Fortunately, the VB editor comes with a robust set of debugging tools that are both easy to use and highly effective. You'll use several of these tools in this chapter to test the Diary program in various ways and uncover the major bug in the program.

We'll also make the Diary program more secure by adding password protection, to prevent somebody else from launching the program and reading your diary.

The Three Types of Errors

Debugging—finding and fixing errors—is an important part of any programming job. Some bugs are easy to fix, others are tough.

Bugs fall into roughly three categories. The easiest bugs to fix are *syntax errors*, and the editor itself will call attention to them while you're writing the code.

The second type of bug is called a *runtime error*, and VB's editor can also often catch these errors as well. In that case, the editor displays an error message and sometimes even recommends a solution. Runtime bugs, as the name suggests, don't show up until you run the program by pressing F5.

The third type of error—the *logic error*—is the most difficult type of bug. Usually, the editor will not even notice this kind of error during design time, while you're writing the code, or during runtime, while you're testing the program. The editor is even unable to tell you *where* a logic error is located in your source code, much less suggest a way to fix it. In fact, a logic error might escape *your* notice for months or years.

Let's start with the easiest bugs: syntax errors.

Handling Syntax Errors

Several times in this book I've pointed out that the editor displays a sawtooth underline if it doesn't recognize a command. Let's say that you mistype the End command like this:

endd

Typos

As soon as you press the ENTER key to submit this line to the editor, it balks and underlines the word endd. Hover your mouse over the offending word and you're told, "Name 'endd' is not declared." See Figure 11-1.

In other words, VB doesn't know what to make of this word. You meant to type end. It's very easy to fix this type of bug. Just delete the second *d* and you're good to go.

TIP

A blue sawtooth underline indicates an error that you must fix. A *green* sawtooth underline, however, is merely a warning and can almost always be ignored. It will likely be a warning about a variable that was declared, but has not been used (this does no harm; see Figure 11-2). Another common warning is about a variable that was declared but not assigned any value before being used (again, no harm done).

Name 'endd' is not declared.

Error Correction Options (Shift+Alt+F10)

Figure 11-1   The editor underlines a simple syntax error with a blue sawtooth line.

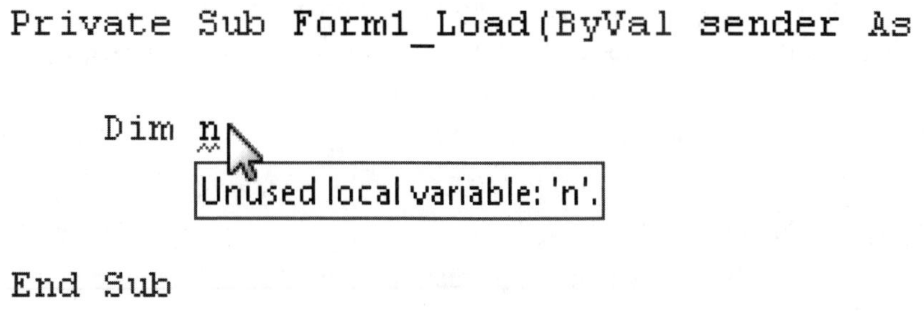

```
Private Sub Form1_Load(ByVal sender As

    Dim n
        Unused local variable: 'n'.


End Sub
```

Figure 11-2 Declaring a variable, but not using it, doesn't cause any problems. It might be a little sloppy, but it's not damaging.

Bad Punctuation

Another kind of syntax error is leaving out a necessary punctuation mark, though the editor will usually help you out here, too. Try typing this line of code, leaving off the final quotation mark:

```
Dim s = "My String
```

The editor won't even allow you to make this mistake. When you press ENTER, the editor automatically supplies the missing end quote. The same thing happens if you leave out parentheses when using a command such as MsgBox. Type **MsgBox "Hello"** and then press ENTER. The editor automatically supplies the needed parentheses.

The UCase (uppercase) command changes a text string to all uppercase letters. Figure 11-3 illustrates the helpful error message displayed if you neglect to add the required close quotes when using this command.

Technically, the text *Norman Bates* in Figure 11-3 is a *string literal* not a *string constant*, but the editor does its best. And you do get the idea, even if the editor doesn't always manage to employ perfect diction.

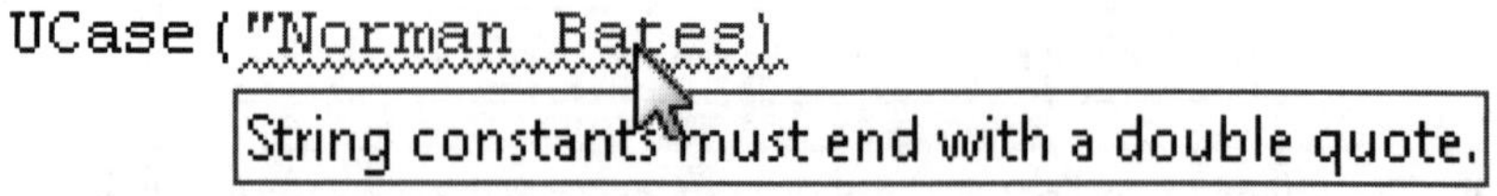

```
UCase("Norman Bates)
        String constants must end with a double quote.
```

Figure 11-3 The editor tells you how to fix this punctuation error.

Syntax Errors

The term *syntax* is used rather loosely when referring to errors in programming. As you've seen, syntax can refer to misspelling or misused punctuation.

But *syntax* in its most strict definition essentially means a problem in the order of words in a statement (line) of code. This type of syntax error can result when an essential command (or operator or other necessary element of a statement) is missing, making the statement impossible for the editor to understand.

Here is an example of bad syntax, because the = command is missing, rendering this statement incomplete:

```
For i 1 to 10
```

The editor underlines this statement and provides *three* error messages. Hover your mouse pointer over the 1, and the editor informs you of a "syntax error." Hover over the For, and you're reminded that you need a matching Next command to end the loop structure. But hover over the i, and you see the complex suggestion shown in Figure 11-4.

The lesson here is that some error messages are totally confusing and not helpful. I don't understand the message shown in Figure 11-4. It says a type can't be "inferred" and something about a "step clause," but who cares? I could probably eventually translate this into English, but it would give me a headache. This kind of arcane error message seems to have been written more for the benefit of those at Microsoft who wrote the VB language than for the programmers, like us, who use VB.

Anyway, it's clear that this line of code has multiple problems, but the primary problem is the missing = and the "syntax error" message shown when you hover your mouse over the 1.

It is important for you to realize that the editor often displays a message *just following* the actual missing command (it can't very well show a message *on* something missing). This same phenomenon occurs with runtime errors, where the line of code following the actual error will be highlighted by the editor. Sometimes you must look for an error in the vicinity of an error indicator (the sawtooth underline or a highlighted line).

Adding an equal sign and a Next statement makes the sawtooth error warning disappear:

```
For i = 1 To 10

Next
```

```
For i 1 to 10
```
Type of 'i' cannot be inferred because the loop bounds and the step clause do not convert to the same type.

Figure 11-4   Don't ask me what this error message is supposed to mean.

As you can see, nearly all of these various syntax errors (ways to garble lines of code) can be pretty easily repaired with help from the editor. These types of errors are indigestible for the editor, and it complains—showing you where the problem is and providing guidance about how to fix it.

Would that syntax errors were the only kinds of bugs. Programmers would get their work done much more quickly. But, alas, more difficult bugs can lurk within code. The second common type of bug shows up only when you execute the program. These bugs are known as *runtime errors* and remember, as the name suggests, the editor can detect them only during runtime (while the program is executing after you press F5).

Catching Runtime Errors with the Try... End Try Structure

With a runtime error, you get the spelling and syntax right, but nonetheless when you execute the code by pressing F5, VB can't accomplish what you've asked it to do. Usually, this type of runtime error involves a problem communicating with peripherals such as the hard drive or printer.

Perhaps your program is trying to print something, but the printer isn't turned on. Or the user is running your program in a notebook in an airport lounge and no printer is available. Or maybe you're trying to save data to a file that's been deleted from the hard drive.

Notice that with runtime errors, your code is correctly written. It's just that what you're asking VB to do is impossible for one reason or another.

Trap Peripheral Errors

These kinds of runtime errors need to *trapped* by your program and handled in a way that doesn't confuse the user or cause other problems such as losing data.

You can trap and manage runtime errors using the `Try...End Try` structure. Whenever a program attempts to communicate with a peripheral, it's almost always a good idea to enclose that communication within a `Try` structure. Here's how.

Start a new VB project and type this code into the `Form_Load` event:

```
Option Strict Off
Option Explicit On

Public Class Form1

    Private Sub Form1_Load(ByVal sender As System.Object, ByVal e As
System.EventArgs) Handles MyBase.Load
Dim bitM
```

```
Dim fName = "c:\temp\zoron.bmp"

'attempt to load the image:

bitM = Image.FromFile(fName)

Me.BackgroundImage = bitM

End Sub
End Class
```

This code is supposed to load a graphics file from the hard drive, and then display it as a background on a form. Press F5 now to see how VB responds to this runtime error when it fails to find the file *temp\zoron.bmp* on your hard drive. Nothing is displayed. This is a bug.

Your program should not fail to carry out an assigned task just because it doesn't find the correct file on the hard drive. And you, the programmer, must anticipate a problem like this.

Perhaps the file has been deleted or renamed. That could happen at any time in the future, and you should handle this possibility. Therefore, you should enclose this hard drive access within a `Try` structure, like this:

```
Private Sub Form1_Load(ByVal sender As System.Object, ByVal e As
System.EventArgs) Handles MyBase.Load

        Dim bitM
        Dim fName = "c:\temp\zoron.bmp"

    Try

            'attempt to load the image:
            bitM = Image.FromFile(fName)

    Catch

            MsgBox("The file named " & fName & " could not be found.
Please save a file by that name to that location. Then re-run this
program.")
            End

    End Try

        Me.BackgroundImage = bitM


End Sub
```

When this program runs, a message box is displayed to the user only if the image cannot be successfully located on the hard drive. In other words, the code between the `Catch` and `End Try` commands executes only if an error occurs.

VB automatically detects errors in these situations, and therefore executes the `Catch` code. In other words, an error flag automatically goes up when VB is unable to find a requested file or detect a printer during an attempt to print, or it finds other similar problems.

Your responsibility is to include a `Try` structure to handle those errors gracefully so the user knows what to do to allow the program to behave as it should. In this case, we display a message telling the user what the problem is and how to fix it.

Sometimes, more than one error is possible during an attempt to contact a peripheral. To deal with that, you can employ multiple `Catch` sections, as well as using the built-in `Err.Number` variable to test for multiple potential errors. That way, each `Catch` section can display a useful, specific message to the user—a message appropriate to that particular error.

If you take this approach to error trapping, you use the `Catch When` command with `Err.Number`, like this:

```
Option Strict Off
Option Explicit On

Imports System.IO


Public Class Form1

Private Sub Form1_Load(ByVal sender As System.Object, ByVal e As
System.EventArgs) Handles MyBase.Load

        Dim bitM
        Dim fName = "c:\temp\zoron.bmp"

    Try

        'attempt to load the image:
        bitM = Image.FromFile(fName)

    Catch When Err.Number = 7
        MsgBox("There's an out of memory error problem:", , _
          Err.Description)
        End
```

```
        Catch When Err.Number = 53
            MsgBox("The file named " & fName & " could not be found.
Please save a file by that name to that location. Then re-run this
program.")
            End

        Catch
            MsgBox("Problem loading file", , Err.Description)
            End

        End Try

        Me.BackgroundImage = bitM

End Sub
End Class
```

That final, generic `Catch` structure displays our general, nonspecific error message, "Problem loading file," only if none of the previous `Catch When` commands were triggered. It's like an `Else` block in an `If...Then...Elseif` stack.

VB responds with error number 7 if the computer's memory is full (a small NetBook portable with little memory, for example, loading a large graphics file). VB responds with error number 53 if a file can't be found.

Use the Built-in Error Numbers

VB contains a whole set of error numbers. To see a list of error codes, type this and press F5:

```
Option Strict Off
Option Explicit On

Public Class Form1

    Private Sub Form1_Load(ByVal sender As System.Object, ByVal e As
System.EventArgs) Handles MyBase.Load

        For i = 1 To 100
                Debug.Print(i & ". " & ErrorToString(i))
        Next i
        End


    End Sub
End Class
```

To see the list of errors, press CTRL-G to open the Immediate window, where results from `Debug.Print` commands are displayed.

Common error codes can be found between 1 and 100. This little program will generate a list of the descriptions of the first 100 error codes. You could copy this list from the Immediate window while executing the program, and then paste it into a text file for future reference.

TIP

This book's tech editor and I were unable to find an official VB.NET error code list, either in Help or online. There *used to be* such lists. Microsoft appears to have abandoned all error codes higher than 93. The likely reason that VB no longer offers a more extensive official error code list is that various namespaces (code libraries) have their own various error code systems—and some code numbers are probably duplicated (used for differing errors in different namespaces).

Remember that the purpose of catching runtime errors is generally to help the user solve a problem that can arise long after the program has been written. You, the programmer, will probably not be around to help. So you build help into the program itself in the form of error messages or other programming that addresses the runtime errors.

TIP

It's usually best for you to write your own custom error messages and display them to the user with a suggested fix—as we've done in the previous examples via message boxes. Although I advise against it, you could just display the official error messages generated by VB itself. These messages are usually a bit technical (sometimes totally tech-speak) and often contain no suggested solution to the problem. Displaying such messages can frighten users.

As I admitted earlier in this chapter, some VB error messages perplex even experienced programmers: I didn't understand VB's message about *step clause inferring* or whatever it was. Now, imagine showing an error message like that to a non-programmer. Not too helpful.

But if you want to give your users a good scare, here's how to display a built-in error message generated by the I/O library, as an illustration:

```
Private Sub Form1_Load(ByVal sender As System.Object, ByVal e As
System.EventArgs) Handles MyBase.Load

        Dim bitM
        Dim fName = "c:\temp\znerktwins.bmp"

        Try

            'attempt to load the image:
```

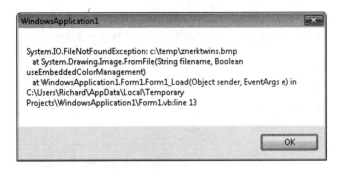

Figure 11-5   VB's own error messages are often fairly technical and are thus often more useful for programmers than for typical users.

```
        bitM = Image.FromFile(fName)

    Catch ex As System.IO.IOException
        MsgBox(ex.ToString)

    End Try

        Me.BackgroundImage = bitM

    End Sub
```

If the file isn't found, VB displays the spooky message shown in Figure 11-5.

TIP
Several years ago it became common among professional programmers to substitute the term *exception* for what most of us would call an *error*. (See Figure 11-5.) My guess is it sounds better to nonprogrammers (such as bosses) to say, "I've been working this week on several *exceptions* I found in my program," than to say, "...*errors* I found...." This is similar to a related euphemism: using the phrase *exceptional students* to describe the sullen group of problem students in detention.

The Official Microsoft Try...Catch Approach

The approach to trapping runtime errors that I've described so far works well. It's a traditional approach, and it has the virtue of simplicity. But Microsoft is now recommending that we move on to a somewhat modified version of that approach: creating a variable for each error type.

Here is the code example I used earlier in this chapter, now modified to demonstrate the approach that Microsoft recommends today. Areas in boldface illustrate the changes:

```
Option Strict Off
Option Explicit On

Imports System.IO


Public Class Form1
    Private Sub Form1_Load(ByVal sender As System.Object, ByVal e As
System.EventArgs) Handles MyBase.Load


        Dim bitM
        Dim fName = "c:\temp\zoron.bmp"

        Try

            'attempt to load the image:
            bitM = Image.FromFile(fName)

        Catch MemoryErr As OutOfMemoryException

            MsgBox("There's an out of memory error problem. The system
error message is: " & MemoryErr.Message)
            End

        Catch FileErr As FileNotFoundException

            MsgBox("The file named " & fName & " could not be found. " & _
            "Please save a file by that name to that location. " & _
            "Then re-run this program. The system error message is: " &
FileErr.Message)
            End

        Catch UnspecifiedErr As Exception

            MsgBox("Problem loading file. The system error message is: " &
UnspecifiedErr.Message)
            End

        End Try

        Me.BackgroundImage = bitM


    End Sub
End Class
```

You create a variable (use whatever name you want) for each error type. In this example, I created variables named `MemoryErr`, `FileErr`, and `UnspecifiedErr`. You also create a `Catch` structure for each error type (much as we did in the earlier example when employing error code numbers).

You can then optionally also display the `Message` property of the exception, as shown in boldface here:

```
Catch MemoryErr As OutOfMemoryException
          MsgBox("There's an out of memory error problem. The system
error message is: " & MemoryErr.Message)
```

Aside from the fact that this approach is Microsoft-approved, it does offer a couple of advantages. The exception names (such as `OutOfMemoryException`) are more readable than error code numbers. Also, IntelliSense displays a list of available exceptions when you type the `As` command, as you can see in Figure 11-6.

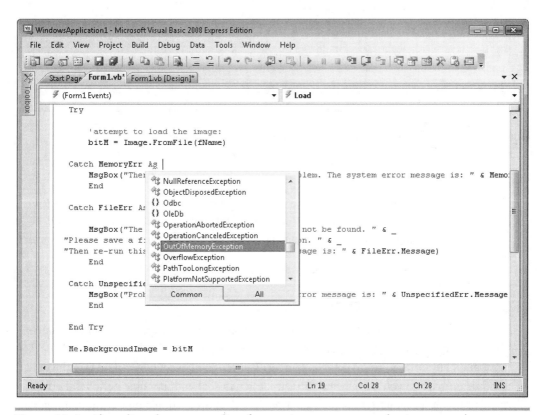

Figure 11-6   The editor shows you a list of exceptions you can employ in your code.

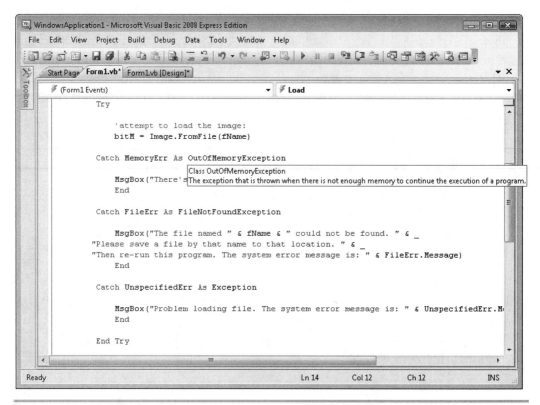

Figure 11-7 IntelliSense describes what the error (exception) means.

Later, when reading your code, you can hover your mouse pointer over an exception name and IntelliSense will display a description of the exception, as shown in Figure 11-7. Note the current lingo displayed in Figure 11-7: Exceptions are thrown to mean errors are detected.

Tracking Down Logic Errors

Now we come to the tough bugs, the errors that challenge even experienced programmers. The third major type of programming error is called a *logic error*. In this situation, all appears normal on the surface: Your syntax is correct. The program executes without flagging any runtime errors, and you've inserted `Try` structures to deal with possible peripheral errors.

But if your program reports that your phone bill is $5 million a month, something illogical is obviously going on.

Logic errors are generally the result of complexity, so the shorter and simpler your program, the less likely that it will contain logic errors. But if you go on to write longer, more elaborate programs, you'll certainly run into logic bugs.

Logic errors can be subtle and difficult to locate. Your debugging efforts can be spent mostly just trying to figure out where the heck in your code the problem occurs.

The bug might be an interaction between two different locations in the code. Perhaps one procedure passes bad data to a second procedure, but the second procedure does not check to see whether the data it gets is outrageously wrong.

The worst kind of logic error is intermittent. A friend of mine wrote a printer procedure that worked just fine 255 times out of 256. But once in a while it would print thousands of *F*s instead of the document it was supposed to print.

OK. Enough hand-wringing. Let's track down and fix a logic error so you'll learn how to work with some of the excellent tools that the editor provides for just this purpose.

Single-stepping

In my experience, probably the most useful of all logic error debugging tools is single-stepping: moving through the program very, very slowly. You go at your own pace, executing only one line at a time and observing the contents of variables or other details.

It's like slowing down a videotape of a bank robbery and viewing the action frame-by-frame. This way, you can perhaps figure out exactly how and when the bad guy got into the bank, and maybe even see details about his appearance or license plate.

Single-stepping is very easy to do using the VB editor. You just press the F8 key rather than F5. (Recall that F5 executes the program at normal speed, just as the user will experience it.)

Each time you press F8, only one line executes, and then the computer stops and waits for further instructions. Often, you'll just press F8 again. And again. Stepping through the lines of the program while observing what's going on.

Maybe the program branches to an unexpected procedure. Maybe a graphic never gets displayed. Most often, the problem involves a variable that for some reason holds a bad value. So you want to pay particular attention to variables.

How do you observe the contents of variables while single-stepping? Just hover your mouse pointer over the variable's name in the code window to see its contents.

While stepping, you could keep looking at the variable `MyPhoneBill` until it suddenly goes up to 5,000,000. This way, you can probably figure out where the logic error is located. The problem will be found just prior to your current location in the code. It's probably in the line just above the current line, where you noticed that the phone bill exploded.

When a program pauses execution (as it does after each time you press F8), you're in a state called *debug mode* or *break mode*. (You can also enter debug mode by pressing CTRL-BREAK while a program is executing at normal speed. Or go into debug mode by setting *break points* within the code, as I'll describe shortly.)

Let's give single-stepping a try: Load the Diary program from your hard drive if you saved it, or just copy and paste it from this book's web site at www.mhprofessional.com/computingdownload into a new project.

Recall that I said in Chapter 10 that there's a logic bug in the Diary program. You may not have used the Diary program enough to have triggered this bug. But I want you to see it now. Delete the diary file from C:\temp\arrDiary.txt so we can start a new fresh diary together.

Commenting Out Lines

Also, *comment out* the lines that call the `Encrypt` and `Decrypt` functions. These functions actually fix the bug, as you'll soon see. But at this point, we want the bug active so we can practice using some debugging tools to locate the bug.

To comment out the lines that execute the `Encrypt` and `Decrypt` functions, just put a single quote in front of each line, like this (the commented line will turn green and *will not execute* when you press F5):

```
Do
    s = ArrReader.ReadLine
    's = Decrypt(s)
    tempArrayList.Add(s)
Loop Until ArrReader.EndOfStream

For Each s In arrayList
    's = Encrypt(s)
    Arrwriter.WriteLine(s)
Next
```

Now press F5 to run the Diary program. On the first blank page, type the word **One**. Then click the Forward button and type **Two** on the second page. Click Forward and type **Three**. Click Exit to save the new diary.

Now, using Windows Explorer, double-click the C:\temp\arrDiary.txt file to open it in Notepad. You should see the following:

```
One
Two
Three
```

All's well. This is what we expected. Each page of the diary (each array item) is stored on its own separate line in the disk file. And the text isn't encrypted because we "commented out" the call to the Encrypt function.

Now, instead of typing only a single line, we're going to type *several paragraphs* in the third page of the diary. That will trigger the bug.

Press F5 again. When the diary displays *Three*, type several lines of text on this page. Press the RIGHT ARROW key to deselect the word *Three*. Now press the ENTER key and type in **New Three** on the next line, and then press ENTER again and type **Last sentence on page three**. Now this page has three lines of text.

Don't click the Forward button. Just type two new lines on page three, so it looks like this:

```
Three
New Three
Last sentence on page three
```

Too Many Diary Pages

Click the Exit button to save this new page three. Then press F5 once again to restart the diary. Click the Back button to view all the pages. Now you see the problem: Each of the lines of text that you typed into page three is now displayed as a separate page. That's not what we wanted.

We want the text lines, these paragraphs, to all remain together on page three. Pressing the ENTER key to create multiple lines in a single page somehow causes entire new pages to be added to the diary.

Press the Exit button to stop the program. Let's try some by single-stepping to figure out how this error happens.

Press F8. You'll see the first line of executable code highlighted in yellow—the declaration of the arrlistDiary array, as shown in Figure 11-8.

Continue pressing F8 a few times until you get down into this loop in the LoadArray function:

```
Do
            s = ArrReader.ReadLine
            's = Decrypt(s)
            tempArrayList.Add(s)
Loop Until ArrReader.EndOfStream
```

This is where the ReadLine method fetches each line of text from the disk file. We're going to examine each line as it comes in. Press F8 to move the yellow highlight just past s = ArrReader.ReadLine, the statement that fetches a line of text from the hard drive.

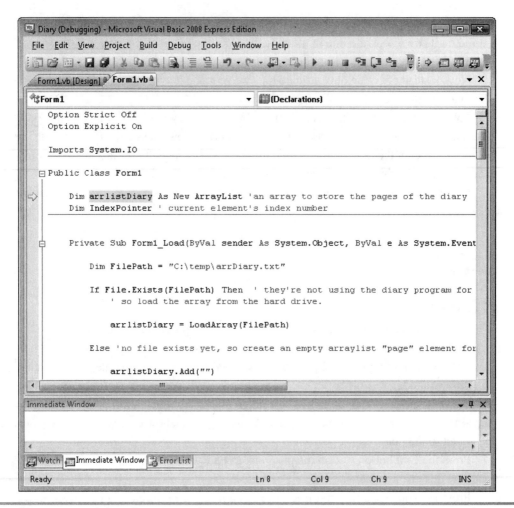

Figure 11-8 Each line that's next to be executed is highlighted in yellow when you single-step.

After you've stepped past this line, the variable s will contain the first datum imported from the disk file. What's in s at this point? Hover your mouse pointer over the variable s to see what it holds. The editor will display the contents of this variable, which currently is "One", as shown in Figure 11-9.

Continue pressing F8, but hover your mouse pointer each time through the loop to see what data is fetched into the variable s.

The second time through the loop you'll see "Two", and the third time you'll see "Three".

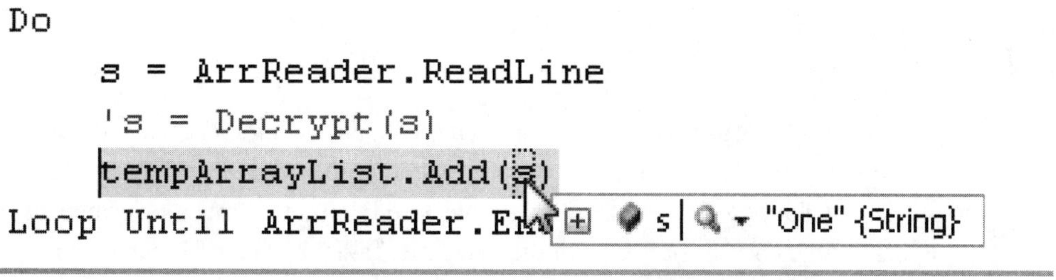

```
Do
    s = ArrReader.ReadLine
    's = Decrypt(s)
    tempArrayList.Add(s)
Loop Until ArrReader.En⊞  ●  s | ⚲ ▾ "One" {String}
```

Figure 11-9   You can see the contents of any variable when in break mode by hovering your mouse pointer over that variable in the code window.

The fourth time you'll see `"New Three"`. This is wrong! You should see the *entire* data that we typed into page three of the diary. You should see multiple lines like this:

```
Three
New Three
Last sentence on page three
```

Instead, you see only `"Three"`, and then the next time you go through the loop you see `"New Three"`. Each time through the loop we're creating a new array element (a new diary page) by executing this line in the loop:

```
tempArrayList.Add(s)
```

What's happening? Why has page three been wrongly subdivided into pages rather than lines?

Nonprinting Characters

Some characters, such as tab or carriage return (caused by pressing ENTER to start a new line of text in a text box) aren't actually visible characters, like *m* or *c*, but you can see their effects.

A tab moves the next printed character over a few spaces; a carriage return moves the next printed character down one line. These nonprinting characters can also be used to *delimit data*.

Understanding Delimiters

Delimiting means separating data. In ordinary English, space characters delimit words, and carriage return characters delimit paragraphs.

Tech Tip

Microsoft Windows uses two characters to indicate a new line: *a carridge return*, which is ASCII code 13, plus a *line feed*, code 10. Together they're referred to as *CRLF*. And together they have the effect of moving down one line on the screen or printer page.

This double code has to do with old-style mechanical printers. A carriage return just moves you all the way to the left on the same line, and then the line feed moves down to the next blank line.

WriteLine Appends Invisible Characters

When the `WriteLine` method stores a paragraph of your diary to the disk, `WriteLine` automatically appends the invisible CRLF characters at the end of the paragraph. In other words, any time you press the ENTER key, an invisible CRLF is entered into the text in a text box. When the `WriteLine` command does its job, each line of text is saved in its *entirety*: the characters you can see, *plus* the CRLF characters at the end of each line. The CRLF characters, in other words, delimit lines of text.

This is how the characters are stored in the disk file:

```
Three[CR][LF]
New Three[CR][LF]
Last sentence on page three[CR][LF]
```

When the `ReadLine` method later fetches these characters from the disk file, `ReadLine` looks for the `[CR][LF]` characters to let it know that it has fetched a complete line. At this point, the line is stored as a diary "page" (an element in the ArrayList), and our loop repeats the `ReadLine` method to see if there are additional pages stored on the hard drive:

```
Do
        s = ArrReader.ReadLine
        's = Decrypt(s)
        tempArrayList.Add(s)

Loop Until ArrReader.EndOfStream
```

The Bug: Each Line Is Seen as a Separate Page

The bug in our program is that each individual line of text is displayed as a separate diary page. We're using the `ReadLine` (read line) comand, so it's behaving correctly—it's reading one line at a time.

But we made the mistake of thinking we could use CRLF as our delimiter for each diary page, when in fact CRLF is delimiting each line of text instead. Our bad.

The Shady Solution

My first thought was the usual sleazy cop-out: just don't let the user press ENTER. Tell them not to. Tell them that each diary page can only be one long unbroken line. No paragraphs allowed.

That solves it. But that was my dark side talking. Or, as they say here in the South, I was *showing myself.*

Finally, my good side won out and I thought: What kind of diary is it if you can't use paragraphs? Why should I burden my user with a stupid restriction when there's an error in *my* code?

We want the user to be able to press ENTER within a diary page. Why shouldn't users be able to employ paragraphs? The truth is that my program should not be creating a new diary page every time it sees that the user has added a new paragraph. It's my problem; I shouldn't make it the user's problem.

The Good Solution

I looked up the `ReadLine` method in Help to see if there was a way to have it overlook [CR] [LF] characters when it loaded data in from the hard drive file. No, that's not possible. `ReadLine` means just what its name implies.

But what if we shift the ASCII characters up by one in the ASCII code before saving them to the disk file? Then, after we fetch the characters back from the file, we shift them back down one to restore them to their normal meaning. This is exactly what our little encryption and decryption functions do:

```
n = Asc(Mid(s, i))
n = n + 1
```

and, in the decrypt function we subtract 1 to restore the original:

```
n = Asc(Mid(s, i))
n = n - 1
```

In this way, the encryption and decryption functions solve our logic bug. The `Encrypt` function shifts the CR and LF characters up one in the ASCII code, so they no longer have their usual effect of delimiting lines of text.

This shifting is just what's needed to avoid creating a new diary page each time there's a new paragraph. The `ReadLine` method now won't see the end of a line, because the character shifting (in `Decrypt`) takes place *after* `ReadLine` executes in our code:

```
s = ArrReader.ReadLine
s = Decrypt(s)
```

Let's see how the `Encrypt` and `Decrypt` functions shift characters and solve our problem. Remove the `'` symbol that you typed earlier in this chapter from the front of the calls to the `Encrypt` and `Decrypt` functions:

```
s = Decrypt(s)
s = Encrypt(s)
```

These lines are now no longer commented out, so they'll execute the `Encrypt` and `Decrypt` functions when we run the program. Also delete the diary file from *C:\temp\ arrDiary.txt* so we can start a new, clean diary file.

We're now going to write several paragraphs on the first page of the diary as a test. We'll find out whether each paragraph is seen as a separate diary page (wrong) or whether the paragraphs are retained within page one (as we want).

Press F5 to run the program. Type something like the following into the first blank page of the new diary. Just be sure to press the ENTER key a few times to create several paragraphs, like this:

```
One
More One
Final paragraph in Page One
```

Click the Exit button. Using Windows Explorer, double-click the *C:\temp\arrDiary. txt* file to see its contents in Notepad. It will look something like the garbled text shown in Figure 11-10.

As you can see in Notepad, or in Figure 11-10, the word *One* has been shifted up to *Pof*. The space character becomes an exclamation point, *!*. And best of all, for our purposes,

```
Pof♫Npsf!Pof♫Gjobm!qbsbhsbqi!jo!Qbhf!Pof
```

Figure 11-10   When shifted up one in the ASCII code, the CRLF characters look like musical notation. And now they won't be interpreted as text line delimiters. Thank goodness.

the CRLF characters are now shifted up and look like sheet music symbols. But we don't care what they look like; we're just happy to have solved the CLRF delimiter problem. Now the user can freely press the ENTER key without penalty. New pages won't be unintentionally created in the diary.

Ask the Expert

Q: Are all logic bugs difficult to track down?

A: Some readers will say, "Wow! Are all bugs as hard to figure out and fix as the logic bug we just wrestled with in the Diary program?"

The answer is no. Sometimes the fix is pretty easy. This one was a bit complex. Other readers are likely thinking, "I'll never be able to figure out a bug like this. You, this book's author, have been programming for almost 30 years, so naturally you knew how to fix this bug."

The truth is I had no idea that the Encrypt and Decrypt functions would fix this bug. I discovered the bug about halfway through writing Chapter 10. And I planned to figure out how to fix it in Chapter 11 as a way of illustrating debugging techniques.

But as soon as I started writing Chapter 11, I discovered that the bug was gone. *Somehow* it had been fixed between when I noticed it in Chapter 10 and when I started writing Chapter 11. Then it took me more than an hour to figure out why the bug had disappeared.

A few brilliant programmers doubtless can just visualize most logic errors and their solutions quite clearly, and without having to employ debugging techniques. Answers come to them while flying kites in thunderstorms or sitting under apple trees.

But not me. I can't visualize logic errors; most programmers can't. Most of us have to fumble around until we locate the bug, and then try various fixes until we find a good solution. Some "solutions" you might try will fix the logic error, but will accidentally cause other bugs to appear. Unintended side effects.

With the diary bug, the opposite happened: I accidentally fixed a bug by adding an encryption feature.

You could fix the Diary program's CRLF delimiter problem in several ways, but I just got lucky. That the encryption functions solved my problem was entirely unplanned.

The primary lesson here is that you should not be ashamed when your programs have logic bugs or that it's sometimes hard for you to locate and fix them. Debugging logic errors is often difficult, particularly if a program is fairly large. That's why companies like Microsoft work for years refining and testing complex software like *Word*. And even after they release the program to the public, the programmers continue to discover "issues that require service packs" (translation: bugs that require fixes).

Setting Breakpoints

I'd like to point out an additional debugging tool that most programmers find quite helpful. Single-stepping is great, as you saw earlier. But you should also add *breakpoints* to your arsenal of bug killers. Breakpoints allow you to jump directly to a suspect area in your code.

Inserting breakpoints in your code is a good tactic as soon as you have an idea where a bug might be located in your program.

Perhaps you think the problem in the Diary program might be in the LoadArray function. So you want to focus your debugging efforts on this particular function. That's where you want to do some single-stepping to see what's happening.

But is it necessary to single-step through *all* the code that executes before this LoadArray function? No: Just put a breakpoint in the LoadArray function, and press F5 to execute at normal, high speed. The editor will automatically halt execution for you where you placed the breakpoint.

When it sees a breakpoint, the editor immediately falls into break mode. Then you can start to single-step, observe the contents of variables, or whatever other sleuthing you want to do in this suspect area of your program.

Here's an example. When debugging our Diary program earlier in this chapter, we single-stepped from the very start of the code (the statements in the Form_Load event). But we could have saved ourselves some time if we had placed a breakpoint in the LoadArray function. We were suspicious of the LoadArray function and wanted to examine its behavior. Putting a breakpoint in the LoadArray function would have caused the editor to take us past the earlier code in Form_Load rapidly, down to the suspect area, and then into break mode.

Try This How to Set a Breakpoint

Let's see how to set a breakpoint. Scroll the code editor until you see the LoadArray function in the Diary program, and then click in the gray area to the far left of the Do statement, as shown in Figure 11-11.

Now press F5. As you see, the program executes at full speed until it reaches your breakpoint, and then it halts and goes into break mode. The code line where the breakpoint is located is now highlighted in yellow, just as if you'd single-stepped to this line.

Now you can press F8 to start single-stepping or employ other debugging tactics. (To remove a breakpoint, just click the red dot and it disappears. To remove all breakpoints in a program, choose Debug | Delete All Breakpoints.)

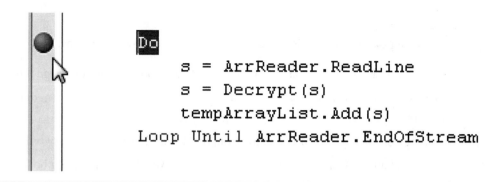

```
Do
    s = ArrReader.ReadLine
    s = Decrypt(s)
    tempArrayList.Add(s)
Loop Until ArrReader.EndOfStream
```

Figure 11-11   When you set a breakpoint, a red dot appears in the left margin.

Now get out of break mode (and return to edit mode) as usual by clicking the blue square on the toolbar (the Stop Debugging button).

There are, of course, various other debugging tools in the VB editor, but at this point your programs are likely to be relatively small and fairly easily debugged. When you're ready to go into more advanced debugging, press F1 and search Help for *debugging in visual studio, debugger, debugging,* and *debugging [Visual Basic].* You'll also find good tutorials online by searching for *debugging visual basic.*

Adding Password Protection to the Diary Program

In Chapter 10 we protected the Diary data file from prying eyes (somewhat) by adding a simple encryption/decryption system to the program. If somebody double-clicks the *arrDiary.txt* file it will open in Notepad (as all .txt files will). But because it's been encrypted, the text is jumbled.

However, an intruder can still find a way to read your secret diary. When anybody runs the Diary program itself, the text is automatically loaded, decrypted, and displayed in the text box.

What's to prevent some nosy person from just executing the Diary program and then giggling and gasping as they read your secret thoughts?

It's Easy

It's easy to add a password-protection feature to a program. Follow these steps:

1. Click the Form1.vb[Design] tab at the top of the code window to return to design mode.

2. Choose Project | Add Windows Form from the editor menu. The Add New Item dialog box appears.

3. In the dialog box, change the form's name from the default Form2.vb to Password.

4. Click the Add button to add the new form and close the Add New Item dialog box.

5. From the Toolbox, drag a Textbox and drop it onto the form.

6. Change the PasswordChar property to * by typing an asterisk in the Properties window.

7. Add a button to the form and change the button's Text property to Submit Password.

8. Resize the form and reposition the text box and button so it looks like a typical, small password dialog box, as shown in Figure 11-12.

9. Double-click the Submit Password button to get to its click event in the code window, and type this into the button's Click event (shown in boldface):

```
Public Class Password

    Private Sub Button1_Click(ByVal sender As System.Object, ByVal
e As System.EventArgs) Handles Button1.Click

        If TextBox1.Text = "raffles" Then

            Me.Hide()
            Form1.Show()


        Else
                End
        End If


    End Sub
End Class
```

Figure 11-12   Create a typical password entry dialog box.

Don't press F5 just yet. We must do one more thing to make this the first form displayed to the user.

But before we do that, here's an explanation of how this code works. It checks to see if the user typed in *raffles*. If so, it hides the password form and shows—makes visible—the original form (Form1) so the diary can be read. The program then executes normally, starting with the code in the Form_Load event in Form1.

But if the password is incorrect, the whole program is shut down with the End command.

Changing the Startup Form

We're nearly finished with the Diary program. One more task.

By default, the first form displayed to the user when a program executes is the first form you created when writing the program. In this case, it's Form1. So we have to tell VB to make our new Password form the startup form instead. Let's do that now.

If the Solution Explorer isn't visible in the code window, press CTRL-R or choose View | Solution Explorer. Right-click the name of our program (*arrListDiary*, which will be shown in boldface in the Solution Explorer). Choose Properties from the context menu that appears.

The Project Designer dialog box appears, as shown in Figure 11-13.

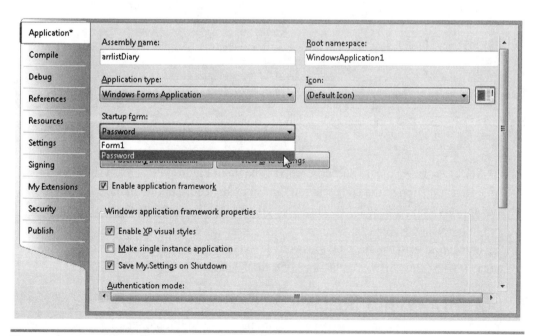

Figure 11-13 Here's where you can change the startup form.

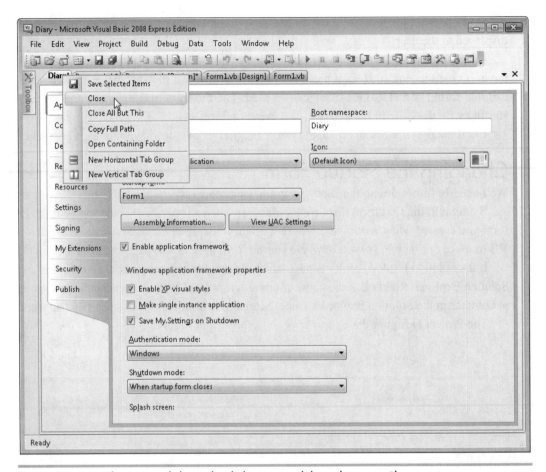

Figure 11-14   Close any tab by right-clicking it, and then choosing Close.

Select *Password* as the Startup Form, as shown in Figure 11-13. Then right-click the Diary tab at the top of the code window, and click the Close option in the context menu that appears (see Figure 11-14). This closes the Project Designer dialog box and returns you to normal code view.

Now press F5 to test the new password-protection feature. You can, of course, choose any password you wish by replacing *raffles* in the code.

Security Within Security

We've added encryption and a password. Are there any additional security issues we need to consider? You bet.

You can never really be totally secure, this side of heaven. For every thicker bunker built, the enemy makes a bigger bunker-buster bomb. Computer security works this way, too: it's a constant back-and-forth between the virus writers and the anti-virus folks trying to protect us.

Even adding the password feature to our program doesn't solve the problem of a persistent or computer-savvy spy who could read the Diary program's source code. The spy could open it in the VB editor by just clicking the .sln file in Windows Explorer.

If the spy read the source code, he or she would be able to figure out your password and gain entry to the diary. You can deal with this threat by storing the program's source code in an encrypted area on your hard drive. Or you could store the password as the first item in the arrDiary.txt file, rather than within the source code. (This second tactic will require that you write additional programming to read the password from the file when the program first executes, and then display the password window.)

But even this defense isn't all that good because somebody reading your source code would see that, in fact, the password is in the arrDiary.txt file, and he or she would also see how your encryption system works. My suggestion is that you just give up and move to a cave in the desert (just kidding).

Your best approach to securing the diary is to add the bank-quality encryption I mentioned in Chapter 10, and also store your source code in an area on your hard drive that's encrypted by using the tools built into Windows itself.

To see how to encrypt a file or folder in Windows, search for *Encryption* in the Windows Explorer Help system, or search Google for *encrypting files.*

Closing the Ghost Window

Before leaving the Diary program, we have one more pretty serious bug to fix. This bug is caused by our having opened two windows—the password-entry window, and the main Diary window. And I call it a serious bug because it can destroy text that the user spent time typing into the diary.

Although we used the `Hide` command to make the password window invisible to the user, that window is nonetheless still lurking around in the computer's memory. Merely hiding a form does not close it.

If the user clicks our Exit button to shut down the Diary program, here's the code that is executed:

```
Private Sub btnExit_Click(ByVal sender As System.Object, ByVal e As
System.EventArgs) Handles btnExit.Click
```

```
        'first store the current page in the arraylist, in case the
user modified it:
        arrlistDiary(IndexPointer) = TextBox1.Text

        Dim FilePath = "C:\temp\arrDiary.txt"

        SaveArray(FilePath, arrlistDiary)

        End


End Sub
```

This procedure first saves any changes the user made to the Diary, and then it shuts down the program using the `End` command. `End` has a global effect—it shuts down the entire program and all its components, including the password window. This is fine.

The Problem of the Red X

There's another way to exit our program, though—one that can cause lost data. What if the user clicks the red *X* in the top-right corner of the main Diary window instead of our Exit button?

The user will assume that she has shut down the program, but this *X* merely closes the particular window that the *X* is on. Any other lurking windows, perhaps invisible (hidden with the `Hide` command), are still lurking.

In other words, each window has a separate red *X*, and clicking its *X* has only the local effect of closing that window—not a global effect of closing the other windows in the program.

Here's the bug. Suppose the user spends an hour writing a long entry in the diary. Then she innocently clicks the red *X*. *All her work will be lost* because the code in the `btnExit` procedure that saves changes to the diary never gets executed. The user didn't click that button, so the most current version of diary is not saved to the hard drive.

We need to do two things, then, to make the Diary program work as it should:

1. First, we have to trap (respond to in our code) the main form's event that triggers when its red *X* is clicked.

2. Second, we have to ensure that if this *X* is clicked, any changes to the diary are saved to the disk file before we `End` the program. In other words, we need to execute the code in the `btnExit` procedure, regardless of whether the user clicks our button or clicks the red *X*.

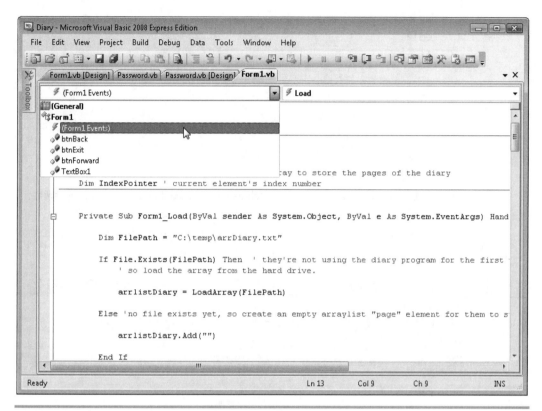

Figure 11-15   Choose (Form1 Events) from this list of objects.

When a user clicks a window's red *X*, the `FormClosing` event is triggered. We need to write some code in the `FormClosing` event handler. To have the editor add this event handler to your code window, open the drop-down list at the top-left of the code window and choose (Form1 Events), as shown in Figure 11-15.

Now open the drop-down list of form events on the top-right corner of the code window, as shown in Figure 11-16.

Select the `FormClosing` event from the drop-down list shown in Figure 11-16. You can now copy and paste the code you wrote for the `btnExit` event handler:

```
Private Sub Form1_FormClosing(ByVal sender As Object, ByVal e As
System.Windows.Forms.FormClosingEventArgs) Handles Me.FormClosing
```

```
        'first store the current page in the arraylist, in case the
user modified it:
        arrlistDiary(IndexPointer) = TextBox1.Text

        Dim FilePath = "C:\temp\arrDiary.txt"
        SaveArray(FilePath, arrlistDiary)
        End

End Sub
```

Avoiding Redundancy

Programmers dislike redundancy almost as much as English teachers, so when programmers see duplicated code they try to figure out a way to eliminate the duplication. This saves computer memory (although these days this hardly matters), but it also simplifies the program, making it easier to read, debug, or modify, and more *elegant*.

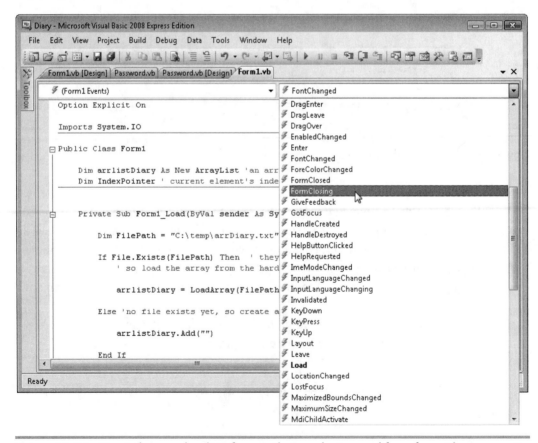

Figure 11-16 Here's the complete list of events that can be trapped for a form. There are quite a few, aren't there?

Programmers want to write a piece of code only once, in a single location, and then just *call* it from any other places in the program that need it. This approach is, in fact, one major reason to use sub and function procedures. You can call a particular procedure as often as you wish, from any location in the code, and it will do its job. This way, you need not repeat the procedure's code every place in the program where you need that job done.

(Of course, you can limit the scope of a procedure with the `Private` command, or other scope-limiting declaration command. Unless you declare it with the global `Public` declaration command, a procedure is available to code only in the range of scope you've specified.)

How can we avoid duplicating the code that correctly shuts down our Diary program? That code is already in the `btnExit` procedure. Can we *call* the `btnExit` procedure, thereby executing its code as if the user clicked that button?

Yes. We can call an event handler procedure like `btnExit`, just as we'd call any other procedure: Call it by using its name, and providing in parentheses any arguments that the called procedure requires. Let's see how that's done.

Event handler procedures require two arguments that I previously told you to ignore. But we *do* need to provide them when calling an event handler. The arguments for all event handlers are `sender` and `e`:

```
Private Sub btnExit_Click(ByVal sender As System.Object, ByVal e As
System.EventArgs) Handles btnExit.Click
```

Ignore the Mechanisms Below
It's simple enough to send these arguments. The sender is `Me` (the form) and `e` is, mysteriously, just `e`.

Exactly what purpose these arguments serve is unimportant to beginners or, in fact, to most VB programmers of any level of experience. Just provide the arguments, and don't bother with the mechanisms down below that require them.

So just type this code to call our `btnExit` procedure from inside the `FormClosing` event handler:

```
Private Sub Form1_FormClosing(ByVal sender As Object, ByVal e As
System.Windows.Forms.FormClosingEventArgs) Handles Me.FormClosing

    btnExit_Click(Me, e)

End Sub
```

Red *X* bug solved.

Chapter 12

Getting Help

Key Skills & Concepts

- Using IntelliSense for immediate assistance

- Pressing F1 for local and online help

- Personalizing how the help system works

- Searching the Internet

A ll programmers need help, most of us quite often, though we are sometimes less than candid about it.

I, personally, was misled by TV chef Julia Child. Although watching her shows improved my cooking skills in most ways, she ruined many of my meals by one, offhand comment she made on a show back in the '70s.

Like other TV cooks, she was quite casual about using teaspoons and tablespoons—implying that a real cook just dumped a certain amount of thyme into the stew, somehow *knowing* that it was a teaspoon. The lesson: Experienced cooks don't need assistance from measuring spoons.

Well, one day—after 30 years of following this practice of blithely guessing—I finally had a bright idea. I decided to actually *test* my measurements to see how my guesses compared to a real teaspoon and tablespoon.

Turned out that I had been under-spicing by about 30 percent compared to the measuring spoon quantities. This means that for decades I had been following recipes in cookbooks and getting results that were significantly too bland—not at all what the cookbook chef had intended.

Since then I always use measuring spoons, and my cooking is spicier, better balanced, and in general much tastier.

So my advice to you is that with programming, as with much else in life, pride cometh before a fall. We shouldn't go around pretending we're such fantastically skilled programmers that we don't need to access the VB Help system, and access it often. We shouldn't act as if we always know instantly how to code a complicated procedure or fix a tough logic bug. Who are we kidding?

In this chapter, I'll suggest several ways to get help—employing the various help systems available to the VB programmer. Let's look at them in order of how often I find myself using them.

Handy IntelliSense

IntelliSense is Microsoft's name for information that pops up automatically while you're writing code in the editor. The IntelliSense tools include auto list members, parameter information, and details about syntax errors that the editor highlights with a sawtooth underline in the code window. These highly useful IntelliSense tools are covered in depth in Chapters 3 and 11.

Pressing the F1 Key

When you become perplexed while writing code, you often need do little more than press F1. The classic F1 Help system in VB can frequently answer a question right away.

When you press F1, the editor looks at the context, the commands at your current location in the source code. The editor sees where the blinking insertion cursor is (or whether you've highlighted any of the source code by dragging your mouse over it to select it). In other words, F1 Help is context-sensitive, so the location of the cursor or selected code tells the Help system what help information to search for and display.

Try This Exploring Context-sensitive Help

To see how the F1 Help system works, click the word .Add in your source code for the Diary program. This will put the blinking cursor on the Add command in this line in the code editor:

```
arrlistDiary.Add("")
```

Then press F1. You should see the following help entry for the Add method of the ArrayList object. I've indicated the important parts of this help entry in boldface:

ArrayList..::.Add Method
Adds an object to the end of the ArrayList.

```
Namespace:  System.Collections

Assembly:  mscorlib (in mscorlib.dll)
 Syntax
Visual Basic (Declaration)

Public Overridable Function Add ( _
    value As Object _
) As Integer

Visual Basic (Usage)
```

```
Dim instance As ArrayList
Dim value As Object
Dim returnValue As Integer

returnValue = instance.Add(value)
```

In addition to providing a useful link to general help about the `ArrayList` object, this entry also shows you how to use the `Add` method in a code example.

TIP

The built-in Microsoft Help system displays *some* information that you should simply ignore. In the previous example of help for the `Add` command, you can ignore the namespace. It's automatically included by the editor, so you don't have to use the `Imports` command to make it available. Ignore the `Assembly`. It's of no value to you. Also ignore the "declaration" that begins with `Public Overridable`. Again, what use is that to us? None. If useless to programmers, why are these items included in the Help system? My guess is that they *are* of use to Microsoft's programming teams, by providing clerical information about which library certain commands are located in. And they are likely needed by some of the other, less accommodating, languages in the .NET family, of which VB is a part.

The important parts of this kind of help entry are the definition of the purpose of the command, and the code example illustrating its syntax in a real VB statement.

Help describes the purpose of the `Add` method as "Adds an object to the end of the ArrayList."

And the code example shows you how you can employ this command in your own code. You can even just copy and paste the help code example into your own program, and then modify it as necessary (usually this means changing variable names). But the syntax and punctuation in the code example are often what you were trying to figure out when you pressed F1.

If the context-sensitive help isn't exactly what you were looking for, type a search term in the *Look For* field in the Index pane at the top-left of the Help window, as shown in Figure 12-1.

And if the Index doesn't provide answers, expand your search by clicking the Search button on the toolbar, as shown in Figure 12-2.

Clicking the Search button opens several sets of links on the right side with which you should experiment: Local Help, MSDN Online, Codezone Community (other programmers online), and Questions. Try clicking these links to become familiar with

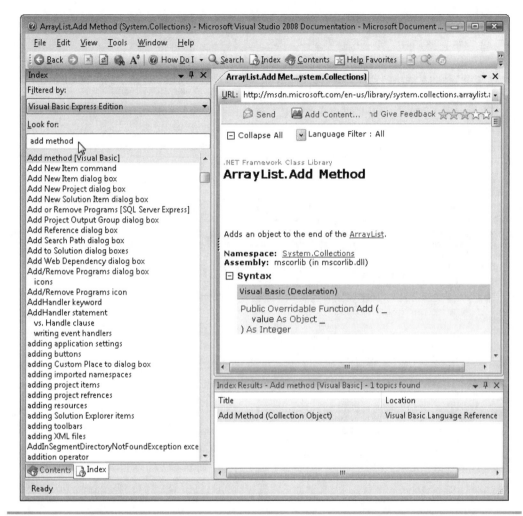

Figure 12-1   Use the Index to search within Help.

the kinds of help each can offer. You can click the Search button to return to the main Search screen. Or click the back or forward button on the toolbar to navigate through recent web pages you've visited within the Search mode. Note that online (and local) help systems are continual works in progress: some areas are rich with understandable assistance,

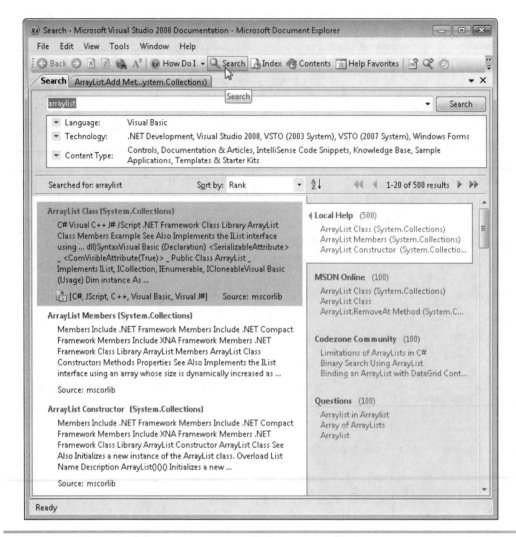

Figure 12-2 The Search button opens up a whole new set of help systems to investigate.

while other areas are rife with tech-speak so obscure as to be useless. Also, the Help system itself can be buggy, displaying script error messages and asking if you want to continue. If this happens to you, just click the Yes buttons until the error messages calm down and go away.

Customizing Help

The Help system can be customized. You can create a list of Favorites; switch between the Search feature, a table of contents, or scrolling through an index; and even specify how searches are conducted and filtered.

If this interests you, spend a little time familiarizing yourself with elements of the VB Help tools. Try working with the various search options, for one thing. Choose Tools | Options in the Help menus. Then click the black arrow next to *Help* in the left pane of the Options dialog box. You now see General and Online options. Click the *Online* option in the left pane to see how you can customize what is displayed and searched when you use the Help system's online resources.

As you see in Figure 12-3, you can select, reorder, or omit the various help features such as MSDN Online (Microsoft's huge Developer Network database) or *local* help (information stored on your computer when you installed VB).

Don't neglect the Codezone Community. This can be a valuable resource. It's where programmers, some expert, gather to share questions and ideas. In the Codezone, you can find useful code examples and, in particular, ask your own questions if other help resources don't provide answers.

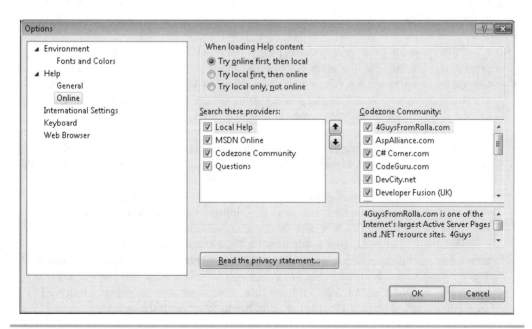

Figure 12-3   The Help system can be customized in many ways.

Be sure to search Google Groups as a supplement to the Codezone. These online user groups are a good place to seek interactive assistance from online gurus. If you really get stuck, write me at earth@triad.rr.com and I'll try to get back to you quickly with an answer.

TIP

Some people prefer that the Help system search through online resources first. They think that the results are more complete, and more up-to-date, than the local help data stored on your hard drive. See the *When loading Help content* choices listed at the top of the Options dialog box, as shown in Figure 12-3.

TIP

If you don't find what you're looking for when searching, be sure to try variations on your search phrase such as *VB ArrayList, Visual Basic ArrayList, VB ArrayList.Add*, and so on.

Ask the Expert

Q: What Help system do you find yourself using most, Microsoft's Help system or just online Googling?

A: It's really a toss-up. I use them both frequently. For quick syntax and code examples, I press F1 most of the time. For more complicated questions, I tend to go immediately to Google for an online search. (Google searches often list MSDN or other Microsoft Help system links anyway. With Google, you're getting several resources at once: user groups, programmers' blogs, online programming sites like DevX, and Microsoft's various online Help systems. And they're all listed in order of relative popularity.)

It is sometimes tempting to skip the built-in help and type some target words directly into Google, such as *VB Add method*. (Putting *VB* first is a good way to tell Google that the most important filter is *VB* followed by the *Add method*.)

When dealing with issues more advanced than simple syntax, Google searches frequently produce clearer, more complete descriptions and better, longer code examples than those in Microsoft's system (whether local or online).

Somebody in an online user group might ask the exact question you're wondering about. For example, you might query Google Groups about *VB Add Method* and Google lists a link to a user group with this: *My question is how do you use the Add method with an ArrayList.* Click that link and you'll see that question on some user group, followed by answers that others provided to this question. Bingo! You've hit the jackpot.

To use Google Groups, just type in whatever search term you want into the Google main page (www.Google.com), and then drop down the list of more options and choose Groups, as shown here:

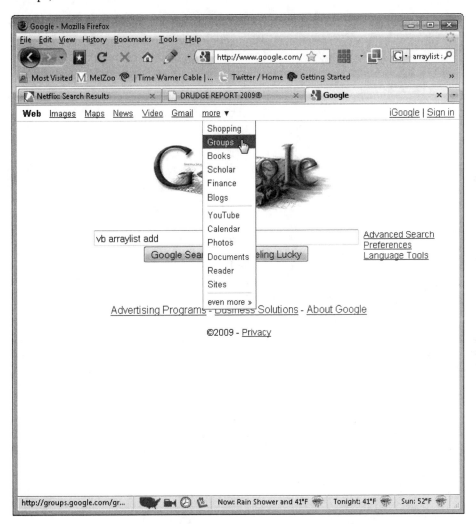

In addition, online information more often than not avoids some of the inessential tech data that is nearly always included in the official Microsoft Help responses (namespaces, assemblies, example code in other languages).

But, on the plus side, F1 can be the quickest way to get answers that are *official* (not some random person's opinion), and you'll usually find links to other areas in the Microsoft system so you can jump around until you get the information you need. It really is a toss-up.

Chapter 13

Where to Go from Here

Key Skills & Concepts

- Defining your goals

- Transitioning via C#

- Translating between VB code and C#

- Introducing OOP

- Considering a career in programming

- Selling shareware

Many people enjoy programming as a hobby, many avoid it, and some see computers as a way to earn a living. It's just like the various ways people approach any art—piano playing, cooking, golf, painting.

Whatever your reasons for buying this book and giving programming a try, in this final chapter we'll explore paths you can take if you're interested in making some money by communicating with computers. You need not turn professional. If you prefer to remain a happy amateur, you can still sell your programs via shareware outlets, as you'll see.

Professional Requirements

What is involved if you do want to turn professional? Increasingly, professional programmers today must have a college degree or at least a degree from a two-year training program. What's more, many employers require that you be academically trained in the C language derivatives such as C++ or Java.

The Rise of C

Although Visual Basic was the most popular language in professional circles in the 1990s, its popularity has declined. Some say the reason for the ascension of the C languages over BASIC is as simple as that name: *BASIC* (Beginners All-purpose Symbolic Instruction Code). For obvious reasons, professionals prefer not to be associated with a synonym for *elementary*. How many dentists describe themselves in the yellow pages as *apprentice dentist*?

But don't be misled by the name *BASIC*. Visual Basic is just as powerful and sophisticated as any other Microsoft language, and VB is still used by many commercial programming groups.

BASIC Is Often the Language of Choice

My guess is that if given a choice, the majority of programmers would switch to BASIC because it's easier to write, read, debug, and maintain than the C languages. Historically, BASIC *has* been the language of choice both for professional and amateur programmers. It remains the language preferred by most amateurs even today. Amateurs, you see, *do* have a choice.

BASIC is also the most accessible language for beginners, which is why I chose to use it in this book.

Becoming Multilingual

If you're a talented computer linguist, there's nothing to stop you from going on to learn several languages and becoming multilingual. Some people excel at this, just as some find it easy to learn multiple human languages. Clearly you'll benefit in the marketplace—at least you'll qualify for a greater number of jobs—if you know how to program in multiple languages.

And, to an extent, different languages are sometimes better for different tasks. VB shines as a teaching language, for general-purpose programming, and when working with databases. But having several arrows in your quiver is clearly an advantage for a professional programmer. You might want to investigate PERL. It's quite flexible, particularly good for manipulating strings, and is sometimes called the "Swiss Army" language because, like BASIC, it is useful in a variety of contexts. And, of course, you might also want to explore C#, a gateway into the C languages.

Introducing C#

Let's look at the C family of languages. In 2000, Microsoft introduced a language it calls C#, which is somewhat easier to learn than others in the C family. The family of programming to which C# belongs includes C, Java, C++, and several others that derive from the original C language—so I'll refer to them as the *C languages*.

Let's take a look at some of the qualities of the C languages, as represented by C#. This way you'll have an idea of what you'll be dealing with if you decide to explore today's most popular alternatives to BASIC.

Computers Don't Care What Words You Use

If you intend to explore the C languages, Microsoft's C# is probably the best place to start. But let's first clear up a common misunderstanding. There is no reason that computer languages can't resemble English. The computer isn't like a Tibetan villager with whom you must learn to communicate in Tibetan if you hope to communicate at all.

Some people think computers have a language built in, as if they were born in Machineland or something. A computer has no native high-level language, merely a simple set of built-in, low-level capabilities such as the capacity to turn memory cells on or off or add numbers together. In this way, the computer is language-neutral like babies: raise a Tibetan in Tucson and she will speak English.

Consider this: In America, we use the word *Christmas*, but it's *Weihnachten* in German, and рождество in Russian. But no matter what word you use, Christmas occurs on December 25. In this sense, words and sentences are simply interchangeable labels and varying syntaxes.

Likewise, it doesn't matter to the computer whether you employ this C# statement to display an input box,

```
EndTime = Int32.Parse(
        Interaction.Input box("Please type in the delay in
minutes...",
                        "", "", 0, 0));
```

or use this BASIC statement:

```
Endtime = InputBox("Please type in the delay in minutes...")
```

The user sees the same input box, just as December 25 is the same day in Russia, Germany, and the United States.

Down Low All Commands Are Equal

Whether you express the concept of input box in C# or BASIC, the idea will be translated by a "compiler" into the same elementary instructions. These low-level instructions display the input box to the user and assign the result to the variable EndTime.

If you're working in the C# language, the C# source code will be translated into low-level commands that the computer can carry out to display the dialog box, get the user input, and assign it to the variable. If you're working in the VB code window, the VB code will be translated into the same low-level behaviors that the computer understands as "display the dialog box," "get the user input," and "assign it to the variable."

Remember that these symbols

Int32.Parse(Interaction.Input box("Please type in the delay in minutes...","","","," 0, 0));

and these

EndTime = Input box("Please type in the delay in minutes...")

have identical effects. They are merely *our* labels, symbols for *our* convenience, an—different ways of saying the same thing: Show an input box and get a value for this variable.

Tech Tip

In the past, compilers *did* produce significantly different low-level behaviors when you used different languages, but since 2000, all .NET languages employ the same underlying framework and can produce the same low-level code. No matter which language use—VB, C#, or the many other .NET languages—they share a common language runtime (core functionality). So no .NET language is faster or more capable than any other. Some of them, of course, are more difficult to program with, but that's a different issue than how well they execute programming on the computer. (By the way, there are lots of .NET languages. Microsoft invented the .NET foundation, but other people have since written their own .NET-compliant languages. See http://en.wikipedia.org/wiki/.NET_Languages.)

Another technical point I need to make is that although it's true that all high-level .NET languages can produce identical low-level behaviors, high-level commands are not always compiled into exactly the same low-level code. In other words, .NET compilers can differ in their implementation details. For example, you might be surprised to know that C#'s `Application.Exit()` command is not literally identical to VB's `End` command when compiled. For example, `Application.Exit()` ensures that the `FormClosing` event is called, while `End` doesn't.

Here are some more details for the technically inclined. The `Application.Exit()` method doesn't accept a numeric value. It can accept a `CancelEventArgs` object, but that's not what we want our program to do: we want it to *end*. In fact, `Application .Exit()` can also cause unintended side effects, so some C# experts recommend you avoid using that command except in case of an emergency. Using C#'s `Close()` or `Environment.Exit(0)` command (where 0 is an integer value providing an exit code) is better. There's also C#'s `Environment.FailFast("Failure Reason")` approach when a catastrophic failure has occurred. Each of these exit strategies has its own purpose.

You could invent your own programming language that used these symbols to display an input box:

F' '&S*a☺ $A = \pi r^2$ (✋)

These human labels are irrelevant to the computer—it will display an input box no matter what programming language you choose to express that idea.

Now you can see why I and many other programming teachers select BASIC as the language to introduce people to programming. BASIC is on the whole easier, though no less powerful, than other languages. BASIC is designed to be English-like in its punctuation, syntax, and diction.

Comparing C# to VB

To give you a taste of C#, let's take a look again at the simple Timer program we created in Chapter 2. We'll see how the VB version compares to the C# version of this same program. Here's the BASIC version we wrote:

```
Option Strict Off
Option Explicit On

Sub TimeIt()

        Dim CurrentTime As Integer
        Dim EndTime



        EndTime = Input box("Please type in the delay in minutes...")

        EndTime = EndTime + Minute(Now)


        Do While CurrentTime < EndTime

           CurrentTime = Minute(Now)

        Loop


        MsgBox("Time's Up!")

        End

    End Sub
```

And here's the translation into C#:

```
using Microsoft.VisualBasic;

public void TimeIt()
{

    int CurrentTime = 0;
    int EndTime = 0;



    EndTime = Int32.Parse(
        Interaction.Input box("Please type in the delay in minutes...",
                              "", "", 0, 0));

    EndTime = EndTime + DateTime.Now.Minute;


    while (CurrentTime < EndTime)
    {

        CurrentTime = DateTime.Now.Minute;
    }

    Message box.Show("Time's Up!");

    Application.Exit();

}
```

For this code to work you must add a *reference* to Microsoft.VisualBasic, described in the following tip.

TIP

C# doesn't offer a built-in input box (and various other VB features), so some C# programmers write C# code to create and display an input box. They hand-code the missing features (such as the input box) or they locate prewritten code online and paste it into their source code. However, you can take a shortcut. Some programmers find it easiest to "import" (reference) the Microsoft.VisualBasic.dll (library) in their C# programs. That way, you can borrow VB's `InputBox`, `Minute` command, and other VB commands—even though you're working mainly in C#. In fact, this ability to import VB functionality into C# makes the transition from BASIC to C-style programming all the more easier. You reference VB's command in a C# program by right-clicking References in the Solution Explorer, and then choosing Add Reference. Scroll within the list of available references and choose Microsoft.VisualBasic.dll. (*Dynamic link library*, or *DLL*, is another word for *namespace, library, or assembly*). Also, you must add this line at the top of the C# code window: `using Microsoft.VisualBasic;`

As you can see in the preceding code example, there are several similarities between BASIC and C#. The main difference between the two is that BASIC tends to use familiar English words, phrases, and syntax, whereas C# (and the other C languages) tend to invert ordinary syntax, abbreviate, or become verbose. Let's take a closer look at these differences.

Inversion and Abbreviation

In this example, let's compare two lines of source code (which, remember, do the same thing in both programs).

Here's the BASIC version that creates a new integer variable named `CurrentTime`:

```
Dim CurrentTime As Integer
```

Here's the C# version. As you can see, C# both inverts and abbreviates this syntax:

```
int CurrentTime = 0;
```

Let's take a closer look at what's happened here. Sometimes it's interesting to visualize computer programming languages as having the same components as human languages: verbs, adjectives, nouns, and so on. What parts of speech do the commands in this line of code most resemble? In this code statement, we want to declare (announce) that the word *CurrentTime* is an Integer type. Here's the grammar:

> Dim (verb)
> CurrentTime (noun)
> Integer (adjective)

This BASIC grammar translates comfortably into a similar English sentence, such as *I pronounce Bob and Ashley married*:

> I pronounce (subject and verb)
> Bob and Ashley (noun)
> married (adjective)

However, the C# version inverts ordinary English syntax order: it puts the adjective first and the noun second, and it leaves out the verb entirely. The C# syntax translates thusly:

> *Married Bob and Ashley.*

Simple Abbreviation

In this next example, C# abbreviates by omitting the word `Do` and also by replacing the word `Loop` with a right curly brace symbol.

Here's the BASIC version of this loop structure:

```
Do While CurrentTime < EndTime

    CurrentTime = Minute(Now)

Loop
```

Versus this C# version (the curly braces are optional when you have only a single statement):

```
while (CurrentTime < EndTime)
    {

        CurrentTime = DateTime.Now.Minute;

    }
```

Verbosity

Finally, C# is more verbose that VB in these two lines:

```
MsgBox("Time's Up!")

End
```

Versus:

```
Message box.Show("Time's Up!");

Application.Exit();
```

Also notice that VB interprets a new line as a new statement. In VB, you specify the end of a line of code by pressing ENTER to move down one line in the code window.

C#, however, ends each line with a semicolon. So the following is perfectly legal C# code:

```
Message box.Show
  ("Time's Up!"); Application.Exit();
```

TIP

If you want to combine two VB statements on the same line, you can do it by separating them with a colon, like this: `MsgBox("Time's Up!"): End`
Or, if you want to break a long line of BASIC code into two separate visual lines, you can use a space character followed by the underline symbol to end the first part of the broken statement. You can break a single line: `MsgBox("Time's up")`

into two visual lines, like this:

```
MsgBox _
  ("Time's up")
```

How C# Handles If...Then

C# If...Then structures are handled in a way that's similar to the way C# handles loop structures, by omitting some words:

```
if (Counter >= TotalSeconds) {

  Timer1.Stop ();

Message box.Show ("Time's up.");
  Application.Exit ();

                          }
```

The BASIC word Then is replaced by a left curly brace symbol, and the phrase End If is replaced by a right brace symbol. Replacing a word with a symbol is a form of abbreviation. In fact, the C# code can be further abbreviated: If only one statement resides within a C# If structure, you can omit the braces, too.

C# For...Next Structures

Most of C#'s abbreviations (omitting words such as Then and End If) only mildly impact readability. You can still read the code and probably get the main idea of what's happening pretty quickly.

But in some structures, such as For...Next, C#'s abbreviation can make reading the code rather difficult—at least until you become experienced enough with the language to make the necessary mental substitutions (substitutions for the way human language expresses these ideas).

In a For...Next...Step structure, for example, BASIC uses four English words—For, To, Step, and Next:

```
For i = 3 To 30 Step 3
  MsgBox (i)
Next
```

The only word that C# employs in this structure is For, and the rest of the structure is expressed symbolically, using <=, +=, and } rather than To, Step, and Next:

```
for (i = 3; i <= 30; i += 3) {
Message box.Show (i);
}
```

How C# Handles Arrays

VB declares an array by specifying *the highest index number*. Here's an example that creates five array elements, Guests(0), Guests(1), Guests(2), Guests(3), and Guests(4):

```
Dim Guests(4) As String
```

C# instead declares *how many elements* the array holds. So here is the C# declaration equivalent. This code creates an array with the same five elements as the VB declaration:

```
string[] Guests = new string[5];
```

Also, C# cannot dynamically resize arrays (as VB's ReDim command can). So if you need to adjust a C# array's size, you must do the job by hand: Create a new, second array of the new size, and then copy the values (the data) from the first array into the second one. You can use C#'s Array.Copy command. However, like VB, C# does have the ArrayList object, which would be easier to work with than the C# array.

Other Differences

Beyond the differences outlined so far, VB and C# also differ in a variety of other ways. Many of the differences relate to *diction*, or choice of words. For example, VB's Imports command becomes Using in C#. Exiting a loop (such as the VB command Exit While) becomes Break in C#. And VB's Select Case becomes Switch.

However, VB and C# *are* relatively similar languages. If you intend to go on to learn Java or some other derivative of C, C# makes an excellent bridge from VB to these C languages that are currently popular among professional programmers.

TIP

VB and C# are so similar that translating code between them has been automated (though the automatic translation can require some manual programmer intervention). If you want to see what some of your VB programming would look like if turned into C#, go to this web site and paste in some of your VB source code: www.developerfusion .com/tools/convert/vb-to-csharp. To go the other way, from C# to VB, visit this web page: www.developerfusion.com/tools/convert/csharp-to-vb.

A Brief Introduction to OOP

OOP—object-oriented programming—has become very popular among professional programmers in the past couple of decades. OOP offers programming techniques that can be useful when more than one person is working on a program, as is so often the case in professional situations. OOP now dominates academic and commercial programming.

OOP is not a language. It's a set of techniques and rules that are implemented in many contemporary languages. VB permits you to employ OOP practices, but doesn't require you to.

OOP is difficult to summarize because it doesn't represent a single concept. Like *philosophy* or *theater*, *OOP* is a broad, generic term that means different things to different people.

For one thing, OOP is differently implemented in different contexts, and even experts are unable to agree on a common definition. But I'll try to give you a brief overview here, a sense of the main ideas. You can find loads of books on the subject if you want to explore OOP further.

Why I Left OOP Out

OOP really isn't for beginners. Although VB allows programmers to employ OOP practices, VB doesn't require it.

I've mostly avoided OOP in this book. A novice programmer in my view needs to absorb the elements of programming first—the editor, the toolbox, variables, arrays, loops, branches, and procedures. Introducing OOP would only complicate things for beginners. After all, many aspects of OOP have been known to complicate things for experts as well.

What's more, if you intend to remain an amateur and only write programs by yourself, OOP just isn't necessary (though some OOP advocates would argue that even casual, personal programming can benefit from following OOP techniques).

At its most elementary level, OOP endeavors to bring these qualities to programming:

- *You can subdivide a program into objects rather than procedures.* Objects tend to contain more lines of code than sub or function procedures. In fact, an object more closely resembles a VB *form* than a procedure. Objects typically contain more than one procedure, just as forms do. But an object *is* a kind of container, a way of keeping related source code together.

- *Objects can contain both data (such as somebody's hire date), as well as code that processes that data (such as calculating the total number of months they've been employed).* You can grasp this idea if you think of the toolbox controls that you can put on a VB form. A text box, for example, contains both *data* (the text box's color, contents, size, and so on) as well as *processing* (the ability to delete all its contents via the built-in `Textbox.Clear` command, for one example).

   VB's controls *are* one kind of objects, so you have been exposed in this book to at least one facet of OOP. A button control, like a text box, contains data (its color property, its text, and so on) as well as behavior (its built-in methods, plus its ability to respond to a user's click via whatever code you write in the button's `Click` event). Note that an object *can* have a visual user interface such as a text box, but it doesn't have to. Many objects are similar to procedures—merely code that performs some task without interacting visually with the user.

- *OOP stresses that objects be self-sufficient, even to the point of containing the data that they process.* Compare this to traditional procedures that often merely *process* data that is located elsewhere, such as in a database. This can be one of the major strengths of OOP. But it is also one of its major weaknesses: when attempting to manage existing, traditional databases using OOP techniques, things often get dicey fast. And there are many traditional (non-OOP) databases in use.

- *Object self-sufficiency also implies that you should avoid using global variables (which necessarily reside outside the objects).* Instead, data should reside within objects, in local variables, and the programmer should pass the data back and forth between objects as needed.

- *A strict set of rules for how objects communicate with each other, by including the ability to send and receive messages.*

The Little Factory

Remember that OOP isn't a single idea: many practices and technologies come under the OOP umbrella. One interesting feature of OOP objects that's not shared by procedures is the ability to create as many clone objects as you want. The clones have (inherit) the data, qualities (properties), and capabilities (methods) of the original. The original is referred to as a *class*, meaning a description or blueprint for creating objects.

In effect, you write code to describe a class, and then that class can turn out as many clone objects as you wish while the program executes. A class is often compared to a factory that turns out objects. For example, you can add as many text boxes as you want to your forms. And although they all inherit the same properties and methods when first cloned, they can be modified so they are no longer exact clones (different text, for example, in different text boxes).

OOP is quite successful in some contexts, most notably in the graphical user interfaces (Windows and others) that are now almost universal in computers. The VB toolbox is filled with objects (controls), and dropping them onto a form couldn't be simpler or more efficient as a way to create a user interface.

OOP can be less effective in other contexts, such as when attempting to manage many kinds of databases. A traditional database contains only data. However, OOP expects data packages to include instructions on how that data should be processed.

And for personal or amateur programming projects, employing most OOP techniques in your own code is often likely to be overkill. Nonetheless, some elements of OOP coding can be both demanding and enjoyable at the same time. And you will surely want to take advantage of the OOP controls on the Toolbox.

If you want to experiment with OOP, no harm done. Start by choosing one of the VB OOP books for beginners.

Do You Want to Program Professionally?

You might end up really enjoying programming, finding it endlessly fascinating (as I do).

True, at times it can be challenging. But like many challenges, it's often rewarding, particularly when you build quality programs that behave precisely as you want them to.

Remember, too, that you can freely customize your own programs: adding improvements, making them communicate with other programs, inserting multimedia audio or video, sending their data to a Kindle, adding custom wallpaper backgrounds, making them run faster or whatever.

But should you write code for personal satisfaction only, or consider a career in programming?

Ask the Expert

Q: What should I bear in mind before launching myself into a career in programming?

A: Many factors are involved: the future of the programming industry, the various career paths available, compensation, working conditions, a typical work day, the rewards, the frustrations, and so on.

I'm always amazed at how casually most people select a college major or drift into their lifelong occupation without doing much research beyond "I like this," "Dad does it," or "suits me."

How do you know you'll like it for a lifetime, or that it will prove a durable and rewarding career? I don't except myself from this all-too-relaxed approach to this significant decision. I wandered into programming and writing books about programming without any investigation at all. I was just good at it and loved doing it. If I were young again, though, I'd be less passive about making such an important commitment.

Luckily, I still enjoy it. But a writer working at home with a view of the lake.... And naps anytime in the bedroom adjoining my study.... Clearly I have it easier than most professional programmers working in teams against communal deadlines.

First, ask a few professional programmers for their opinions of the job—the pros and cons of this career.

Also, investigate whether a career in program development is wise. Will the profession be the same five years from now? Does it suit your personality? Are most programmers wellpaid?

Although programming itself can be quite enjoyable, programming as a career can have serious drawbacks, many of which are discussed in this interesting article: www.halfsigma .com/2007/03/why_a_career_in.html. But for balance, also read the comments below the article—some of which present intelligent counterarguments.

My feeling is that, before you actually join a company, it's essential that you first investigate how the company views and treats its programmers. Does the corporate culture see programmers as brilliant but childlike? Or as experts, valued as an essential part of the team? Talk to people who work there.

And don't forget that programmers increasingly work freelance. You can find companies that manage outsourced programming jobs. RentACoder and oDesk are two:

- www.rentacoder.com

- www.odesk.com/w/

Amateur Programming Is Alive and Well

If you decide to pursue programming alone, as a hobby, you can nonetheless still make good money at it. A thriving community of independent programmers publish shareware.

If you write a program that does something useful and you think others might be interested in buying it, the tradition is to offer customers a free trial. Then after, say, 30 days, request payment. Alternatively, you can disable a key feature in the program (saving files, for example) until payment is sent.

In any case, opportunities for generating income via amateur programming are out there. Take a look at www.download.com or www.majorgeeks.com.

Some famous commercial programs—generating millions of dollars year after year—started out as shareware. *WinZip*, *Paint Shop*, and the McAfee security programs all began as shareware.

Part **IV**

Appendixes

Appendix A

The 17 Primary Visual Basic Express Commands

This appendix describes core commands used most often in this book. There are of course other core commands in the VB language, but they are either less frequently used or a bit advanced.

In addition, thousands of other commands are available to you in various libraries devoted to such specialized computing as security, Extensible Markup Language (XML), database programming, and so on. These libraries can be added to VB by using the `Imports` command (described in Chapter 9) or, for some libraries, by using the Project | Add Reference option.

However, for this book's purpose—introducing you to programming—the following is a pretty good starter list of the fundamental BASIC commands you'll most often employ.

For...Next

The `For...Next` structure creates a *loop* that repeats any code you write within the structure (within the *code block* as it's sometimes called). Loops continue to repeat a certain behavior until a job is done.

It's typical to employ `For...Next` when a loop's exit condition is known during programming. This loop repeats 20 times:

```
For i = 1 to 20
```

It repeats 20 times because *20* is specified as the *end condition*, the trigger that stops the looping. But when you don't know the specific number of times to loop, you'll generally employ the `Do...Loop` structure. It loops while some condition remains *true* (such as `Do While CurrentTime < EndTime`).

In any loop, the program repeats the code within the loop until the loop condition is satisfied. Then the program continues on to execute whatever code is below the loop structure. Loops are similar to many human jobs, such as *keep driving your truck until you reach Seattle,* or *keep selling donuts until the store closes.*

Do...Loop

A `Do...Loop` structure repeats, just as a `For...Next` structure does, but the `Do...Loop` has no specified literal number of iterations (repetitions). Instead, a `Do...Loop` iterates until some condition changes from true to false. The literal number of loops is normally known only while the program is running (not while you're writing the program). For example, in the Diary program we wrote in this book, the diary pages are stored in a file. When it first starts running, the program has to fetch these pages in from the file, one by one. This is accomplished in a `Do...Loop` because the diary contains no set, predictable number of pages—the diary will grow larger over time as the user adds new entries.

After you have fetched all the items (the "pages in the diary" in this case) from a disk file, the `EndOfStream` property of the `StreamReader` object changes to *true*. There are no more stored pages in the file. This `EndOfStream` is our trigger to exit the Do...Loop. Here's the code, with the exit condition shown in boldface:

```
Do
    s = ArrReader.ReadLine
    s = Decrypt(s)
    tempArrayList.Add(s)
Loop Until ArrReader.EndOfStream
```

Note that `True` and `False` are *values* in VB, just like `132` or `"New York"`. So you can test for True or False. In this code, we could have written this:

```
Loop Until ArrReader.EndOfStream = True
```

But it's perfectly legal and common practice to leave off the `= True` as we did in this code:

```
Loop Until ArrReader.EndOfStream
```

Do...Loop structures come in a variety of flavors. You can place the exit condition at the beginning of the loop:

```
Do While CurrentTime < EndTime

    CurrentTime = Minute(Now)

Loop
```

Or you can put it at the end of the loop:

```
Do

    CurrentTime = Minute(Now)

Loop While CurrentTime < EndTime
```

Moving the exit condition test to the end of the loop structure ensures that the loop *will always execute its inner code at least once*. Put another way, if the test is at the start of the loop and the test fails as soon as the loop structure is first reached, the code within the loop will never execute (VB will just skip past loop).

A Do...Loop also permits two kinds of exit conditional tests: `While` and `Until`. You can say Do...While or Do...Until. This distinction is only semantic, a matter of how you want to express things. It's like the difference between "Sweep *until* the porch is clean" and "Sweep *while* the porch is dirty." In both cases, you're performing the same task, but you're just describing the end point differently.

But the way you express the exit condition can sometimes make your meaning clearer to you and other programmers who might read your program. For example, you could reword the previous example to replace While with Until, like this:

```
Do Until CurrentTime = EndTime

    CurrentTime = Minute(Now)

Loop
```

If

The If...Then structure is the most common decision-making tool in a VB program. Your program asks itself a question: If something is true. Based on the answer, Then the program responds appropriately. In this simple example, if the variable *X* contains *51*, the program ends:

```
If X = 51 Then
    End
End If
```

Else

Else is used with If...Then to specify two responses: one way the program will respond if the condition (such as X = 51) is true, and a second response if the condition is false. In other words, your program asks itself a question: If something is true, Then the programming code between the If and Else commands is carried out. However, If the answer is false, Then the other code between the Else and End If commands is carried out, like this:

```
        X = UsersWeight

        If X > 200 Then

            MsgBox("It's time to diet.")

        Else

            MsgBox("Have another cookie!")

        End If
```

With the If...Then...Else structure, the program asks itself only a single question. In this example, the question is: *Is the user's weight greater than 200?*

However, sometimes you want the program to ask itself multiple questions and respond in a different way to each possible answer. In that situation, you can use the `ElseIf` command (also see `Select Case`).

Each `ElseIf` command allows you to ask a different question and respond by writing code directly below the `ElseIf`. In the next example, your program asks if the user's weight is greater than 200, between 100 and 200, or between 60 and 100. Different code (different programming instructions) is used for each possible answer. Different answers result in the display of different messages:

```
Dim X As String

        X = InputBox("What's your weight?")

        If X > 200 Then

            MsgBox("Maybe it's time to diet")

        ElseIf X > 100 Then

            MsgBox("Have another cookie!")

        ElseIf X > 60 Then

            MsgBox("Please eat something!")

        End If
```

Select Case

The `Select Case` command (which can be abbreviated to `Case`) is quite similar to using multiple `ElseIf` commands, as in the preceding example. `Select`, like `If...Then`, is a branching structure (the program can take more than one path when it comes to a branching structure). Like `If...Then`, `Select` makes a decision and then executes code you've written that is appropriate for each possible `Case` (answer).

`Select Case` is often easier to read than a complex `If...Then` structure. `Select Case` is also often simpler and clearer than a stack of multiple `ElseIf` statements.

Here's how you would rewrite the example we used in the preceding `If...Then` section as a `Select Case` decision structure rather than a set of `ElseIf` statements:

```
        Dim X As String

        X = InputBox("What's your weight?")

        Select Case CInt(X)
```

```
Case Is > 200

    MsgBox("Maybe it's time to diet")

Case Is > 100

    MsgBox("Have another cookie!")

Case Is > 60

    MsgBox("Please eat something!")

End Select
```

Note that If...Then decision structures end with End If, and Select Case structures end with End Select.

Is there a command you can use in a Select...Case structure to respond if "none of the above" cases is true (the same way that the Else command works in an If...Then structure)? Indeed there is. You use Case Else, like this:

```
Dim X As String

X = InputBox("What's your weight?")

Select Case CInt(X)

    Case Is > 200

        MsgBox("Maybe it's time to diet?")

    Case Else

        MsgBox("Have another cookie!")

End Select
```

Another way to program this same Select Case example is to use the To command that allows you to specify a range, like this:

```
Case 200 To 1000

    MsgBox("Maybe it's time to diet")
```

Sub (Subroutine)

A *subroutine* is a section of code that usually ranges from 1 to 30 statements (lines). It is a self-contained unit that performs a single task. In this way, a subroutine is similar to an ordinary paragraph in a book. A paragraph is a unit composed of sentences that all work together to make a single point.

The sub is one of two common types of *procedures*—the other being the *function* (see "Function").

Procedures help organize a program, subdividing it into component parts. Because subroutines are essentially self-contained units devoted to a single purpose, they are easier to test. If your program were one large block of uninterrupted code, it would be disorganized, difficult to read, and hard to debug.

In VB, all event handlers (such as Sub Button1_Click) are subroutines. An event handler is a sub in which you write programming code to handle various events that can happen while a program is running. Usually these events are things the user does, such as click a button.

For example, if you put a button on a form, you can make the button carry out its task by typing the End command in the button's Click event, like this:

```
Private Sub Button1_Click(ByVal sender As System.Object, ByVal e As
System.EventArgs) Handles Button1.Click

        End

End Sub
```

Event handlers are a special kind of sub and are automatically inserted for you by VB when you select an event from the two drop-down lists at the top of the code editor window.

However, you can write your own subs as well. In the code editor, just type the word Sub and provide a name for the sub, such as Sub Markdown, and then press ENTER. (Use a name that describes what the sub does.) VB will then fill in the complete sub structure for you, like this:

```
    Sub Markdown()

    End Sub
```

And inside this structure you write programming code to handle the task of marking down.

You *call* (execute) a sub or function merely by using its name. Here's how you would call the Markdown sub:

```
Private Sub Form1_Load(ByVal sender As System.Object, ByVal e As
System.EventArgs) Handles MyBase.Load
```

```
    Markdown()

End Sub


Sub Markdown()

End Sub
```

When any program starts executing, the `Form_Load` event is automatically triggered, even before any window (user interface) is displayed to the user. What happens here is that the word `Markdown` matches the name of a sub, so VB knows this is a "procedure call" to `Markdown`, and VB jumps out of the `Form_Load` event. VB proceeds to execute the code in the `Markdown` sub. Then when all the code in the `Markdown` sub has been executed, VB returns to `Form_Load` to execute whatever code remains below the procedure call.

Function

A *function* is similar to a sub; both are *procedures* and they help organize a program into manageably small zones. There's only one main difference between them: A sub normally does not return any data to whatever procedure called the sub. A function, however, carries out its task and then returns a *datum*, a value, to the procedure that called it. To return the value, the function uses a `Return` command, described next.

Return

The `Return` command is used within a function to send back a value to the caller. Normally, the `Return` command is the last statement in the function, executed after the function has done its job and is sending back a result.

In this example, a string is sent to a function. The function itself, named `RaiseCase`, accepts a string, changes it into all uppercase letters using the `UCase` command, and then send the resulting string back to the caller:

```
Option Strict Off
Option Explicit On

Public Class Form1

    Private Sub Form1_Load(ByVal sender As System.Object, ByVal e As
System.EventArgs) Handles MyBase.Load

        Dim strName, strResult

        strName = "Macon County"
```

```
        strResult = RaiseCase(strName)

    MsgBox(strResult)

        End
    End Sub


Function RaiseCase(ByVal s)

        s = UCase(s)

        Return s

End Function

End Class
```

After this code executes, a message box displays,

```
MACON COUNTY
```

+ − * /

These are *operators*. In particular, they are arithmetic operators and they do math—addition, subtraction, multiplication, and division, respectively. This line

```
MsgBox(5 * 12)
```

results in 60. Several other arithmetic operators are described in Chapter 5.

Operators are frequently used to specify how variables interact. You often need to examine, test, or modify variables in a program, and operators assist in these jobs.

Arithmetic operators aren't the only type of operators. A set of relational (comparison) operators can also be used:

- < Less than
- <= Less than or equal to
- > Greater than
- >= Greater than or equal to
- <> Not equal
- = Equal
- **Is** Do two object variables refer to the same object?
- **IsNot** Opposite of the Is operator
- **Like** Used to match patterns in strings

Sometimes you need to compare two variables. Maybe you need to find out, for example, which holds the smaller number, or whether they are equal (hold the same data), or some other relationship.

Here's an example that uses the less than operator (<) to see if one variable contains a smaller number than the other:

```
Dim Num1 = 68
Dim Num2 = 77

        If Num1 < Num2 Then

            MsgBox("Num1 is less")

        End If
```

The set of logical operators include these three: And, Or, and Not. You can use them pretty much the same way you would in English, and with them you can create longer, compound comparisons:

```
If 5 + 2 = 4 Or 6 + 6 = 12 Then MsgBox ("One of them is true.")
```

Finally, the special operator & is used to join (concatenate) two pieces of text:

```
Dim Str1 As String = "Mark "
Dim Str2 As String = "Twain"


MsgBox(Str1 & Str2)
```

This results in *Mark Twain* because the two strings are concatenated thanks to the & operator.

String and Other Data Types

A *string* is a data type. It means text data. (It's the *only* data type for text.) For example, if you specify that a variable is a string type, it will hold text. Even it you assign a number to it, such as "15115", the string variable is holding only five *digits* (actually just characters, like the alphabet). This variable named *strAddress* is not a number, it's *text*:

```
Dim strAddress As String
```

In this book, we turn Option Strict Off, allowing VB to manage data typing issues automatically for us. This makes it easier for us to focus on the other elements of programming. See Chapter 5 for details on the pros and cons of programmer versus automatic data type management.

Here are the most commonly used data types, in addition to the string type:

- **Integer**   For most programming involving numbers, you'll use integer types. It's by far the most common type of number. It means there's no fraction. In other words, 12, 24000, 1, 0, −88, and 530543 are all integers. But 4454.6 and 1.222233 are not integers because of that floating point.

- **Long**   If you need a larger range, but still can use integers, the Long type is the choice. It ranges from −9,223,372,036,854,775,808 to 9,223,372,036,854,775,807. Long, too, doesn't use decimal points, but it holds bigger numbers than its brother, the integer type.

- **Double**   Some special situations (calculating laser specs, for example) require more precision than integers offer. You must use fractions. In that case, you'll use the *double* type. This data type can hold a huge range of numbers (about 4.94×10^{-324} to $1.798 \times 10^{+308}$) for both positive or negative numbers. So just remember that you'll be using the double type if you work with highly precise fractions. Otherwise, you'll stick to the integer type, which has a range of −2,147,483,648 to 2,147,483,647. (Whole numbers only, remember.) There's also a single type, which is like double, but holds a smaller range of numbers.

- **Date**   Another type you might want to take note of is the *date* type. It stores time and date information.

Dim

The Dim command is the most common way to declare a variable:

```
Dim strAddress
```

Or you can simultaneously declare a variable and assign it a value:

```
Dim strAddress = "Norton"
```

A third option is to declare multiple variables in the same statement:

```
Dim strAddress, strTown, strState
```

Static

Use the Static command instead of Dim when you want to declare a local variable that will retain its contents even when execution moves outside the variable's own procedure:

```
Static Toggle
```

A static variable is a local variable (it's declared inside a procedure, not up near the top of the code window in the "General Declarations" section). So, being local, `Toggle` still cannot be accessed by other source code outside its own procedure. However, declaring a variable `Static` expands its *lifetime*—meaning that it retains its value until the user shuts down the program.

UBound

The `UBound` command tells you the upper boundary (the highest index number) of an array. Using `UBound` can make your programs more flexible, more easily modified. For example, if you later change the size of an array, you need not also change any `For...Next` loop that manipulates that array. It's the difference between hard-coding the number of loops with, for example, a literal *12* to match the array's declared size like this:

```
Dim arrGuests(12) As String

For i = 0 To 12

Next
```

Or, instead replace the *12* with `UBound` to calculate automatically how many times to loop, like this:

```
Dim arrGuests(12) As String

For i = 0 To UBound(arrGuests)

Next
```

With `UBound`, no matter what size the array is (or may later become if you modify the program), the loop will always execute the correct number of times.

MsgBox and InputBox

Both of these commands display dialog boxes, but the `InputBox` command also returns some information that the user types in:

```
s = InputBox("How old are you")

MsgBox(s)
```

In addition to its use as a way of displaying information to the user, the message box is also used quite a bit by many programmers as a debugging tool. The programmer temporarily adds a message box to test an assumption. Perhaps you're not sure what the UBound command will report about an array. Is it the highest index number (*12* in this example) or the total number of elements in the array (*13*, because there's a zeroth element)? Just insert a temporary message box, press F5, and the message box will show you that the answer is in fact *12*. Then delete the message box:

```
Dim arrGuests(12) As String

MsgBox(UBound(arrGuests))
```

' (REM)

When you type a single-quote symbol at the start (or within) a line of code, everything following that symbol is ignored by VB. You have created a *comment* for you and other programmers to read, but it's not intended to be executed as part of the program. The VB editor cues you visually by changing the color of remark text to green.

Commenting allows you to clarify what your code and procedures are supposed to do. This can make it easier for you to read and maintain (debug and customize) the code later, and it will almost certainly be appreciated by anyone else who later tries to modify or understand your programming.

You can alternatively replace the ' symbol with the REM (for remark) command, though few people do this.

Try

The Try...End Try structure is generally employed when your program attempts to interact with a peripheral, most often the hard drive. Perhaps you're trying to save data to a file that has been deleted or renamed on the hard drive. Or perhaps your program is trying to print something, but the printer isn't turned on.

The prudent programmer encloses such potentially risky zones of a program with a Try...End Try structure that can catch (detect) when an error occurs, identify the type of error, and either solve the problem or inform the user of what the problem is and ask the user to fix it. For example, you might use a message box to display "We are unable to detect the printer. Your printer appears to be either turned off or unplugged from the computer. Please fix this, and then try to print again." (See Chapter 11 for more details.)

End

The End command shuts down a program, just as if the user had pressed ALT-F4, or clicked the close box X in the upper-right corner of the program's window. When you use End, all the program's windows are closed and execution quits.

Appendix B

Variable and Control Naming Conventions

This appendix shows you two ways to make your programming code more readable, more easily understood if you return to it later to debug or improve the program. And it's also always possible that other programmers might work with your source code as well.

Following is a list of suggested prefixes, such as *str* for *string*, or *int* for *integer*, that some programmers employ when naming variables, arrays, and controls. It's thought that prefixing a variable's or control's name with these lowercase abbreviations makes it easier to identify the variable's data type, or the purpose of a control.

And unless you're dealing with extremely brief programs (such as some of the illustrations in this book), remember that it also helps to use descriptive names for your variables and controls. For example, name a button `btnExit` or `btnNextPage` rather than simply using the default `Button1`.

The following is a list of the prefixes I've found most useful, but you can see Microsoft's complete list of suggested naming conventions for VB at http://support.microsoft.com/kb/110264.

Prefixes for Variable Names

To use any of these prefix abbreviations in your code, simply prepend the abbreviation to the name of the variable. So `int` indicates the integer data type—for example:

```
Dim intMilesDriven
```

- **arr** Array
- **bln** Boolean
- **dat** Date and time
- **dbl** Double
- **dec** Decimal
- **err** Error
- **int** Integer
- **lng** Long
- **obj** Object
- **sng** Single
- **str** String

Naming Controls Descriptively

VB provides default names when you add a control to a form from the toolbox. But these names are generic and merely describe what kind of control it is: *Label3*, *Textbox1*, and so on.

Use the Properties window to change the Name property of each control you add to your program. Pick a name that expresses what the control *does*—it's job in the program.

For example, when a button is first added to a form, VB supplies the default name *Button1*, so its event handler Sub looks like this:

```
Private Sub Button1_Click(ByVal sender As System.Object, ByVal e As
System.EventArgs) Handles Button1.Click
```

But you should give your controls better, more descriptive, names than the defaults. For example, if you changed a button's Text property to *Exit*, because clicking it shuts down the program, change the button's Name property to btnExit. If the button prints some text, use btnPrint, and so on. Making these changes improves code readability because VB automatically uses a control's Name property to name its event handler in the source code, like this:

```
Private Sub btnExit_Click(ByVal sender As System.Object, ByVal e As
System.EventArgs) Handles btnExit.Click
```

One final point about naming. If you change the default name *Button1* to *Exit*, you lose some important information: what kind of a control it is. So, over time people have developed a set of prefixes you should use that describe the control's type. Instead of just using the name *Exit* for a button, use btnExit.

Here's the list of control prefixes:

•	**cbo**	ComboBox		
•	**chk**	CheckBox		
•	**dag**	DataGrid		
•	**dat**	DataSet		
•	**fra**	Frame		
•	**frm**	Form		
•	**grd**	Grid		
•	**hsb**	Horizontal scroll bar		
•	**lbl**	Label		
•	**lst**	ListBox		
•	**mnu**	Menu		

•	**nud**	NumericUpDown
•	**pgb**	ProgressBar
•	**pic**	PictureBox
•	**pnl**	Panel
•	**rdb**	RadioButton
•	**rtb**	RichTextBox
•	**spn**	Spin control
•	**tmr**	Timer
•	**txt**	TextBox
•	**vsb**	Vertical scroll bar

Appendix C
Keyboard Shortcuts

This appendix provides a list of keyboard shortcuts that you might find handy when working in the VB editor. If you've read this book, you already know at least two shortcuts: F5 executes the program currently in the editor, and F8 single-steps through the source code. But here is a list of additional useful shortcuts.

My Favorite Shortcut Keys

Like a word processor, the VB editor is designed to make the job of writing easier. One way to do that is via what are sometimes called *accelerator keys* or *keyboard shortcuts*—function keys, or key combinations, that trigger some feature in the editor.

Here is a list of the shortcut keys I've found most useful over the years. But perhaps you would prefer to employ a different group of shortcut keys. At the end of this appendix you'll learn how to see *all* the available default shortcut key combinations and how to redefine the key combinations if the defaults don't suit your programming style.

F5	Execute the program currently in the editor
F8	Single-step through the program
F2	Open the Object Browser
F3	Find Next (during a search of the code)
F4	Open the Properties window
F7	Switch to the code editor (from the design window)
SHIFT-F7	Switch to the design window (from the code editor)
F9	Toggle a breakpoint
TAB	Move to the next control on the form (based on the `TabIndex` properties of the controls)
CTRL-Z	Undo whatever you last did in either the code window or the form design window
CTRL-Y	Undo CTRL-Z (reverses whatever CTRL-Z did)
CTRL-N	Start a new project

Typical Word Processor Key Assignments

Many familiar word processing shortcuts such as CTRL-HOME, DEL, CTRL-V (to paste), CTRL-C (to copy), SHIFT-END (to select text to the end of a line), CTRL-A (to select all), and so on, behave exactly the same way in the VB code editor as they do in a word processor and other Windows applications.

Manipulating Controls on Forms with the Arrow Keys

When designing a form, it's helpful to be able to reposition controls via the keyboard rather than dragging them with the mouse. This is because the keyboard offers finer control than the mouse.

Repositioning

Click a button or other control to select it, on the form and then press the left-, right-, up-, or down-arrow keys to maneuver the button to whatever position looks best. This moves controls in the smallest increments, but if you want to move the control around more quickly, hold down the CTRL key while pressing the arrow keys. In this mode, you'll also see lines appear on the form when your control is properly aligned with another control (these same lines appear when you use the mouse to drag controls). Aligned controls make a form look more polished, more professional.

Resizing

The arrow keys can also be employed to resize controls. Hold down the SHIFT key while pressing the arrow keys. The SHIFT-CTRL-arrow will resize in larger increments and also display the lines on the form that indicate alignment with other controls.

Viewing or Modifying the VB Express Shortcut Keys

As you're doubtless discovering, VB's editor is remarkably sophisticated, full-featured, capable, and efficient. It should be. It's the culmination of two decades of user input, focus groups, and talented programmers and designers. Here are two of the many benefits of all this effort:

- The editor contains shortcut keys for many more features than those that appear in my personal favorites list.

- The keyboard shortcuts are fully customizable by the user.

Looking at the Existing Key Combinations

To see all the possible shortcut options, or what any *particular* key combination triggers, follow these steps:

1. Choose Tools | Options. The Options dialog box opens.

2. If necessary, click the Show All Settings checkbox in the lower left of the Options dialog box to ensure it is checked.

3. Under Environment in the left pane of the Options dialog box, click Keyboard.

4. Now you can see the list of available keyboard shortcuts and scroll the list to see all of them. Notice that most keyboard shortcuts represent menu options in the editor. And the shortcuts are named after these menus and options, such as *View.FullScreen* or *File.SaveAll.*

5. If you want to see what a particular key combination does, type the combination into the Press Shortcut Keys field. For example, press CTRL-J and you'll see that this key combination is currently assigned to the Edit | ListMembers feature (part of the IntelliSense system described in Chapter 3). To the left of the | symbol is the menu where this option can be found. (IntelliSense, for example, is located on the Edit menu.)

Customizing Key Combinations

To change any of the existing key combinations, just type in the shortcut key combination (as described in step 5) that you want to modify. Then scroll the list of available features (also described in step 5) and click the feature you want to assign to this shortcut key combination. Click the Assign button to complete the reassignment.

Shortcuts can include the CTRL, SHIFT, and ALT keys (in any combination), plus a letter or function key. However, you can't employ the following keys in a shortcut: CAPS LOCK, END, ESC, BREAK, HOME, INSERT, PAGE UP, PAGE DOWN, PRINT SCRN, SCRLK, TAB, the Windows logo keys, any arrow keys, or CLEAR, DEL, ENTER, or NUM LOCK (on the numeric keypad).

Appendix D

The ASCII
Character Codes

ere is a list of the ASCII character codes discussed in Chapter 10.

Group 1: The Nonprinting Characters

The characters from 0 to 31 are called *control characters* or *nonprinting characters*. Their purpose is to send control codes to devices such as the printer or monitor.

0	Null character	16	Data line escape
1	Start of heading	17	Device Control 1 (oft. XON)
2	Start of text	18	Device Control 2
3	End of text	19	Device Control 3 (oft. XOFF)
4	End of transmission	20	Device Control 4
5	Inquiry	21	Negative acknowledgment
6	Acknowledgment	22	Synchronous idle
7	Bell	23	End of transmit block
8	Back space	24	Cancel
9	Horizontal tab	25	End of medium
10	Line feed	26	Substitute
11	Vertical tab	27	Escape
12	Form feed	28	File separator
13	Carriage return	29	Group separator
14	Shift out / X-On	30	Record separator
15	Shift in / X-Off	31	Unit separator

Group 2: The Keyboard Set

The set of characters from 32 to 127 is the *meat* of the ASCII code. Here you find all the ordinary keyboard characters. Called *printable characters*, this set includes the letters of the alphabet, the ten digits, punctuation marks, and a few miscellaneous symbols such as the pipe symbol | and the lovely tilde ~.

32		Space	35	#	Number
33	!	Exclamation mark	36	$	Dollar
34	"	Double quote	37	%	Percent

38	&	Ampersand
39	'	Single quote
40	(	Open parenthesis
41	)	Close parenthesis
42	*	Asterisk
43	+	Plus
44	,	Comma
45	-	Hyphen
46	.	Period
47	/	Forward slash (compare to backslash) or arithmetic division symbol
48	0	Zero
49	1	One
50	2	Two
51	3	Three
52	4	Four
53	5	Five
54	6	Six
55	7	Seven
56	8	Eight
57	9	Nine
58	:	Colon
59	;	Semicolon
60	<	Less than
61	=	Equal
62	>	Greater than
63	?	Question mark
64	@	At symbol
65	A	Uppercase A
66	B	Uppercase B
67	C	Uppercase C
68	D	Uppercase D
69	E	Uppercase E
70	F	Uppercase F

71	G	Uppercase G
72	H	Uppercase H
73	I	Uppercase I
74	J	Uppercase J
75	K	Uppercase K
76	L	Uppercase L
77	M	Uppercase M
78	N	Uppercase N
79	O	Uppercase O
80	P	Uppercase P
81	Q	Uppercase Q
82	R	Uppercase R
83	S	Uppercase S
84	T	Uppercase T
85	U	Uppercase U
86	V	Uppercase V
87	W	Uppercase W
88	X	Uppercase X
89	Y	Uppercase Y
90	Z	Uppercase Z
91	[	Opening bracket
92	\	Backslash
93	]	Closing bracket
94	^	Caret (aka circumflex)
95	_	Underscore
96	`	Accent grave
97	a	Lowercase a
98	b	Lowercase b
99	c	Lowercase c
100	d	Lowercase d
101	e	Lowercase e
102	f	Lowercase f
103	g	Lowercase g
104	h	Lowercase h

105	i	Lowercase i
106	j	Lowercase j
107	k	Lowercase k
108	l	Lowercase l
109	m	Lowercase m
110	n	Lowercase n
111	o	Lowercase o
112	p	Lowercase p
113	q	Lowercase q
114	r	Lowercase r
115	s	Lowercase s
116	t	Lowercase t

117	u	Lowercase u
118	v	Lowercase v
119	w	Lowercase w
120	x	Lowercase x
121	y	Lowercase y
122	z	Lowercase z
123	{	Opening curly brace
124	|	Pipe symbol (vertical bar)
125	}	Closing curly brace
126	~	The tilde
127		Delete

Group 3: The Extended Code Set

The characters from 128 to 255 are called *extended character codes*. This set includes bizzaro symbols you're unlikely to use, such as the Å—a "Latin" capital letter with a "ring" on top. (There are actually several versions of this set of extended character codes. However, this is the one used by Visual Basic.)

128	€	Euro
129		Unassigned
130	,	Single low-9 quotation mark
131	ƒ	Latin small letter f with hook
132	„	Double low-9 quotation marks
133	…	Horizontal ellipsis
134	†	Dagger
135	‡	Double dagger
136	ˆ	Modifier letter circumflex accent
137	‰	Per mille sign
138	Š	Latin capital letter S with caron
139	‹	Single left-pointing angle quotation
140	Œ	Latin capital OE
141		Unassigned

142	Ž	Latin captial letter Z with caron
143		Unassigned
144		Unassigned
145	'	Left single quotation mark
146	'	Right single quotation mark
147	"	Left double quotation mark
148	"	Right double quotation mark
149	•	Bullet
150	–	En dash
151	—	Em dash
152	˜	Small tilde
153	™	Trademark sign
154	š	Latin small letter S with caron
155	›	Single right-pointing angle quotation mark

156	œ	Latin small oe
157		Unassigned
158	ž	Latin small letter z with caron
159	Ÿ	Latin capital letter Y with diaeresis
160		Nonbreaking space
161	¡	Inverted exclamation mark
162	¢	Cent
163	£	Pound
164	¤	Currency
165	¥	Yen
166	¦	Pipe or broken vertical bar
167	§	Section
168	¨	Spacing diaeresis or umlaut
169	©	Copyright
170	ª	Feminine ordinal indicator
171	«	Left double angle quotation marks
172	¬	Not
173		Soft hyphen
174	®	Registered trademark
175	¯	Spacing macron or overline
176	°	Degree symbol
177	±	Plus-or-minus
178	^{2}	Superscript 2 (squared)
179	^{3}	Superscript 3 (cubed)
180	´	Accent acute
181	µ	Micro
182	¶	Paragraph or pilcrow
183	·	Middle dot or Georgian comma
184	¸	Spacing cedilla
185	^{1}	Superscript 1
186	º	Masculine ordinal indicator
187	»	Right double angle quotataion marks

188	¼	One quarter
189	½	One half
190	¾	Three quarters
191	¿	Inverted question mark
192	À	Latin capital letter A with accent grave
193	Á	Latin capital letter A with accent acute
194	Â	Latin capital letter A with circumflex
195	Ã	Latin capital letter A with tilde
196	Ä	Latin capital letter A with diaeresis
197	Å	Latin capital letter A with ring
198	Æ	Latin capital letter AE
199	Ç	Latin capital letter C with cedilla
200	È	Latin capital letter E with accent grave
201	É	Latin capital letter E with accent acute
202	Ê	Latin capital letter E with circumflex
203	Ë	Latin capital letter E with diaeresis
204	Ì	Latin capital letter I with accent grave
205	Í	Latin capital letter I with accent acute
206	Î	Latin capital letter I with circumflex
207	Ï	Latin capital letter I with diaeresis
208	Ð	Latin capital letter ETH
209	Ñ	Latin capital letter N with tilde
210	Ò	Latin capital letter O with accent grave
211	Ó	Latin capital letter O with accent acute

212	Ô	Latin capital letter O with circumflex
213	Õ	Latin capital letter O with tilde
214	Ö	Latin capital letter O with diaeresis
215	×	Multiplication sign
216	Ø	Latin capital letter O with slash
217	Ù	Latin capital letter U with accent grave
218	Ú	Latin capital letter U with accent acute
219	Û	Latin capital letter U with circumflex
220	Ü	Latin capital letter U with diaeresis
221	Ý	Latin capital letter Y with accent acute
222	Þ	Latin capital letter thorn
223	ß	Latin small letter sharp s
224	à	Latin small letter a with accent grave
225	á	Latin small letter a with accent acute
226	â	Latin small letter a with circumflex
227	ã	Latin small letter a with tilde
228	ä	Latin small letter a with diaeresis
229	å	Latin small letter a with ring
230	æ	Latin small letter ae
231	ç	Latin small letter c with cedilla
232	è	Latin small letter e with accent grave
233	é	Latin small letter e with accent acute

234	ê	Latin small letter e with circumflex
235	ë	Latin small letter e with diaeresis
236	ì	Latin small letter i with accent grave
237	í	Latin small letter i with accent acute
238	î	Latin small letter i with circumflex
239	ï	Latin small letter i with diaeresis
240	ð	Latin small letter eth
241	ñ	Latin small letter n with tilde
242	ò	Latin small letter o with accent grave
243	ó	Latin small letter o with accent acute
244	ô	Latin small letter o with circumflex
245	õ	Latin small letter o with tilde
246	ö	Latin small letter o with diaeresis
247	÷	Division
248	ø	Latin small letter o with slash
249	ù	Latin small letter u with accent grave
250	ú	Latin small letter u with accent acute
251	û	Latin small letter u with circumflex
252	ü	Latin small letter u with diaeresis
253	ý	Latin small letter y with accent acute
254	þ	Latin small letter thorn
255	ÿ	Latin small letter y with diaeresis

Glossary

This glossary describes various terms and acronyms used throughout the book. A glossary not only helps you quickly remember a concept, but also clarifies terminology used in this book where it differs from common use.

For example, I use the word *command* as a general-purpose term describing the words in the BASIC language (such as `If` or `Return`) or words found in libraries available for your use while programming in BASIC (such as `StreamWriter`). Other writers employ the terms *keyword*, *reserved word*, and *instruction* for what I call a *command*.

(These words are "reserved" because they have meaning to the Visual Basic language itself. They are commands that tell VB what you want it to do. Because they're reserved, they can't be employed by you as names for your procedures, variables, and so on.)

Also, computer terminology changes rapidly. Dozens of synonyms exist for what I'm calling a *library* in this book (such as *assembly, dynamic link library [DLL], namespace*, and on and on). In this glossary, you'll find the specific terminology used in this book.

What If a Term Isn't in This Glossary?

You can find programming terms defined in various online locations and of course in the built-in VB Help system. Chapter 12 goes into detail about how best to use the Help system. And here are some good places to look online for explanations and definitions of programming terminology:

- **Webopedia** A solid search engine for programmers
  www.webopedia.com/

- **The Sharpened Glossary** A general glossary of computing terms
  www.sharpened.net/glossary/

- **StartVB.Net** A good, searchable guide to various elements of VB and the .NET foundation on which it rests
  www.startvbdotnet.com/

- **Glossarist** A glossary of glossaries (and dictionaries) for programmers
  www.glossarist.com/glossaries/computers-internet/programming.asp?Page=2

- **Acronym Finder** A large compendium
  www.acronymfinder.com/

+ − operators Plus and minus; used for math just as they are in ordinary arithmetic.

/ operator Used for division.

* operator Used for multiplication.

^ operator   Used for exponentiation. Raises a number to a power.

& operator   Concatenates words. For example, `"The"` & `"Ocean"` becomes `"The Ocean"`

ANSI   American National Standards Institute. A code used to represent alphabetic and other characters. *See also* ASCII, character code, and Appendix D, which contains a complete list of the ASCII codes and their descriptions.

argument   Data (such as numbers or text) that is passed to a procedure (a function or sub). Sometimes the word *parameter* is also used to describe this. Arguments are listed in an *argument list* contained within parentheses following a *call* (*see* call) to a procedure. The following code calls a function named `Flix` and passes an argument (a variable named `strNet`):

```
Flix(strNet)
```

arithmetic operators   The operators + – * / and ^ that are used to do arithmetic.

array   A way of grouping variables to make their data easier to manipulate as a unit. Arrays are often searched or otherwise manipulated within loops. The elements of an array are distinguished by index numbers because all elements of an array share the same array name. For example, `Coins(22)` is an array containing 23 elements (there is a zero element). Arrays are declared, usually with the `Dim` command, like variables. *See also* ArrayList and fixed-size array.

ArrayList   An ArrayList is similar to a traditional array, but an ArrayList simplifies and streamlines some tasks. An ArrayList can automatically resize itself while a program runs. An ArrayList can also manage data in other ways that require extra programming with traditional arrays. ArrayList capabilities include `AddRange`, `Insert`, and `InsertRange` methods. And removing items is easy with methods such as `Remove` and `RemoveAt`.

array subscript   The number that specifies how many items are in an array, such as 112 here:

```
Dim MyArray(112) As String
```

Also, the index number that identifies a specific element in the array, such as 42 here:

```
MyArray(42) = "Carole"
```

ASCII   American Standard Code for Information Interchange. A popular code used to represent alphabetical and other characters. *See also* ANSI, character code, and Appendix D, which contains a complete list of the ASCII codes and their descriptions.

assignment operator   The equals sign, used to assign a value to a property or a variable: `strState = "Nevada"`.

binary comparison   Comparing text using a case-sensitive comparison. For example, `"nancy"` would not equal `"Nancy"`.

```
Dim s As String = "nancy"
Dim s1 As String = "Nancy"

If s = s1 Then MsgBox("They are identical")
```

This "binary" way of comparing strings is the default in VB. *See also* textual comparison.

block   An area of code, often called a *structure*. For example, an *If...Then* block begins with an `If...Then` statement and concludes with `End If`. Other lines of code are written within a block (or structure).

Boolean   A variable type that can hold only two possible values—true or false:

```
Dim Toggle As Boolean
```

break mode   Pausing a program's execution while that program is running in the VB editor. This mode is employed when debugging to allow you to single-step through each line of code or observe the contents of variables while the program's execution is suspended. Putting a breakpoint or `Stop` command in your source code, or pressing the break key, can halt execution and put the editor in break mode.

bug   An error that causes a program to misbehave, to act in inappropriate ways. There are three primary types of bugs: syntax, runtime, and logic bugs. Locating and fixing bugs in your source code is called *debugging*.

by reference   You can pass arguments to procedures in two ways: by reference or by value. By default, VB employs the `ByVal` command to pass arguments by value:

```
Private Sub Form1_Load(ByVal sender As System.Object, ByVal e As
System.EventArgs) Handles MyBase.Load
```

When you pass data by reference (`ByRef`), the target procedure can change the data in the variable because the target procedure is given access to the memory location where the original variable stores its value. In VB programming, you'll probably always employ the default `ByVal` approach to passing data. When passed a variable `ByVal`, the called procedure cannot change the value of the variable.

by value   Always the default in VB, this is the way data is passed to a procedure. In this case, the target procedure is not given permission to change the actual value of the passed variable. In other words, it is not given the actual memory address where the value is stored. The target procedure is merely sent a *copy* of the data in the variable.

The rarely used alternative, `ByRef`, does pass the address of the stored value, so the called procedure is capable of modifying the value.

call   To execute a procedure. Sub and function procedures are called in your source code when you want them to do their job. You call a procedure by using its name and passing any necessary parameters to it. The following calls a function named `Flix` and passes an argument (a variable named `strNet`):

```
Flix(strNet)
```

character code   A computer refers to each alphabetic character by a special code, typically either the ASCII or ANSI code. The ANSI character code for a capital A is 65 and for a capital B is 66. There are also codes for symbols like @$& and for nonprinting characters such as the tab. *See also* ASCII, ANSI, and Appendix D, which contains a complete list of ASCII codes and their descriptions.

class module   A specialized VB module that contains the definition of a class. Classes are used in object-oriented programming. Modules are similar in VB to forms, but modules have no visible user interface. Modules are used internally by a program. Like forms, they contain code. Unlike forms, they have no design mode and they cannot contain controls from the toolbox.

clean   A file whose contents have not been changed while a program runs. The programmer need not save a clean file (for example, the user has not modified the contents of a text box). Clean is the opposite of dirty (*see* dirty).

code   Programming another word for *source code*. Whatever you write in the code editor—commands, data, and statements that make your program do what you want.

combo box   A combination box. A control in the Toolbox you can put on your forms. It combines the functionality of a list box with a single-line text box. The user can either select an existing entry in the list or type a new entry into the text box portion of this control.

command   Throughout this book I use the term *command* as an all-purpose name for words in the VB language itself (such as `End` or `Loop`) as well as for object methods (such as the `Hide` or `Close` methods of a form object). Commands are highlighted in this book's text by using a different font than the ordinary body text. The font looks like `This`.

Many other books on programming employ the term *keyword* or *reserved word* for the commands in the VB language, and the term *method* for objects' methods. I find the word *command* useful because it suggests that you're telling the computer what to do. Your *source code* (the programming you write in the editor to tell the computer how to behave) is filled with commands.

A complete instruction in your program to the computer is called a *statement*—a group of one or more commands that, taken together, express a single concept (*see* statement).

comment   Also sometimes called a *remark*, a comment is an explanation that you type into your source code, usually to describe what the code is supposed to do. Comments are not executed by VB; they are merely there for the programmer's future reference—to make the code more easily understandable and easier to modify. In VB, anything following a single quotation mark (') on a line of code is a comment.

comment out   To put a single quotation mark (') at the start of a line of code to prevent it from being executed. This technique is sometimes used by programmers while debugging to cause execution to skip over some code. You get to see what happens if this section of code is temporarily removed from the program. The lines can later be restored to executability by removing the single quotes.

comparison operators   Also called *relational operators*, these are a set of operators that are used to compare values. You often need to examine, test, or modify variables in a program. Operators are frequently used to test how variables compare to each other (is the datum in one variable larger, are they equal, and so on). Here's an example that employs the > (greater than) operator to see if one variable contains a larger number than the other:

```
Dim Num1 As Integer = 14
Dim Num2 As Integer = 7

        If Num1 > Num2 Then
```

The primary comparison operators are

- < Less than
- <= Less than or equal to
- > Greater than
- >= Greater than or equal to

- <> Not equal
- = Equal

compile error   This error occurs when you press F5 in the code editor to execute your program, but VB halts execution because it can't figure out how to execute one of the statements in your source code. It's more often called a *runtime error.* When you press F5, VB translates (compiles) your source code into a lower-level language that the computer understands. If VB can't translate a line of your code, you've got a compile error. VB will display an error message to let you know where the error happened in your code, and VB will also describe the error to you.

component   *See* control.

concatenate   Joining two pieces of text together, using the & operator. *See* & operator.

concatenation operator   The & operator that joins two strings together.

constant   Similar to a variable, but in a constant, the value doesn't change while a program is executing. You can define your own constants, though most people just use variables even if the data isn't going to change. For example, Dim Nev As String = "Nevada" defines a variable, but this can be used in the program as if it were a constant. The variable name Nev can always mean *Nevada.* Nowhere in your code do you replace the datum *Nevada.*

A more frequently used type of constant is the set of built-in constants, part of the VB language itself. These generally begin with the letters vb. For example, the built-in constant vbCr stands for the carriage return (ASCII code 13), indicating that the ENTER key is pressed. To see a complete list of the built-in constants, type **vb** in the code window. *See also* intrinsic constant.

context menu   When you right-click something in a Windows program such as Windows Explorer, you'll often see a menu pop up, displaying options relating to the clicked item.

control   An object from the Toolbox that you place on a form. Most controls are visible to the user, such as buttons or text boxes, but some controls are only visible to the programmer in the editor while the program is being designed. A timer control, for instance, has no visible user interface, but instead works behind the scenes while a program executes.

Technically, most programmers would call a timer a *component* rather than a control because it doesn't have a user interface. A discussion at the Visual Studio 2008 Developer

Center at http://msdn.microsoft.com/en-us/library/0b1dk63b.aspx is helpful concerning this usage. If you look under the "Control" heading, you'll see that Microsoft specifically states that controls have a user interface. On the other hand, the `Timer` class specification doesn't say that the `Timer` class implements *IComponent*, which is theoretically one of the requirements for a component. Interestingly (to the technically inclined), the `Timer` class doesn't implement *IControl* either—one of the requirements for a control.

data type The kind of data (usually referring to the contents, the value) held in a variable. For example, text is of the *string* data type, and nondecimal numbers can be of the *integer* data type. When you declare a variable, you can specify its data type so VB knows how you want it managed. In this example, the variable `strParty` is declared to be a string data type:

```
Dim strParty As String
```

In this book, we simplify our programming job by allowing VB itself to deal with data typing and data type conversions. This topic is covered in Chapter 5.

Note that some programmers like to prepend a variable name with an abbreviation of the data type (the *str* in `strParty` is an abbreviation for *string*). Appendix B lists the common VB naming conventions that I've found useful, and you can find a complete list of Microsoft's suggested conventions at http://support.microsoft.com/kb/110264.

debug To test your source code and attempt to catch all the errors (bugs) in your program.

design mode The mode in which you are working while in the editor's design window—creating the visual user-interface by adding controls to a form, resizing them, adjusting their properties, and so on. This phrase can also refer to when you're working on the program in general, even in the code window (as opposed to execution mode, or *runtime*).

design time A synonym for design mode.

dirty A file whose contents have changed while your program runs (such as when the user modifies a text box's contents), but the changes have not yet been saved to the disk file. The opposite of clean (*see also* clean).

double A variable type that permits the use of decimal points: double-precision floating point number. This type can hold numbers as large as 1.79769313486231570E+308. *See also* single.

dynamic array   An array that can change its size as needed while a program runs. In earlier versions of VB, some arrays could not be resized. In VB Express, all arrays can be redimensioned with the `ReDim` command. *See* fixed-size array.

edit box   Another term for text box. Not often used.

elegant   Scientists and programmers employ this term to describe something they admire. When used to describe programming, it generally means code that's both simple and effective.

error handler   An area in your source code that is designed to detect and analyze errors, and then respond. Sometimes called an *error trap*, error handlers are frequently located within a `Try...End Try` structure. VB itself provides an error code when something goes wrong, so you can write programming that responds to whatever error code is triggered. Error handlers are most often employed when the program contacts a peripheral, such as the hard drive, and therefore unpredictable situations can arise (the drive is full, a disk file cannot be located, and so on).

event   Events are such things as mouse clicks or keypresses—actions that happen while a program runs. For example, you the programmer write some code that is executed if the user clicks a button labeled Print. Your code (located in a sub procedure referred to as that button's *click event hander*) prints something in response to that button click. Most controls have a set of built-in events—things that can happen to the control—such as a text box's `TextChanged` event. This event is triggered whenever the contents of the text box change. *See also* Event Procedure.

event procedure   Programming code that you write to respond to an event. You write that code within an event procedure (also called an *event handler*). In VB, an event procedure is a `Sub...End Sub` structure that also includes some arguments and a `Handles` command. Following is an example of an event procure. Each VB form has a `Form_Load` event procedure. Programmers often put code in this procedure to perform any necessary housekeeping (such as filling a list box control with options) before the form is displayed to the user:

```
Private Sub Form1_Load(ByVal sender As System.Object, ByVal e As
System.EventArgs) Handles MyBase.Load

End Sub
```

expression Some elements in a program hold a value (a datum, such as the number 22 or the text "Veronica"). Variables, constants, properties, and literals all can hold a value. When you combine two variables or a variable and a constant (or some other combination of these value-holding elements) by using an *operator* (such as + or <), you have created an *expression*. Think of an expression as a compound value-holding unit. For example, `5 + 2` is an expression that holds two values. The 5 and 2 are literal numbers and the + is the operator that describes their relationship in this expression.

`5 + 2 = 4 Or 6 + 6 = 12` is a longer, more complicated expression, employing the `Or` operator.

Even though an expression holds two or more values, the expression as a whole has its own, single value. For example, the expression 5 + 2 *evalutates to* (has a value of) 7. The expression 8 > 12 (eight is greater than 12) evaluates to *false*.

fixed-iteration loop A loop that repeats a specified number of times. Most `For...Next` loops are fixed-iteration loops because you specify how many times they iterate (repeat execution of the loop). `For i = 1 to 10` is fixed: it will iterate ten times.

fixed-size array Any array in which the number of elements is specified when you declare the array and cannot be automatically resized. In earlier versions of VB, some arrays were fixed. In VB Express, you can use the `ReDim` command to resize any array. An ordinary array is declared using a specific number that specifies its size:

```
Dim arrQuestions(12) As String
```

Or, if you prefer, you can declare an array but not specify its size, of the array, like this:

```
Dim arrQuestions() As String
```

The `ArrayList` object is an array that allows you to employ an `Add` method to increase the array size dynamically (and employ other methods to remove elements and decrease its size). With an `ArrayList`, you need not employ the `ReDim` command.

form A container in which you can put controls, such as buttons and text boxes, that the user will interact with. A form also serves as a container for source code, when you switch to the code editor. You use the VB editor's design window to design forms. A form becomes a window when the program executes. A form, in other words, is the graphical user interface for your program. A large program may contain multiple windows (forms) to display to the user based on the tasks in which the user is currently engaged. Compare the form to a module. *See also* module and class module.

function A type of procedure. A function is code you write within the `Function` and `End Function` commands. Typically, a function uses the `Return` command to send back a result to the code that calls it (*see* call). A Sub (the other primary type of procedure) does not normally return a result.

get   To return a value, usually of a variable or property. As in the phrase, *This command gets the value in the variable* `strName`. The term "read" is often used to mean get. Get is the opposite of set (which means to change the value, not merely access it). *See also* set.

group box   Another word for the frame control. This control is used to create zones visually within a form, so the user can see that certain controls belong together and work as a unit. One common use for a frame is to place a set of radio (option) button controls on the frame. When you do this, each radio button becomes part of the set, and only one of the radio buttons can be selected (clicked and turned dark) at any given time while the program is executing. You group a set of radio buttons to provide the user with a set of mutually exclusive choices, such as a choice between several font sizes.

hard-coding   Specifying literal values rather than, say, allowing the user to input a value. For instance, if you write a program that calculates state tax, you might *hard-code* the tax within the program, like this:

```
Dim StateTax = 1.07
```

However, it's all too likely that the state will at some point raise this tax. If your program has hard-coded the state tax, the user will be unable to enter the new tax rate, so the program will no longer be accurate. For information that might change, you should provide a way for the user to modify that data. Perhaps you could provide a button or menu item that opens a dialog box where the user can optionally update information such as the current tax rate.

If...Then structure   An area of code that begins with an `If...Then` statement and concludes with `End If`. This is the most commonly used decision-making (or branching) structure in VB programming. It allows your program to take alternative paths through the code, based on current conditions. For example, if a user enters their age as less than 18, your quiz program might display a different set of questions than it would for persons over 18. Chapter 8 covers branching.

indefinite loop   The opposite of fixed-iteration loop. An indefinite loop repeats a flexible number of times. A `While` loop, for example, continues to repeat until some condition in the program is satisfied. By contrast, a fixed-iteration loop such as a `For...Next` loop typically specifies the number of iterations it can perform. *See* hard-coding, fixed-iteration loop. Also see Chapter 7.

integer variable   The most commonly used type of numeric variable. An integer is a number that has no decimal point (no fractional part). The number *243* is an integer. However, add a decimal point like this, *243.6*, and you cannot use the `Integer` variable type. (You must use a `Single` or `Double` variable type.)

Integers execute the fastest of any numeric data type, and they are the most common type of numeric variable. However, if you need to work with really large whole numbers, use the big brother of the integer called the `Long` (*see also* Long). In this book, though, we're allowing the VB language to manage variable types for us. See Chapter 5.

intrinsic constant   A constant whose value VB already knows as part of the VB language (also called a "built-in constant"). Using built-in constants can be a convenient and more readable approach than simply supplying values to a property or variable.

VB includes various sets of intrinsic constants, including, for example, a set of message box styles or character codes. So, rather than typing

```
Dim s As String = Chr(13)
```

to assign the carriage return character to this variable, you can use the built-in constant for this character, which is named `vbCr`:

```
Dim s As String = vbCr
```

When you type **vb** in the code window, the VB IntelliSense feature will display a list of VB's built-in constants, as shown here:

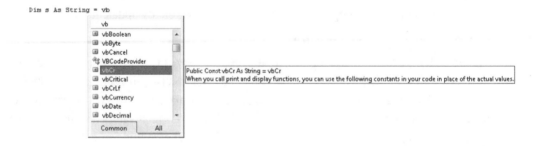

iteration   An iteration means executing a loop one time. A loop such as this one will iterate fourteen times:

```
For i = 1 To 14
```

See also fixed iteration loop.

keyword   A word that is part of the VB language—for example Dim, End, or Next. In this book, I've used the word *command* rather than *keyword* to indicate a built-in capability of the language. Note that command words (or keywords) are also known as *reserved* words because VB must reserve them for its own use. This means you, the programmer, can't use these words for your own purposes. You can't name one of your program's variables (or arrays, procedures, constants, and so on) using a command name like this:

```
Dim End
```

If you attempt to declare a variable named, for instance, End, VB will respond with an error message: "Keyword is not valid as an identifier."

language error   *See* syntax error.

library   In this book, I use the term *library* to mean a collection of prewritten functions, methods, objects, and commands that you can add to the commands built into the core VB language. Libraries are called by many names: assemblies, dynamic link libraries (DLLs), namespaces, and so on. You can add a library to your VB project (and thus make its collection of commands available to that project) by using the Imports command. In some cases, however, you must instead *reference* a library using the editor's Project | Add Reference menu option. *See also* reference.

lifetime   *Local* variables (variables declared within a procedure) have a lifetime only while that procedure is executing. They are not in existence when other procedures are executing (as opposed to a global variable that is declared at the top of a form—outside any procedure—and thus has a lifetime while *any* procedure in that form is executing). A variable's lifetime is tied to its *scope*.

You *can* force a local variable to retain its contents (the datum it holds) by using the Static command. To understand the distinction between lifetime and scope, *see* static variable and scope. These issues are covered in Chapter 5.

local scope   Another name for procedure-level scope. *See also* static variable, scope, and public (and private).

logic error   This is usually the most difficult kind of error to track down and fix. A logic error causes an incorrect result (such as a diet program reporting that your personal target weight should be 14,480 pounds). However, there is no typo (syntax error) in your source code.

A logic error produces incorrect results, although there are no syntactical problems and the code compiles and runs successfully.

A good debugging tool when tracking down a logic error is the single-step feature of the VB editor. *See* single-step.

logical operators   Operators such as And, Not, and Or, which are used pretty much as they are in English. The logical operators are employed in *expressions*. *See* expression for an example that uses the Or operator. There's also the interesting XOR operator that you could use in this book's Diary program to improve the encryption/decryption security functions. One reason XOR is handy for scrambling text is because it is quite symmetrical in its behavior: XOR a character once and it's encrypted; XOR a second time (the encrypted character) and it returns to the original plaintext character you started with. And if you employ a randomized key of the same length as the text you're scrambling, XOR can produce an unbreakable encryption (it's assumed). For those interested in this topic, check out a good brief introduction at http://en.wikipedia.org/wiki/XOR_cipher.

loop   A structure in a program that repeats. Within a loop structure you write code that will execute the number of times that the loop iterates (loops). *See* iterate. A For...Next structure is a commonly used loop.

member   Collectively, an object's methods, events, properties, enumerations, and other components are known as its *members*. *See also* method and property.

method   This term is used with objects to describe their capabilities, actions they can take. For instance, the button control has a Hide method. This means it has the ability to become invisible. If you employ this method in a button's Click event,

```
Button1.Hide()
```

when the user clicks this button, it disappears. Don't confuse an object's methods with its properties. Although some overlap can exist (a button has the ability, for example, to change its color property when the user clicks it), a property generally refers to a *quality* such as its size or caption rather than an *action* (or behavior) such as hiding itself.

Collectively, an object's methods, properties, and other components are known as its *members*. *See also* property.

modal   A modal dialog box or form halts execution of a program, forcing the user to click OK, Cancel, or some other button to close the dialog box before program execution can resume. A message box is modal.

modeless   The opposite of *modal*. A modeless dialog box (which is rare) can be displayed while a program continues to permit the user to do other things. Or it can be closed by the program automatically, rather than requiring the user to close it. *See also* modal.

modular   Subdividing a program into relatively small, manageable units. Nearly all contemporary programming is modular (a procedure or event is a subsection within a larger structure, such as a form or module). In VB, a group of forms that collectively make up a given program are known as a *project* (another name for *program*). You can view your project's component forms by looking at the editor's Solution Explorer window.

module   A storage container for code which, unlike a form, has no visible user-interface components. In larger programs, it can be useful to subdivide your source code into various modules to hold code that doesn't need to be located within an event procedure. Object-oriented programming (OOP) classes are also written inside a module, specifically a *class module. See* class module.

object   A unit of source code and data bound together. Objects have methods and properties (known as the object's *members*) and can respond to events. A text box control is an object—like all the other items in the VB Toolbox. But you can also create your own objects by employing class modules. Chapter 13 explores object-oriented programming, or OOP. *See also* class module.

object-oriented programming (OOP)   As opposed to *procedure-oriented* programming, OOP creates a program by designing classes (blueprints that describe objects). See Chapter 13.

object variable   A type of variable that instead of containing a typical datum (like the number contained by a numeric variable) contains (or technically "references") an object. When you declare an object, you give it a name, just as you would any other variable. Thereafter, when you access that object in your code, you employ the object variable name.

An object variable can store any type of data. It has no specific data type such as integer or string. An object variable can hold any value, text, numeric, decimal numbers, and so on. In earlier versions of VB, the variant was the default data type. Now the object variable is the default type. So if you don't specify a data type when declaring a variable, it becomes an object by default. VB will make all variables object types, and it automatically handles data typing or data type conversions for you, as long as you have `Option Strict` off. For example, if you want to display a numeric variable in a message box, VB will automatically convert the numeric type (such as integer) into the string type that message boxes require.

You can, however, force the programmer to deal with data typing and conversions by turning on the `Option Strict` feature. You can have VB automatically enforce `Option Strict` by right-clicking the project's name (it's in boldface) in the Solution Explorer, choosing Properties from the context menu, then clicking the Compile tab (on the left), and then setting `Option Strict` on. See Chapter 5 for a fuller explanation of variable types.

OOP *See* object-oriented programming. See Chapter 13.

operator A programming element that is used in an expression. In this expression, the + is the operator:

```
2 + 13
```

See expression, logical operator, comparison operator, and arithmetic operator.

option button *See* radio button.

point A unit of measurement, 1/72 inch. The point is commonly used to specify the size of text. When you add a label control (or other control that has a text property), the default point size will be 8.5 points, which is usually too small on today's monitors. So I usually go to the Property window and open the Font options, and then change the font size to 11 points. (You can also refuse to use points if you wish by changing the Font Unit property to another measurement system, such as inches.)

procedure A section of code contained within a `Sub...End Sub` or `Function...End Function` structure. Usually ranging from a single line of code, to perhaps as much as 30 lines, a procedure is supposed to perform a single task. Procedure-oriented programming, as opposed to object-oriented programming (OOP), subdivides a program into individual tasks that are described by the source code contained within various procedures. OOP, on the other hand, subdivides a program into classes.

Except for form-wide variables and a few other kinds of global declarations, all the code in most programs is contained within procedures (unless you choose to approach programming employing OOP techniques, as described in Chapter 13).

procedure call *See* call.

procedure scope Also called *local* scope or *procedure-level scope*. *See* scope.

property A quality or attribute of an object, such as its size, typeface, position, or color. VB includes a Properties window, for example, that you can use to adjust the properties of controls on a form while you're designing the user interface. But you can also write code that modifies or reads the value of properties dynamically (during program execution). This example dynamically changes the background color of this label during runtime (when the program is running):

```
Label1.BackColor = Color.DarkSalmon
```

The other primary attributes of an object are called its *methods*. Properties are usually descriptive qualities such as adjectives (blue, boldface, and so on). Methods are more like verbs (stop, hide, move, and so on). *See also* method.

public (and private)   When you use the command `Private` with a procedure, its scope is limited to the form or module within which it resides. Use the command `Public` and code inside other forms or modules can access the procedure. *See* scope and lifetime.

```
Private Sub Form1_Load(ByVal sender As System.Object, ByVal e As
System.EventArgs) Handles MyBase.Load
```

By default, VB makes its event procedures private, though you can delete `Private` and make the event `Public` if you are writing a multi-form program and want to communicate among the forms.

The scope of procedures can also be specified using specialized commands instead of the common `Public` or `Private`—such as `Friend` or `Protected Friend`. This kind of scoping, though, is pretty much limited to object-oriented programming (OOP).

radio button   Sometimes called an *option button*. A button that is part of a group (or set) of choices. Only one option button in a group can be selected at a time. If the user clicks a different button in the group, the currently selected button is deselected. That's why VB calls the option button control a *radio button*. They work like the set of buttons on a car radio—when you press one, the previously selected button pops out and is deselected. *See also* group box.

read-only property   A property whose value you can fetch (*read* or *get*) but cannot change (*write* or *set*).

read-write property   A property whose value you can both read and modify. *See* read-only property.

redimension   To use the `ReDim` command to change the size of an array.

reference   Referencing a code library (*see* library) allows you to add new sets of commands and capabilities to the VB language (such as commands available in other languages, specialized tasks such as DirectX, mobile web programming, and so on). You can reference (make available) a library by right-clicking your project name (it's in boldface) in the editor's Solution Explorer (press CTRL-R). Then choose Add Reference. An Add Reference dialog box opens. Scroll within the list of available references and choose the one you want. (Alternatively, choose Project | Add Reference from the editor's menus.) Referencing is similar to using the Imports command. Some code libraries are added to a program using Imports, and others require referencing.

remark   Another name for *comment*. *See* comment.

return   This term has several meanings in computing:

● Signifies that execution is has reached the end of a called procedure and is returning to the location in the code that originally called that procedure.

● The `Return` command sends data back from a function procedure to the caller.

● To fetch the current value of a variable, property, or other value-holding programming element. When used in this sense, *return* means the same as *get*, *fetch*, or *read*.

run mode   This mode means that your program is currently executing in the editor. For example, when you press F5, you enter run mode because the program starts running. (As opposed to *design mode*, when you are writing the source code in the code editor, or designing a form in the VB editor's design window.) *See* design mode.

run time   A synonym for run mode. The opposite of *design time*. This distinction is important: between being in the VB editor and writing the program, as opposed to pressing F5 to force the editor to *run* the program. For example, different types of errors can occur depending on which mode you're in. An error that shows up only when you execute the program is called a *runtime error* or *compile error*. An error that shows up while you are writing code (design time) is called a syntax error.

scope   A variable's (or procedure's) range of influence within the programming code. When you declare a variable *inside* a procedure, the variable has only *local scope*. It can be used only by the code in the procedure where it is declared. Code in other procedures simply can't "see" (access) this variable at all. Code in other procedures cannot "read" (find out the value) or "write" (change the value of) a local variable. This is because when the program is executing other procedures, that local variable is simply not in existence. It lives only while its own procedure is executing, then is destroyed. *See* lifetime.

Procedures also have scope. When you use the command `Private` with a procedure, its scope is limited to the form or module within which it resides. Use the command `Public`, and code inside other forms or modules can access the procedure.

Many programming experts advise that it is a "best practice" (the way you should write programs to avoid errors or otherwise achieve the best results) to employ private procedures and local variables if at all possible.

You *can* force a local variable to retain its contents (the datum it holds) by using the `Static` command. This command extends the lifetime of a variable to the entire duration of program execution. However, it does not extend the variable's scope (which remains local to its procedure). For further details about the distinction between lifetime and scope, *see* static variable. *See also* public (and private).

set *See* get.

single   A variable type that permits the use of decimal points: single-precision floating point number. This type can hold numbers as large as 3.4028235E+38. If you need to manipulate even larger numbers involving decimal points, use the `double` variable type.

single-step   To execute a program's code one statement at a time (by pressing F8 repeatedly). This is one of the most powerful debugging tools you can employ when wrestling with the worst type of bug, the logic error. *See* logic error.

Solution Explorer   This is a small window (pane) usually displayed on the right side of the editor. The Solution Explorer lists the current projects you're working on and their components, such as forms and modules. It gives you an overall, large-scale view.

Clicking a form in the Solution Explorer is also a quick way to display the form in the editor. Or right-click a project's name (it's in boldface) to reference a code library (*see* reference). Or right-click and choose Properties to open an extensive tabbed dialog box where you can specify a variety of options for your program including security, debugging, the startup form, and many others.

source code   The lines of programming you type into the VB editor. Collectively, these lines are your program.

statement   A line of source code. A statement specifies a complete action. For example, if you're declaring a variable, you are specifying a complete action:

```
Dim s
```

That's a statement. But the command `Dim` by itself is not a complete action, so it's not a statement:

```
Dim
```

Usually in VB, each statement is on its own, separate line of code in the editor.

The programmer can force a statement to break in two and move down a line by dividing the statement with a space character followed by the underline character, like this:

```
Label1.BackColor = _
  Color.AntiqueWhite
```

As opposed to the usual single-line version of that same statement:

```
Label1.BackColor = Color.AntiqueWhite
```

A programmer can also force two statements to share a single visual line in the editor line by joining them together using a colon (:). Here are two statements on the same line, separated by a colon:

```
If x = 0 Then MsgBox("We're finished.") : End
```

static variable   A local variable whose value (contents) you want to preserve even when execution moves outside the variable's own procedure. You create a static variable by replacing the usual `Dim` command with the `Static` command when declaring the variable, like this:

```
Static Toggle
```

Now, this local variable named `Toggle` will retain its contents, even when execution is taking place outside its procedure. However, `Toggle` still cannot be accessed by other source code outside its procedure. This is the key distinction between *lifetime* and *scope*. Making a variable static expands its lifetime to the duration of program execution (in other words, until the user shuts down the program). But making a variable static does not expand its scope, which remains local. *See* lifetime and scope.

step out   Press CTRL-SHIFT-F8. Similar to single-stepping, this debugging technique resumes normal-speed execution for the remaining statements in a procedure that you've been single-stepping through. When you employ step out, VB halts normal execution and reenters break mode when it leaves the current procedure. So it *steps out* of the entire current procedure, but then breaks. Use this if you don't feel that the logic error you're tracking down exists in the current procedure and you want to move quickly to the next procedure in the program's execution path. If you're single-stepping through a lengthy loop, for example, you might want to move on rather than press F8 10,000 more times to finally single-step through that loop.

step over   Press SHIFT-F8 if you want to execute *without stepping* a procedure that is called from the procedure you're currently stepping through. Got it? Let me restate the concept: If you know that a particular function works OK, there's no need to single-step through it. So when you reach a place where that known-good function is called, use the step over feature so you can resume single-stepping at the statement below the call. Saves time while debugging.

string   A data type used to store text (as opposed to numeric data types such as the `Integer` variable type).

subprocedure   *See* subroutine.

subroutine   A procedure that starts with the command Sub and ends with the command End Sub. Unlike a function, a subroutine does not normally return a result to its caller. *See* function.

subscript   *See* array subscript.

syntax error   The VB code editor can detect this type of error and will display a sawtooth error indicator in the code window under the offending code. VB will also refuse to compile your program (when you press F5 the program will not execute). A syntax error is a misuse of the VB language: mistyping a word, leaving out some punctuation, or leaving out part of a structure (such as the End If command). Sometimes called a "language error."

TabIndex   A property of some controls that allows users to move quickly between the controls by pressing the TAB key. Formerly known as *tab order*. For example, say you're asking the user to fill in a set of text boxes on a form: name, address, phone, and so on. You can adjust the tab order so users never have to waste time by taking their hand off the keyboard to click the mouse to move focus to the next text box. The user can just press TAB to move to each subsequent box and continue filling in the information.

Each control's TabIndex property specifies the order in which VB gives them the focus (can be typed into) as the user moves through the controls by pressing the TAB key to move forward or SHIFT-TAB to move backward.

VB automatically assigns a unique TabIndex property to each control as you add the control to your form. So by default, the property merely reflects the order in which you put the controls on the form. Use the Property window to change the controls' TabIndex properties.

Ensuring the proper TabIndex order can be helpful to users, particularly in programs involving data entry that require that somebody sit at a computer for hours typing information into the same form over and over again. If users had to keep reaching for the mouse every time they filled in the next field in the form, they would go barking mad.

textual comparison   A comparison of strings (text) that is not case-sensitive. *See also* binary comparison.

trap   To catch an error while a program is executing. You use the Try...End Try structure to trap runtime errors. *See also* compile error.

user-defined constant   A constant created by the user (as opposed to an *intrinsic constant*). VB programmers rarely create their own constants, generally preferring to use variables for the same purpose. *See* constant and intrinsic constant.

variable   A location in memory set aside for storing a single piece of information (a datum or value) that can be changed while the program runs.

variant variable   In earlier versions of VB, the variant was the default type. It has been removed from VB and replaced by a new default: the object type.

    The object type of variable can store all types of data. It has no specific data type such as integer or string. An object can hold any value, text, numeric, decimal numbers, and so on.

XOR   Useful for encryption. *See* logical operators.

Index

T